LOVE AND
NARRATIVE FORM
IN TONI MORRISON'S
LATER NOVELS

LOVE AND NARRATIVE FORM IN TONI MORRISON'S LATER NOVELS

JEAN WYATT

The University of Georgia Press

ATHENS

Most University of Georgia Press titles are
available from popular e-book vendors.

Printed digitally

Library of Congress Cataloging-in-Publication Data

Names: Wyatt, Jean, author.
Title: Love and narrative form in Toni Morrison's later novels / Jean Wyatt.
Description: Athens : The University of Georgia Press, 2017. |
Includes bibliographical references and index.
Identifiers: LCCN 2016028177| ISBN 9780820350868 (pbk. : alk. paper) |
ISBN 9780820350608 (cloth : alk. paper) | ISBN 9780820350592 (ebook)
Subjects: LCSH: Morrison, Toni—Criticism and interpretation. |
Love in literature. | Narration (Rhetoric)
Classification: LCC PS3563.O8749 Z96 2017 | DDC 813/.54—dc23
LC record available at https://lccn.loc.gov/2016028177

For Bob, John, and Lisa

CONTENTS

ACKNOWLEDGMENTS

I have been enormously fortunate in having readers who generously contributed their own ideas to expand my interpretations of Toni Morrison's works. This book would certainly not have existed without the urging and constant support of the following readers. Mirin Fader worked on Toni Morrison with me first as student, then as research assistant and friend. Her tireless, scrupulous bibliographic work, her astute comments on my chapters, and her insights into Morrison's novels sustained me through all the years of writing. Todd McGowan read drafts, sometimes two drafts, of every chapter; his keen eye for structure helped me to rethink, refocus, and organize my arguments. Sheldon George generously shared his own ideas on Morrison's work as he went through each of my chapters, enabling me to complicate and expand my interpretations. Frances Restuccia used her critical and practical acumen to help me out of many an impasse in the writing. Doreen Fowler read the whole book and contributed helpful suggestions for improving it. Elizabeth Abel, ever a generous reader of my work on Morrison, substantially broadened the scope of this study (especially the introduction) through several suggestions for contextualizing the later novels. Naomi Morgenstern read three versions of my introduction, each time moving my writing a bit nearer to her own high level of critical sophistication. Sharla Fett brought her expertise on slavery to my chapter on *Beloved*, opening up the historical scholarship to me through many fruitful recommendations of recent feminist studies on slave mothering. Megan Obourn's original thoughts on Freud's uncanny enabled me to complicate and extend my argument on repression and the uncanny in *Home*.

Jame Phelan's many creative suggestions broached the scope and sharpened the theortetical focus of my analysis of *Love* (chapter 4). Hilary Jones studied *Paradise* with me as a student and then used her editorial skills to expertly condense my chapter on *Paradise*. Roberta Rubenstein read the chapter on *Jazz* and shared the seminal ideas of her article on *Jazz* with me. Shirley Stave catalyzed my interest in *A Mercy* and encouraged me to write on it. Kate Nash made key suggestions for analyzing character narration in *A Mercy*. The late Victor Wolfenstein and I shared our ideas on *Jazz*, *A Mercy*, and *Love* in generative and inspiring conversations that enriched my book. Cristina Escobar and Forrest Havens read many Morrison novels with me, first as students, then as friends, then as colleagues who critiqued my chapters in very useful ways.

I am grateful to the Lovis and Hermoine Brown Humanities Support Fund of Occidental College for funding Amy Stewart's work on the index. A portion of chapter 1 was published in *PMLA* 108.3 (May 1993). An analysis of *Beloved* with a different focus appeared in my book *Risking Difference* (State University of New York Press, 2004). A version of chapter 4 was published in *Narrative* 16.2 (May 2008). A different version of chapter 5 appeared in *Modern Fiction Studies* 58.1 (Spring 2012). I thank the editors of these journals and SUNY Press for permission to use the materials here.

LOVE AND
NARRATIVE FORM
IN TONI MORRISON'S
LATER NOVELS

Love and Narrative Form

The structure is the argument.
TONI MORRISON

Since Peter Brooks wrote *Reading for the Plot* in 1984, psychoanalytic narrative critics have explored, critiqued, and suggested variations on Brooks's contention that desire generates the energy of a novel, keeping the narrative moving and a reader moving with it. In this study of Toni Morrison's later novels, I ask, What is the effect on narrative structure if it is love, not desire, that moves narrative forward—or, perhaps, imposes stasis and brings narrative momentum to a halt? Or pushes the parameters of narrative convention to reflect heretofore unrepresented kinds of love? Morrison often points to love as a central focus of her novels: "Actually, I think, all the time that I write, I'm writing about love or its absence. I think that I still write about the same thing, which is how people relate to one another and miss it or hang on to it . . . or are tenacious about love. About love and how to survive" (Bakerman 40). Increasingly in her later period, Morrison emphasizes that her central interest in composing a novel lies in creating narrative structure: "For me as a writer it is the structure. All of the meaning lies in the structure, the way it is told" (Ashbrook). *Love and Narrative Form* brings these two writerly preoccupations together, focusing on the later novels' structural and stylistic innovations and on Morrison's successive models of love. Where the two converge, where love inflects narrative structure—which it often but not always does—I ask how narrative form reflects and enriches the novel's particular conception of love.

In many of the later novels, starting with *Beloved* (1987) and ending with the latest, *God Help the Child* (2015), the peculiarities of the narrative structure—its gaps, discontinuities, and surprises—bring a reader to question his or her own fixed beliefs about love. How do Morrison's narrative techniques invite readers into an ethical dialogue with the text such that they are provoked to reexamine fixed convictions? I use the term "ethical" in a specific sense in this study to evoke the narrative techniques through which these later texts implicate the reader, often by drawing out a reader's preconceptions about love, race, and gender—and then inducing the reader to rethink and reevaluate those ideas. Whereas Morrison's earlier novels (*The Bluest Eye*, *Sula*, *Song of Solomon*, and *Tar Baby*) are also didactic, as Morrison herself has said of them (Koenen 74), they educate a reader in straightforward ways, through plot and character—and, at important junctures, through explicit declarations on race or love made by a narrative voice difficult to distinguish from the author's. The later novels call forth the reader's own concepts through an active interplay with a text that withholds judgment until the reader's customary values are engaged—and then calls them into question. This complex, subtle, and flexible technique is Toni Morrison's variation on the tradition of call-and-response central to African American art forms.

Methodology:
Psychoanalysis, Rhetorical Narrative Theory,
and Close Reading

I use psychoanalysis to think about narrative form. That approach differs from the more usual literary critical mode of deploying psychoanalytic theory to explain the psychic processes of individual characters. I bring psychoanalytic categories to bear on Morrison's narrative strategies in order to show how the later novels work on readers.

Sometimes Freud and his contemporary interpreters Jacques Lacan and Jean Laplanche present a crucial subjective process in the form of an anecdote or parable.[1] Aligning such a psychoanalytic narrative with the structure of a Morrison text can illuminate its narrative structure and how it affects a reader.

Lacan's and Laplanche's extensions of psychoanalytic concepts into the realms of language, temporality, and desire are particularly useful to my understanding of how the novels' formal properties work on readers. For example, I use Lacan's parable of the *Fort! Da!* to illuminate, in *Beloved*, Sethe's troubled relationship with language as well as the troubled narrative discourse that reflects it. Laplanche's notion of the enigmatic parental message helps explain the peculiarities of Florens's relation to language both as character and as narrator of *A Mercy*. Reconceptualizing Freud's notion of *Nachträglichkeit* (afterwardsness), Laplanche tells the story of "Emma" to illustrate the deferred time of trauma, and his paradigm enables me to think through the consequences of the deferred disclosures in *Love*.

Indeed, several of Morrison's novels have a belated, or deferred (*nachträglich*), structure, meaning that a crucial event is dislodged from its place in the chronological order of events and disclosed late in the novel. Laplanche's schema of *Nachträglichkeit*—which is very much indebted to Freud's *Project*—enables me to speculate on the necessarily complex responses of readers to the deferred disclosures in *Beloved, Love,* and *A Mercy*. Laplanche understands the shape of trauma as a temporal displacement: an initial scene, when the child is young, consists of an adult invasion of the child's space, usually a sexual invasion; a second scene, after the child has gone through puberty, triggers the now-adolescent child's memory of the event through some trivial similarity to the original incident. She or he realizes now, for the first time, that the initial incident was sexual and feels the horror and excitation proper to a trauma—emotions appropriate to the earlier scene but out of place now in the present. The trauma itself cannot be tied to a specific moment, but rather the knowledge and affect generated by the trauma relay back and forth between the two scenes in a temporal loop.[2] I argue that in processing the delayed disclosures of *Beloved, Love,* and *A Mercy*, a reader experiences a similarly complex back-and-forth movement between past and present text, between the two scenes of her reading. Thus in *Love*, for instance, it is only at the end that we discover that Heed and Christine, whom we have known as crabbed and mean-spirited elderly women, loved each other as eleven-year-old children. It is not just that the deferred revelation of childhood love causes the reader to reconfigure the whole text she has read (as any surprise ending is likely to do), but rather that meaning ricochets from past text to present text and back again. And, as in the psychoanalytic pattern of *Nachträglichkeit*, affect too moves from present text to past text and back again: we feel a new pity for the barren lives of the two women we have been witnessing through the body of the novel as we realize the early tragedy of their separation; and that accrued sense of wasted lives makes the present rediscovery of love seem all the more tragic (for Heed is now on the verge of death).

Such chronologically dislocated revelations in Morrison's oeuvre have ethical effects on readers, calling into the light and into question the assumptions that have been governing the reader's processing of events up to the textual moment of disclosure (such as the assumption that a man must be the center of any love story). Narrative structure by itself thus provokes a reassessment of readers' values and beliefs—about love, about gender, about race.

Rhetorical narrative theory is also useful to my analysis of Morrison's complex narrative strategies: this school of thought emphasizes the intersection between the aesthetic and the ethical and considers the intricacies of communication among author, implied author, narrator, implied reader, and flesh-and-blood reader. To a rhetorical narrative theorist, as James Phelan and Peter Rabinowitz explain, a narrative is not so much an object to be interpreted as an act of communication between author and reader (3). The emphasis on communication implies that both sides are important, the reader an active participant along with the author.[3]

Thus the rhetorical approach has some affinities with the call-and-response patterns of African American oral art forms—which, Morrison insists, form "the culture out of which I write" ("Rootedness" 342). Elsewhere, Morrison enumerates the "principles of Black Art" that she strives to incorporate in her writing: "If my work is faithfully to reflect the aesthetic tradition of Afro-American culture, it must make conscious use of the characteristics of its art forms and translate them into print: antiphony, the group nature of art, its functionality, its improvisational nature, its relationship to audience performance" ("Memory" 388–89). Morrison is listing characteristics of African American oral traditions, originating in work songs, spirituals, black church practices, and storytelling. As Maggie Sale explains, "Function, improvisation, and audience performance can all be thought of as part of the group or communal nature of art. . . . Call-and-response patterns provide a basic model that depends and thrives upon audience performance and improvisation, which work together to ensure that the art will be meaningful or functional to the community" (Sale 41). In the essay "Rootedness," Morrison further aligns her style with African American traditional practices that build meaning collectively: she "calls" on her reader to supply the meaning that the gaps and obscurities of her prose leave expressly for his or her imaginings to fill—"in the same way that a Black preacher requires his congregation to speak, to join him in the sermon, to . . . accede or to change and to modify—to expand on the sermon that is being delivered" (341). To be sure, Morrison invents her own idiosyncratic version of call-and-response in what I have been calling the texts' ethical dialogues with the reader. The reader is invited to fill in the many ellipses in the text with her preconceptions about race or love or gender—with "her own politics," as Morrison says in the essay "Home" (7)—and is thus brought to confront her own implication in or co-optation by systems of oppression. Involving the reader as co-creator of a text is an integral part of the later novels' strategies for critiquing systems of oppression.[4]

I also trace the effects of the novels' open endings: by avoiding closure, by ending on a note of ambiguity, the later novels—especially *Beloved, Jazz,* and *Paradise*—continue the "call" of the text on the reader, inviting her to keep on reinventing the story even after she has closed the book. "Morrison's point in creating [these] endings . . . is to keep meaning in motion, to keep the story going on and on in the reader's mind and heart" (Cutter 61). In interviews, Morrison makes clear that her open endings are grounded in the same African American oral tradition: "You don't end a story in the oral tradition—you can have the little message at the end, your little moral, but the ambiguity is deliberate because it doesn't end, it's an ongoing thing and the reader or the listener is *in* it" (Christina Davis 419; emphasis in the original).

Rhetorical narrative theory, with its emphasis on the intricacies of communication among author, implied author, narrator, and reader, is particularly helpful in thinking about Morrison's complex use of narrators. For example, in *A Mercy,* Florens is a first-person narrator telling her story to her narratee, the blacksmith who is her lover, for her own purposes—to explain her violent attack on him, perhaps. Morrison is using both Florens's story and the idiosyncrasies of her telling for Morrison's own purposes (see Phelan and Rabinowitz 3). Morrison's choice to make the character Florens a narrator enables us to see the damage done to her by the separation from her mother in the very forms of her language—its broken sentences and fragmented syntax.

Narrative theory thus combines with psychoanalysis and traditions of call-and-response to provide the theoretical background for my analysis of Morrison's narrative forms and their effects on readers. Most important to a description of my method, however, is that I work from the inside out—from a close reading of particular passages and their linguistic anomalies to an overview of the narrative structure to a judgment about the implied rhetorical effects on a reader.

Among the many books written on Morrison's novels, Evelyn Schreiber's *Race, Trauma, and Home in the Novels of Toni Morrison* resembles the present study in its consistent use of a psychoanalytic frame to analyze Morrison's work. In recognition of the many-leveled complexity of trauma and its effects, Schreiber expertly integrates perspectives on trauma drawn from contemporary trauma theories, Lacanian accounts of subjectivity, neurobiological work on trauma and the brain, attachment theory, and historical accounts of cultural trauma. Schreiber uses psychoanalytic theory to focus on individual characters, especially on the intergenerational transmission of traumas from slavery through all the generations of Morrison's characters. By contrast, my book uses structural models of subjectivity, language, and desire drawn from Freud's, Lacan's, and Laplanche's work to think about Morrison's narrative forms and how they affect readers.

Philip Page's *Dangerous Freedom* most closely aligns with my focus on the formal aspects of Morrison's novels. (His book ends with a chapter on *Jazz*, while the present study covers not only *Beloved* and *Jazz* but the succeeding five novels as well.) Arguing that a postmodern orientation is necessary for understanding Morrison's methods, Page foregrounds her use of postmodern techniques such as nonlinear sequence, circular narrative structure, multiple narrators, and lack of closure.[5]

Situating Morrison's texts within a contemporary context of postmodern narrative innovation is useful. But a broad contextualization of her experiments with style and form ought to include, as well, her early intimacy with modernist texts, especially those of William Faulkner and Virginia Woolf, on whom Morrison wrote her master's thesis at Cornell. Faulkner and Woolf broke with tradition to present the self as multifaceted and the narrative as many-voiced. And Woolf's discovery, while she was writing *Mrs. Dalloway*, of what she called her "tunneling process," a method of interrupting a character's consciousness of the present with scenes from his or her past (*A Writer's Diary* 61),[6] may well have contributed to Morrison's experiments with retrospective narration. Woolf's complication of a character's consciousness through the interpolation of a moment from the past—as on *Mrs. Dalloway's* opening page—becomes in Morrison's *Beloved* the involuntary, unwanted intrusion of traumatic memory on Sethe's awareness, as in the following passage: "suddenly there was Sweet Home rolling, rolling, rolling out before her eyes" (7)—"not 'she remembered,' but 'there it was,'" as Naomi Morgenstern observes ("Mother's Milk" 111). Or it becomes, in *Love*, Heed's momentary glimpse of a repressed lost love, "something just out of reach, like a shell snatched away by a wave" (*Love* 27)—a memory so evanescent it hardly breaks the surface of consciousness.

As Gurleen Grewal reminds us, "In [Morrison's] writing the confluence of two streams of narrative tradition is made visible and audible: one the oral tradition of storytelling passed down over generations in her own family and community, custodians of a history far removed from the world of the bourgeois novel, whose narrative tradition is the other Morrison appropriates. . . . Morrison studied the stylists of modernist memory Virginia Woolf and William Faulkner" (Grewal 1). She took the lessons of high modernism home, as Grewal says, to blend with her own African American literary traditions of storytelling and call-and-response.

Style, Early and Late

To provide a context for my claim that *Beloved* represents a radical shift to more experimental narrative forms, I review here the early novels' more conventional narrative discourse. I then turn to a review of the early novels' depictions of love in order to give perspective to the increased complexity and novelty of love in the later novels, beginning with *Beloved*.

There is by no means a consensus among Morrison scholars that *Beloved* is the pivotal novel in the arc of her career. Among those who have written on a sequence of Morrison novels and thus have an interest in the periodization of her works, Philip Page and Malin Pereira select *Tar Baby* as "pivotal" (Page 108), and Valerie Smith sees *Song of Solomon* as the "pivotal text" because of "its expansion of [Morrison's] artistic vision and range" (42).

I would argue that the language of *Song of Solomon* remains, like that of *The Bluest Eye, Sula,* and *Tar Baby*, largely mimetic realist discourse. This is not meant to disparage, or dismiss, the structural innovations of the earlier novels—in *The Bluest Eye*, for example, the structural dialogue between the epigraphs taken from the Dick-and-Jane reading primer that idealize white family norms and the text of Pecola's wretched childhood; or the alternation between mythic and realist presentations of diaspora in *Tar Baby* (see Goyal). But the prose of the four early novels remains realist—a discourse recognizable and familiar to the reader, offering little resistance to comprehension. *Beloved* marks a turning point in that its elliptical, ambiguous language is not readily masterable but "calls" on the reader to do the hard work of interpretation, to become an active partner in creating meaning.

A quick look at the prose that greets Milkman's discovery of the vernacular form of oral transmission—the song the children of Shalimar are singing—will illustrate what I mean by the mimetic realist language of Morrison's early novels and thus provide a contrast to the revolution in narrative style that I claim for *Beloved*. Toward the end of Milkman's journey south in quest of his roots, he hears the children in Shalimar singing a song as part of their game. It dawns on Milkman as he listens that what he hears is the story of his own ancestors, Solomon and Ryna and their twenty-one children. When he tries to write down the words, he realizes he has no pen—so "he would just have to listen and memorize it. . . . And Milkman memorized all of what they sang" (303).

For a young man indoctrinated by his father with the values of Western capitalism, the song functions as a tie to African American oral and musical traditions that "lead back through time and relate individuals to their collectivity and history" (Brenkman 68). Through careful listening and memorizing, Milkman rejoins the oral tradition of his ancestors; having memorized the song, he is positioned to retell it and pass it on. The call of the oral tradition is there, and Milkman hears it. But where is his response? And where, indeed, is the response of the text's language to the call? The passage that describes Milkman's response is representative of *Song of Solomon*'s textual discourse:

> He was grinning. His eyes were shining. He was as eager and happy as he had ever been in his life. (304)

In *Song of Solomon*, the children's song, encapsulating two African American oral and vernacular forms—storytelling and the blues (Mobley 60)—challenges the written forms of white Western literary traditions. Yet the prose that describes Milkman's response to his sudden access to a whole new linguistic and cultural tradition—his own—continues in the Western mimetic mode, pretending to a transparent transmission of Milkman's feelings. The flat realist idiom does not match up to the revolutionary potential of Milkman's experience, nor to his excitement about it.

Jazz, the novel that followed and carried forward *Beloved*'s breakthrough into a new narrative idiom, also revolves around a musical theme (jazz), and again the music represents an African American cultural form. But consider the contrast with *Song of Solomon*'s discourse: "Here comes the new. Look out. There goes the sad stuff. The bad stuff. The things-nobody-could-help stuff" (*Jazz* 7). Here the language itself is animated by the rhythms, repetitions, and variations of jazz. The dancing rhythms of the language convey the excitement of the city's denizens as they respond to jazz and to the new liberating culture of the urban North that the music represents.

The passage from *Song of Solomon* is representative of the early novels' mimetic prose. Realist discourse, because over time it has become the language of narrative normativity, appears to render reality—and to render it comprehensible and therefore manageable, as Peter Brooks says (*Realist* 2–3). "Already naturalized by its audience" (Weinstein 72), mimetic language does not pose a challenge to the reader but rather delivers the promise of mastery over an easily graspable reality. The transparent prose makes for smooth and stumble-free reading, for it does not disrupt a reader's conventional understandings nor exercise his or her ingenuity nor demand that he or she think in new ways—as the language of the later novels almost always does.

By way of contrast with the passage from *Song of Solomon*, here are the famous opening words of *Beloved:*

124 was spiteful. Full of a baby's venom. (1)

We are no longer within the familiar and easily masterable narrative world of realist prose. Here a number functions as the subject of a sentence and we enter a narrative world where that same number (124) is a subject complete with strong emotions, agency, and the capacity to effect change in its world. We are given fair warning that the relationship between the reader and the text will not be an easy one, that it will "require the audience to stretch, even struggle, to keep up with the narrator and the implied author," as James Phelan says of *Beloved*'s opening ("The Beginning" 202). If we are to make sense of this kind of language, we will have to supply meaning ourselves. Morrison herself has said that the opening of *Beloved* is meant to disorient the reader, as the slaves thrown onto slave ships were disoriented, cast into an oceanic space with no markers of place, time, or direction ("Unspeakable Things" 32). What makes a reader's hard work seem worthwhile, I think, is that the language which baffles the desire for meaning also, as Morrison indicates here, expresses something fundamentally meaningful about the characters' experience.

Beloved as Turning Point

Why did this move toward more expressive language and experimental form occur at the moment of composing *Beloved*? Usually one can only speculate on what goes into a novel's creation, but in the case of *Beloved*, Morrison herself provides a generous window onto her writing process.

Well, this book was difficult for me because I had done different things with other books, and posed certain technical obstacles for myself in order to stay interested in the writing. . . . And from one book to the next I learned a lot about how to do certain things.

For *Beloved* though, there was almost nothing that I knew that I seemed sure of, nothing I could really use. All of my books have been different for me, but *Beloved* was like I'd never written a book before. It was brand new. . . . I thought, more than I've thought about any book, "I cannot do this." I thought that a lot. And I stopped for long, long, long periods of time and said, "I know I've never read a book like this because who can write it?" But then I decided that was a very selfish way to think. After all, these people had lived that life. This book was only a tiny little part of what some of that life had been. ("A Bench by the Road" 49)

Morrison draws a firm line between the early novels and *Beloved*—and the distinction pivots on literary technique. The skills learned from writing the earlier novels proved useless: "There was nothing I could really use."

Why? In a 1986 talk at Yale University attended and described by Adrienne Davis, Morrison specified that the sticking point in her creative process was language.

[Morrison] talked about the paucity of language to describe the horror of American slavery. What language can we use to represent human bondage, to describe the conversion of humans into property, to capture the experience of being possessed or, even more grimly perhaps, of *possessing* another? (Adrienne Davis 103–4)

Morrison's thoughts are of course filtered through Davis's words, but despite this mediation we can see that Morrison was finding the resources of the language she had inherited from both white American and African American literary traditions unequal to the task of "captur[ing] the experience of being possessed." As she says in the *World* interview quoted above, "*Beloved* was like I'd never written a book before. It was brand new."

It was the subject matter of slavery that demanded new forms of language and narration commensurate with the traumatized lives "these people had lived." To express the troubled inner lives of ex-slaves penetrated to the bone by slavery, Morrison troubles the narrative discourse, disrupting grammar and syntax. (Of course, large stretches of *Beloved* deploy realist modes of language, else the story could not be told.) And Morrison's ambition for *Beloved* was large: she aimed to represent the collective sufferings of slaves over the generations. So she invented the figure of Beloved, who encompasses several generations of daughters cut off from their mothers by the Middle Passage and slavery. How inadequate the methods of psychological realism would be, as Philip Weinstein remarks, to the task of representing such a collective figure—one who "shadowily figures forth the tragedy of a race" (Weinstein 73).

"What I wanted [the reader] to experience . . . was what it *felt* like [to be a slave]," Morrison says ("Toni Morrison: The Art" 77). In order to convey the disorientation of the Africans captured and thrown onto the slave ships in the Middle Passage, and of the slaves moved around by the vagaries of the slave market, Morrison had to invent a language that would disorient the reader in turn. And the discontinuous narration, full of jumps into different time periods, had to be invented to make a reader feel something akin to the dislocations of temporality endemic to those marked by trauma. Through both temporal and spatial distortions, a reader is brought to feel unsettled, displaced from the familiar terrain of conventional narrative continuity, in a readerly imitation of the disorientation the slaves "*felt.*"

Lapses in chronological order and narrative discontinuities continue, in the texts that follow *Beloved*, to reflect the multiple dislocations of African American history. As Houston Baker has said, "PLACE as an Afro-American portion of the world begins in a European DISPLACEMENT of bodies for commercial purposes" (108). And the significance of "place" continues with African Americans' quest for a livable place to be, through an American geography that excludes them. The later novels follow this path of successive upheavals. As the Middle Passage, with its massive collective rupture of the captive Africans' connection to their families, their homeland, and their culture, is at the traumatic heart of *Beloved,* so in the novel *Home* Frank's journey across a hostile America in search of a "home" reflects African Americans' quest for a place in a land that excludes them. Necessarily, then, each of my readings of the later novels pays attention to the historical context. And some chapters include a supplement on history that but extends Morrison's intention to show how history shapes each individual's story.

The Later Novels' Experiments with Narrators

So far, I have mapped the progression of Morrison's narrative techniques to foreground the radical shift in form that took place in the writing of *Beloved*. Extending the line of development past *Beloved*, we can perceive a secondary shift in Morrison's narrative structures after *Paradise*, with the publication of the three consecutive novels *Love, A Mercy*, and *Home*.

In *Beloved, Jazz*, and *Paradise,* Morrison draws the reader into "co-creating" the text not only through ambiguous discourse, such as the opening words of *Beloved* quoted above, but also by conundrums that are solved only late in the novel, or not at all. Thus the pivotal question, "Who killed the baby ghost?" teases the reader through the first half of *Beloved*. And readers are baffled by *Jazz*'s narrator—where is she positioned, within the fictional world or outside it? Does she speak narrative truth or is she confused? The reader is called upon to exercise her ingenuity, and the burden of making meaning shifts from author to reader.

With *Paradise*, the delicate balance between withholding information and keeping readers involved falters, and with it Morrison's call-and-response relation with the reader falters, too. In *Paradise*, enigmas proliferate at such a rate that they outrun readers' signifying capacities and patience, evoking exasperated responses like that of Scott Turow: "I have had a violent reaction against a couple of Toni Morrison's novels, which I deemed deliberately opaque" ("By the Book," *New York Times Book Review*, October 10, 2013). The ethical dialogue between reader and text characteristic of Morrison's later novels is impeded. For if a reader cannot discern the call within the dense obscurity of a text, she or he cannot frame an appropriate response.

Perhaps because Morrison recognized that the method of baffling the reader in order to call her to the task of providing meaning had reached its limit in *Paradise*, she turned in the trio of novels written after *Paradise* (*Love*, *A Mercy*, *Home*) to a different model of call-and-response. These three novels are structured by the artful use of two narrators: a character narrator and a third-person, apparently omniscient narrator. The question of reliability or unreliability shifts back and forth between them, so that the reader is (ideally) made to think and judge for herself. In *Love*, the third-person narrator, whom by convention we credit with the objectivity of omniscience, turns out to be biased toward patriarchal values. If we take his narrative at face value, we are made to reflect, by the turnabout in the final pages, on our unexamined tendencies to accept a man-centered, male-dominant vision of things. *Home* stages a battle between narrators, in which a character narrator accuses the omniscient third-person narrator (the "writer," implicitly Morrison herself) of not knowing anything about love, or about him. That charge has the potential to make a reader question not only his or her own convictions about love but also his or her faith in lessons learned about love from earlier Morrison novels. Maybe, a reader might think, the models of love set forth in earlier Morrison narratives should be interrogated now that they have become "master narratives" of love in the culture, with hegemonic power to compel belief. (See Stephen Best for evidence that Morrison's *Beloved* has indeed become a master narrative; he argues forcefully, as I describe in the conclusion to this study, that *Beloved* has set the tone and the agenda for an entire generation of scholars of slavery.) While each of these three novels deploys its dueling voices toward a different end, Morrison uses the narrators to play upon readers' conventional belief systems, puzzling and provoking readers toward an examination of their entrenched convictions about gender, race, and love.

Love in the Early Novels

Turning from form to content, I offer here an overview of love in Morrison's early novels, with the aim of situating within the arc of her career the later novels' more radical experiments with varieties of love.

Love comes in a different and surprising shape in each of Morrison's novels, both early and late. And each character's way of loving is embedded in a historical context. Not only the character's personal past, but also the collective past of African Americans, shapes, or more likely warps, a character's form of loving. Already in her first novel, *The Bluest Eye*, Morrison distinguishes different modes of loving: "Love is never any better than the lover. Wicked people love wickedly, violent people love violently, weak people love weakly, stupid people love stupidly" (206). Writing against the prevalent cultural assumption that loving is by definition a good thing, Morrison de-idealizes love. The statement on love quoted above follows the sentence, "Cholly loved Pecola." Since Cholly's repeated incestuous rapes of his daughter have destroyed her sanity, it may surprise a reader that Cholly's form of attention receives the accolade of "love." In Morrison's storyworlds—quite provocatively—even incest and rape are not to be judged out of hand but understood in the context of all the character's life events and historical circumstances. Thus, in this first novel, the U.S. social context of white supremacy, denigration of black masculinity, and mockery of black sexuality have shaped Cholly's chaotic and destructive form of loving.

The next three novels—*Sula, Song of Solomon,* and *Tar Baby*—are consistent in providing one overriding message on love: possessiveness destroys love. This is true of Hagar's obsessive "anaconda love" for Milkman in *Song of Solomon*. And the intense reciprocal passion between Son and Jadine in *Tar Baby* is strangled when each turns to controlling the other, trying to mold the beloved into the shape of the lover's ideal. In *Sula*, Ajax and Sula are lovers who enjoy each other freely and creatively. The relationship thrives, until one day Sula has a new feeling: "possession" (131). She anticipates Ajax's visit by tying a green ribbon into her hair and cleaning the house. Noting the green ribbon and the spotless bathroom, Ajax detects "the scent of the nest," and he is out of there—for good (133). One small step over the line from love to possessive love—all Sula did, after all, was put on a green ribbon—and Sula is punished by losing the one man who could interest and please her. Likewise, when Nel, assuming that marriage gives her exclusive rights to her husband Jude's body, rages at her best friend Sula for having sex with Jude, she is excessively punished for her possessiveness. It is not just that she loses both Jude and Sula, but that without Sula, who had been the source of Nel's vitality, Nel lives out a barren and colorless existence.

Thus love in Morrison's early novels is quite demanding, harshly punishing the slightest taint of possessiveness. Yet it is also clear that the isolated self cannot make it, that to be a self at all one needs to be in relationship. Sula strives to be the consummate self-created individualist: she says, "I don't want to make somebody else. I want to make myself " (*Sula* 92). And Sula does not survive. Halfway through the novel, she dies, leaving us to miss her presence through the remainder of the novel named for her. It is as if Sula is able to be physically as well as emotionally healthy only when she is developing and growing through her deep relationship with her friend Nel. Solitary, she cannot even sustain a life. In the early novels, then, Morrison's idea of love is rigorous: one needs to be in relationship with an other; but the narrative severely punishes the slightest all-too-human slippage from love into possessive love.

Looking back on the four early novels from the vantage point of the fifth novel, *Beloved*, we can discern one possible reason for Morrison's abhorrence of possessiveness in love. When in *Beloved* Sethe says to her daughters "You are mine" and each responds "You are mine," they are expressing love, to be sure. But the novel's context of slavery reminds us that "You are mine" is also what the slaveholders said—and in the latter case the violence immanent in any claim to possess a human being is manifest. The profession of love, "You are mine," reminds us that property relations can creep into family relations supposedly outside the realm of buying and selling, with violence as a result (see Christopher Peterson).

The one entirely positive vision of love in the early novels is in *Song of Solomon*. Guitar, a friend of the protagonist Milkman, is talking to Hagar after Milkman has broken off his relationship with her.

> You think he belongs to you because you want to belong to him. Hagar, don't. It's a bad word, "belong." Especially when you put it with somebody you love. Love shouldn't be like that. Did you ever see the way the clouds love a mountain? They circle all around it; sometimes you can't even see the mountain for the clouds. . . . [But they] never cover the head. His head pokes through, because the clouds let him; they don't wrap him up. They

let him keep his head up high, free, with nothing to hide him or bind him. Hear me, Hagar? (306)

Although I have seen no such conjecture in the scholarship on *Song of Solomon*, I believe that Morrison is drawing her inspiration for this model of love from Zen Buddhist philosophy, namely from *Zen Mind, Beginner's Mind*, by Shunryu Suzuki:

> The blue mountain is the father of the white cloud. The white cloud is the son of the blue mountain. All day long they depend on each other, without being dependent on each other. The white cloud is always the white cloud. The blue mountain is always the blue mountain. . . . There may be many things like the white cloud and the blue mountain: man and woman, teacher and disciple. . . . They are quite independent, but yet dependent. (Suzuki 13–14)

The Suzuki parable clarifies the terms of Guitar's speech. The cloud hovers close to the mountain, but it does not impinge on the mountain's space, leaving it free to be what it is. Likewise, the mountain does not interfere with the cloud's autonomy. Each demands nothing of the other, yet each depends on the other being there.

Guitar's model of nonpossessive love is inspiring, but it remains in the abstract form of a lecture; there is no relationship in *Song of Solomon* that puts it into practice. The ideal of nonpossessive, nonintrusive love hovers over the early novels, but it never takes concrete shape as a relationship between two people. It is known only through its negation: novel after novel portrays characters who wreck their relationships through possessiveness.

As in the case of *The Bluest Eye*'s concluding aphorism on love, Guitar's lesson on love is delivered as a lecture, a lecture that appears to come straight from implied author to reader—although Guitar acts as its mouthpiece. Morrison's novels are meant to teach: she says so quite explicitly in interviews: "My mode of writing is sublimely didactic. . . . At the end of every book there is epiphany, discovery, somebody has learned something that they never would have otherwise" (Koenen 74). But there is a clear distinction between the pedagogical strategies of the early novels and those of the later novels. The early novels educate the reader directly, informing him or her about systems of oppression—especially the evils of racism and internalized racism—through plot and character as well as through an occasional direct commentary from the implied author. For example, in scene after scene of *The Bluest Eye*, Pecola is battered by racist acts. And the concluding wisdom on love in *The Bluest Eye* quoted above abandons the character narrator Claudia's voice to pronounce what seems to be authorial opinion: "Love is never any better than the lover. Wicked people love wickedly, violent people love violently, weak people love weakly, stupid people love stupidly" (206). The reader is given a lesson for sure—about racism, then about love—but the lesson calls for no response. A reader need take no responsibility for the wisdom, nor need she contribute her own ideas on the subject, for the hortatory text is complete in itself. The later novels' methods engage the reader in a dialogue between his ethical convictions and the structures of the text that call them into question. The subtle literary techniques Morrison employs to draw out and expose the reader's values and beliefs and then provoke a reevaluation of them is a central topic of the chapters that follow.

Love and Narrative Form in the Later Novels:
The Sequence of Chapters

My chapters follow the chronology of Morrison's later novels, showing how in each novel (with the exception of *Paradise*) Morrison reconceptualizes love and how narrative form bends to accommodate and reflect the idiosyncrasies of love or to challenge a reader's preconceptions about race, gender, and love.

Chapter 1. In *Beloved*, the protagonist Sethe's response to the many traumas of slavery is to enact a belated version of the nursing connection between herself and her now-grown daughters. The narrative structure is similarly belated (*nachträglich*), as Sethe's infanticide, a causal event that happened long before the fictional present, is revealed only after the novel has passed its midpoint. The narrative form of deferred disclosure causes a reader to rethink, and perhaps revise, a range of assumptions about maternal love. *Beloved* thus inaugurates a series of novels that cause the reader to do considerably more work than Morrison's previous novels required—the work of becoming a partner in an ethical exchange with the text that requires her both to contribute her own meanings to the text and to reassess her own convictions.

Chapter 2. Love and narrative technique are perhaps most integrated in *Jazz*. The leap in technical proficiency that Morrison achieved in *Beloved* somehow freed Morrison to play with, and mock, a range of narrative conventions and a range of conventional understandings of love. The changes that Morrison rings on the persona of the narrator constitute perhaps the most comic and elaborate play with narrative form in her works. *Jazz* plays with many different formulations of love, some in the white Western tradition of the love-death plot, some suggested by the improvisational style of jazz and other African American forms of art; the novel creates a narrative form to express each version of love.

Chapter 3. The exception to the later novels' preoccupation with love is *Paradise*. In *Paradise,* there are brief love stories—Connie's love for Mother and then Connie's love for Deacon. But these loves are both conventionally structured and peripheral to the main interest of the story. Gender politics is foregrounded in place of love, as if to suggest that where relations of dominance and submission are of primary importance, love gets squeezed out. Displacement—both geographic and psychic—is the force that moves both plot and character. Narrative form echoes the thematics of displacement, sometimes by transporting the reader into an unknown fictive world lacking all signposts of time, place, and character, sometimes by baffling, through an overabundance of enigma and paradox, a reader's search for meaning.

Chapter 4. *Love* is structured by a surprise ending that pushes us to revise our previous assumptions about what love is. The retrospective shift in our understanding—it is not, after all, Bill Cosey's wandering desire that the title *Love* refers to, but the deep friendship between two eleven-year-old girls—can cause a reader to question the lens of preconceptions about love through which she has been reading the novel.

Chapter 5. The absence of mother-love governs the story of the slave daughter Florens in *A Mercy*. That absence is doubled on the formal level by messages that are sent but cannot be received—crucially, messages of love. The story narrated by Florens is itself a message that cannot be received or read by its designated recipient, the blacksmith who is her lover. The last pages of the novel contain the mother's address to Florens, which explains that giving Florens away to the slaveholder Jacob was an act of maternal protection in a world where there was no protection. This message, which the mother urgently addresses to Florens and Florens urgently needs to hear, can never reach its destination. Because of the conditions of slavery, the separation between slave daughter and slave mother, tied to plantations in different states, is absolute and irremediable. Jean Laplanche's theory of the enigmatic signifier enables a reading of *A Mercy* that highlights the interconnection of narrative form (the mangled language of Florens as narrator) with political reality—specifically, the damage done a child's psyche by the forced separations of slavery.

Chapter 6. *Home*, whose limpid prose appears at first to constitute a reversion to the realist discourse of Morrison's early novels, is actually artfully crafted to reflect, through its structure, layers of repression both personal and national as well as the return of the repressed as the uncanny. Images of body parts dot the narrative, referencing while simultaneously hiding the body part that the protagonist Frank is invested in forgetting: a severed hand holding an orange. Love disturbs Frank's repression and brings up the image of the murdered girl that he has been avoiding. It is the difference of the beloved other (Frank's sister Cee) and the discomfort occasioned by her different desire that precipitate Frank's likewise discomfiting confrontation with the uncanny memory of the girl he killed. The novel endorses this model of love as difference, challenge, and discomfort for its potential to trigger deep psychic change.

Chapter 7. A tone of urgency permeates Morrison's latest novel, *God Help the Child*. The overriding idea of the novel is that people should not cling to past trauma but work through it quickly and get on with the business of loving—because, as the wise woman Queen says, love is so difficult, and lovers so selfish, that loving requires all one's emotional energies. The (rejected) temptation to stay mired in early trauma is expressed in the form of Bride's surreal devolution into the body of a little girl (parallel to the "poor little black girl" of Morrison's earlier fiction) and in Booker's phantasmatic preservation of his dead brother as an incorporated part of his own body. The forms of the novel reflect the urgency of the text's overriding message. The novel is brief, and each of the first several narratives is brief, opening up the trauma that governs the focalizing character's life and then moving on to the next character, as if reflecting the theme that people should move on to new loves. The language is spare and direct (except for the language of Booker's meditations, wherein metaphor and poetic prose reflect the complexity of the character).

Any attempt to chart a traditional arc of career through the course of the later novels runs into the fact that Morrison "breaks [her] mould" with each novel, in Virginia Woolf's phrase (*A Writer's Diary* 202, 220), inventing a new narrative form to express the new complexities of her subject.

CHAPTER 1

Maternal Language and
Maternal History in *Beloved*

Beloved (1987) represents a radical shift in Toni Morrison's literary techniques.[1] Abandoning the largely chronological ordering and realist discourse of her early novels, Morrison introduces disruptions of syntax and grammar that reflect the troubled psychic worlds of the ex-slaves who are her characters.[2] For example, the narrative discourse mirrors Sethe's idiosyncratic view of herself as a maternal body inseparable from her children through linguistic innovations like literalization and the erasure of the separation between subject positions. And Morrison deploys a temporally convoluted narrative structure that reflects Sethe's disrupted temporality. The narrative structure has ethical effects as well. We do not know until we have read more than half the novel that it was Sethe who killed her baby; so we are likely to view the murder within the context of her life experience. The structure of deferred disclosure thus discourages a rush to judgment and trains a reader to make contextual judgments. *Beloved* launches a series of late novels that, through subtle structural means, provoke an ethical dialogue between text and reader.

This chapter focuses on Sethe's mother-love. Sethe rescued her four children from slavery some eighteen years before the novel opens; she then killed one of them in order to prevent her being returned to slavery. In the present day, the baby's ghost returns to Sethe in the figure of Beloved, and mother and daughter (along with Sethe's second daughter, Denver) withdraw from the world into a maternal fusion that imitates the closeness of a nursing connection between mother and infant. The scholarship on Sethe's maternal love includes many astute interpretations of her overclose connection to her children (see footnote 10). I extend both psychoanalytic and historical approaches to Sethe's mothering. On the one hand, I use a Lacanian framework to connect Sethe's troubled relation to language to her stubborn maternal resistance to the principles of separation and substitution necessary to symbolization. On the other hand, I supply an extratextual historical background for Sethe's relation to her own slave mother drawn from the archival work of contemporary historians of slavery.

Sethe's mother-love is complicated, unfolding layer by layer as a reader makes her way through the novel. Even at the surface, on a superficial reading, a reader can plainly see that Sethe is overattached to her children and unwilling to acknowledge even a minimal separation from them. But it is only as the narrative progresses that a reader gradually uncovers the multiple dimensions of slavery that have shaped Sethe's attitudes toward her children. At first unable to put into words (or even conscious thought) her feelings of being neglected by her own mother, Sethe begins to recover, under Beloved's relentless questioning, the memory of her mother's scar and the memory of her mother's hat. It is up to the reader to pull together these material signs of a maternal body and so compose the story of Sethe's childhood, a story of maternal distance. Behind the sparse textual references to Sethe's mother is the historical context of slave mothering. As contemporary scholars of slavery tell us, motherhood under slavery was structured by a conflict between the master's demands for slave mothers' labor and the slave child's needs for nurturing. The historical supplement on the actual practices of slave mothers in this chapter extends Morrison's own oblique references to the history of slave mothering. And it fills in gaps in Sethe's story, giving shape to her childhood experience of maternal absence. It is in part as compensation for that maternal absence that Sethe insists on an uninterrupted closeness to her own children.

And then, beyond the practices of slave mothering lies the still more obscured history of the Middle Passage. The scholarship on *Beloved* has fully acknowledged the relation of Beloved to the Middle Passage, but it has not yet sufficiently explored the link between Sethe and the Middle Passage—yet it is important. The Middle Passage has cut Sethe off from the African maternal culture that would have guided her in mothering her own children. One factor contributing to the lacks and excesses of Sethe's mothering, then, is the linguistic and cultural rupture with Sethe's African maternal legacy.

Ambiguity has ethical force in *Beloved*. In the effort to pull together the scattered clues to Sethe's deprived childhood, to the conditions of slave mothering, and to the cultural losses attendant on the Middle Passage, and to think through how all these dimensions of slavery have led to Sethe's excessive mothering, a reader must perforce invest her own powers of synthesis and imaginative reconstruction. That personal investment in a constantly widening understanding of the deprivations and impossible choices of mothering under slavery has the potential to broaden the reader's range of empathy to encompass even an understanding of Sethe's choice to kill her child, rather than let her be taken back into slavery.[3]

Similarly, the narrative structure itself offers a lesson in ethics. The narrative disclosure that Sethe killed her baby daughter reaches us belatedly, so that we have to read the infanticide within the context of the absolute maternal devotion that Sethe has displayed throughout the first half of the novel. That structure of deferred disclosure prevents a too quick knee-jerk reaction to the fact of infanticide and trains us to defer judgment on a person's action till we know all the details of his or her life situation. What George Eliot tries to do through direct moral exhortation—telling her reader that "moral judgments must remain false and hollow unless they are checked and enlightened by a perpetual reference to the special circumstances that mark the individual lot" (*Mill* 521)—Morrison accomplishes through the workings of narrative structure on the reader.[4]

The Maternal Body in Language:
A Discourse of Presence

Sethe pictures her relation to her children as a nursing connection; long after they are weaned, her bond with them remains so strong that she continues to think of it as a nursing relationship. I want to pursue the effects of Sethe's perseveration in the role of maternal body on language—both on Sethe's own capacity for language and on the language of the text.

The description of Sethe's escape from slavery highlights several competing dimensions of her maternal subjectivity. First, her commitment to her children undeniably gives her courage. In presenting Sethe's journey from slavery in Kentucky to the free state of Ohio as a maternal quest, Morrison is elaborating the figure of the heroic slave mother that in many female slave narratives replaces the figure of the heroic male fugitive.[5] Harriet Jacobs's *Incidents in the Life of a Slave Girl*, for instance, turns the rhetoric of heroic resolve common to male slave narratives into a discourse of maternal courage: "I was resolved that I would foil my master and save my children, or I would perish in the attempt"; "Every trial I endured, every sacrifice I made for [the children's] sakes, drew them closer to my heart, and gave me fresh courage" (84, 89–90). If Jacobs (and other female slave narrators, like Lucy

Delaney) appropriates the conventions of male heroism for the celebration of motherhood, Morrison in turn reconstructs the acts of maternal heroism as the reproductive feats of the female body. Jacobs writes, "It was more for my helpless children than for myself that I longed for freedom" (89); Sethe turns Jacobs's spiritual commitment to her children into a physical connection to the nursing baby she has sent on ahead: "I had to get my milk to my baby girl" (16). Sethe, like Jacobs, experiences the wish to give up the fight for survival and die, but while Jacobs says she was "willing to bear on" "for the children's sakes" (127), the reason that Sethe gives for enduring is the presence of the baby in her womb: "[I]t didn't seem such a bad idea [to die], . . . but the thought of herself stretched out dead while the little antelope lived on . . . in her lifeless body grieved her so" that she persevered (31).

As Sethe reports the triumphant close of her maternal quest, "I was big, Paul D, and deep and wide and when I stretched out my arms all my children could get in between. I was *that* wide" (162; italics in original). Later, her claim is that "she had milk enough for all" (162, 100). Thus the "nurturing power of the slave mother" that Henry Louis Gates finds in female slave narratives (Gates, "Introduction" xxxi) becomes literal in Morrison's account: Sethe's monumental body and abundant milk give and sustain life. But despite its mythic dimensions, the maternal body appears to lack a subjective center. During the journey, Sethe experiences her own existence only in relation to her children's survival. As she feels she is dying from her wounds, she is "concerned" not for herself but "for the life of her children's mother"; she thinks, "I believe this baby's ma'am is gonna die" and pictures herself as "a crawling graveyard for a six-month baby's last hours" (30, 31, 34). Identifying the self only as the ground of her children's being—the container of her unborn baby and the carrier of her nursling's milk—Sethe loses sight of her own sufferings and her own need for survival. While celebrating the determination and courage that Sethe draws from her attachment to her children, Morrison's narrative also dramatizes the problematic aspects of Sethe's maternal self-definition, which is so embedded in her children that it allows her to kill the nursing baby that she continues, long after its birth, to perceive as "part of her" (163).

Sethe's sense of continuity with her children also makes it difficult for her to take the position of narrating subject and tell her story.[6] Her troubled relation to language can be read as a carryover from a nursing mother's attitude toward separation. When she engineered her family's escape from slavery, Sethe had to send her baby ahead of her to Ohio: "I told the women in the wagon . . . to put sugar water in cloth to suck from so when I got there in a few days [the baby] wouldn't have forgot me. The milk would be there and I would be there with it" (16). Sethe would not compromise with absence, overlooking the potentially life-threatening lack of food for her baby "for a few days" to insist on presence: her milk would be "there," and the mother would be "there with it." For Sethe, the standpoint of nursing mother precludes separation and the substitutions that any separation would require.

Sethe's embrace of a relational system of presence and connection, her reluctance to accept the principle of substitution, extends to her refusal to invest in words and helps explain the link between her failure to tell the story of her baby girl's death and that baby's embodiment in Beloved. Lacan's account of a child's entry into language opposes bodily connection and verbal exchange in a way that clarifies Sethe's attitude. To move into a position in language and the social order according to Lacan, an infant must sacrifice its imaginary sense of wholeness and continuity with the mother's body. (Sethe is of course in the mother's position rather than the child's, but her physical connection with her nursing baby resembles the infant's initial radical dependency on the mother's body.) In "The Function and Field of Speech and Language in Psychoanalysis," Lacan borrows from Freud a mother-child anecdote that crystallizes the either-or choice between maternal bodily presence and abstract signifier. Freud's grandson Ernst becomes a speaking subject in the same moment that he acknowledges his mother's absence. Ernst's one game, Freud says, is to throw a spool attached to a thread far away from him and bring it back to the accompaniment of sounds ("ooo! aaa!"); Freud interprets these sounds as the signifiers "*Fort*! *Da*!" ("Gone! There!"). Initially using the spool as a symbol for the mother, Ernst then moves to a higher level of symbolization when he substitutes signifiers—"*Fort*" and "*Da*"—for bodies. He thus assumes a symbolic mastery over what he cannot control in reality—his mother's absence and return (Freud, *Beyond* 8–10). Lacan adds that the child "thereby raises his desire to a second power," investing desire in language ("Function" 103). By acknowledging that he must put a signifier there where his mother's body used to be, the child both recognizes absence and accepts loss. The word "manifests itself first of all as the murder of the thing" ("Function" 104)—or, in John Muller's gloss, "the word destroys the immediacy of objects and gives us distance from them" (29).

It is this distance, this loss, that Sethe rejects. Just as she declined any mediation between her body and her nursing baby, she now refuses to replace that baby with a signifier and tell the story of the baby's death. (Sethe is never able to tell the story of the infanticide, leaving it to be narrated first through the demeaning focalization of the slave-owner and then through the more

sympathetic focalization of Stamp Paid.)⁷ Sethe refuses to accept the irre-
vocability of absence by putting the child's death into words. Her denial of
loss is fundamentally antimetaphorical—that is, the refusal to displace libido
onto words is a refusal to let one thing stand for another and so impedes the
whole project of speech. Sethe remains without a narrative but with the baby
ghost—there, embodied, a concrete presence.

Textual practice seconds Sethe's emphasis on presence by rejecting metaphorical substitutions for the maternal body. In the opening scene Paul D,
an ex-slave from the same plantation as Sethe, finds her after a separation of
eighteen years. After Sethe has told Paul D about her escape from slavery, on
a quest to get her milk to the baby in Ohio, he cups her breasts from behind
in a display of tenderness: "What she knew was that the responsibility for her
breasts, at last, was in somebody else's hands" (18). The reader does a double
take: the phrase "in somebody else's hands" usually functions as a metaphor
meaning "someone else's responsibility": here the hands are literally there,
and what rests in them is not an abstract concept but flesh. The same slippage
occurs in the next sentence, as Sethe imagines being "relieved of the weight of
her breasts" (18). Because *weight* appears within the usually figurative phrase
"relieved of the weight of," readers assume that it is a metaphor for care or
responsibility, but the modifying phrase "of her breasts" gives *weight* back its
literal meaning. When the maternal body becomes the locus of discourse, the
metaphorical becomes the actual, a move that reinforces Sethe's definition of
motherhood as an embodied responsibility: there are no substitutes, metaphorical or otherwise, for her breasts.

In the same passage, Paul D "reads" the story of slavery engraved on
Sethe's back by a final savage beating. Because the scar tissue is without sensation—"her back skin had been dead for years"—Sethe's back is, in a sense,
not her own; it has been appropriated and reified as a tablet on which the
slave masters have inscribed their code, marking Sethe as slave. Sethe cannot
substitute for this discourse of violence her own version of the event, in spite
of Paul D's repeated insistence that she tell him about it (17). Instead, Sethe
repeats Amy Denver's description of the wound left by the whipping as "a
whole tree on my back . . . that's what she said it looked like. A chokecherry
tree" (15–16). Unable to seize the word and thus become master of her own
experience, Sethe remains "a body whose flesh . . . bears . . . the marks of a
cultural text" that inscribes her as slave (Spillers 67).

Sethe does not begin to take a position as speaking subject in the symbolic
order until the end of the narrative, where with the encouragement of Paul D

she starts to accept the loss of the baby: "She left me," she says of her baby Beloved, finally acknowledging absence and substituting a word ("she") for the baby's body.

The Nursing Connection and Language

The action of *Beloved* gets underway when Paul D, an ex-slave from the same plantation as Sethe, finds his way to her Ohio home. After Paul D, Sethe, and Denver live together for a time, a figure named Beloved joins them; Denver, and the reader too, pick up on clues that the nineteen-year-old woman embodies the ghost of the baby Sethe killed. For some time the adults try to maintain the configuration of a nuclear family—mother, father, two daughters—but finally Beloved's jealous desire to be the sole object of Sethe's love and attention drives Paul D from the household. Soon after, Sethe begins to understand that Beloved is the dead baby "come back to [her] in the flesh" (200), and mother and daughters retreat to a state of undifferentiated maternal union.[8]

"Nobody will ever get my milk no more except my children," Sethe declares as she closes the door on the outside world. The imagery of mother's milk governs this section of part 2, as mother and daughters live out a nursing fantasy writ large. Sethe does not actually breastfeed Beloved, but, ecstatic that her murdered baby girl has returned to her in the figure of Beloved, she overfeeds Beloved while "Beloved lapp[ed] devotion like cream" (243). Beloved becomes "bigger, plumper by the day" while Sethe's "flesh" grows "thin as china silk" (239), in a grotesque exaggeration of the mother feeding the baby with her own substance.

Nursing imagery represents the willed regression of the three participants to a maternal merger in which identities are inseparable and indistinguishable.[9] Sethe is primed for such a regression by her resistance to the separations and substitutions required by the symbolic order and her stubborn adherence to the dead nursling. Beloved embodies a nursing child cut off from life before the entry into the symbolic and is consequently unable to distinguish self from other: "I am not separate from her there is no place where I stop" (210). Even Denver voices the amorphous boundaries between herself and her mother and sister: "I swallowed [my sister's] blood right along with my mother's milk" (205). For Denver, too, at least for the moment, bodily fluids overrun the boundaries between self and other, conflating identities.

How can there be a dialogue among those who resist the ground rules of language, who refuse separation and the substitution of words for bodies? Yet a dialogue among the three provides the centerpiece of part 2. Since many critics have written, and written well, on the mother-daughter relationships in *Beloved* and the language that characterizes them,[10] I will confine my remarks on the mother-daughter dialogue to the subject of the present inquiry: the linguistic innovations that attempt to capture feeling states not usually entered into literary discourse and the range of possible reader responses to them.

The speakers in the three-way dialogue in *Beloved* reject the separation of persons required by the subject positions of language, where "I" is separate from "you" and "she": they insist on the interpenetration of identities. Consequently, their language erases linguistic demarcations between self and other:

I have your milk. . . .
I brought your milk (216).

It is impossible to determine who is speaking: Does the "I" in "I have your milk" refer to Sethe, who might be saying that she "has" (is carrying) Beloved's milk, or to Beloved, who could just as well be the "I" who speaks, saying that she "has" Sethe's milk inside her? The dedifferentiation of possessive pronouns dramatizes the impossibility of separating what belongs to the one body from what belongs to the other when the two are joined by the milk that flows between them.

Dialogue among speaking subjects (ideally) moves toward the discovery of something new; the exchange of ideas gives each speaker the opportunity to move toward the different position of the other, enabling change. The dialogue among Sethe, Beloved, and Denver, however, exists not to stimulate a movement of ideas but to reassure the speakers of stability.

I will never leave you again
Don't ever leave me again
You will never leave me again. (216)

The technique of repetition, each speaker using the same phrase as the other, annuls difference and reassures the speakers that they are the same. Instead of moving the speakers toward the emergence of something new, dialogue reiterates stasis.

The phrase "You are mine," which recurs in the dialogue, bends toward fusion: "You" stands only for a moment as a separate pronoun before sliding into "mine," which signifies an extension of me—as my hand is mine, my ear is mine. The dialogue ends in repetition:

You are mine
You are mine
You are mine. (217)

It is impossible to distinguish who is speaking: there is no difference. Language operates more like interreflecting mirrors than like dialogue: it exists to assure the speakers that they are there and they are the same. There is no absence and there is no difference.

How does a reader respond to this lack of definition and boundary? Different readers will of course experience it differently, but it seems safe to say that the lack of punctuation and the lack of distinction between speakers baffle a reader's ordinary reading habits. Do we experience the inability to distinguish one thing from another as a block on literacy, a block on reading comprehension? That would perhaps locate the reader temporarily in a position at the threshold of language, before the stage of the *Fort*! *Da*! and thus in a position analogous to Sethe's. Our conventional means of connecting with a text through identification is also blocked: there is no single protagonist to identify with when all three are merged and indistinguishable; that might confound a reader accustomed to immersing herself in identification with a human figure. Another reader might associate the dominance of rhythm and repetition with the cadences of a lullaby, appropriate to the rhythmic interrelationship of mother and baby that the text is imitating. Or perhaps a different reader might respond to Morrison's lyricism, to the aesthetic pleasure of a language that relinquishes conventional sense in favor of rhythm and repetition; thus a reader attuned to African American religious discourse could find the repetitions familiar, for Morrison is doubtless drawing, as she often does, on the call-and-response rhythms of African American church services.

We have a record of at least two readers' reactions to this passage, in the articles of Cheryl Hall and Lars Eckstein. Both respond to structures familiar from African American music, most notably jazz. Hall sees in the mother-daughter dialogue the "theme-and-variation" structure of jazz, wherein the musicians improvise a series of solos, each "riffing" on the previous soloist's theme (90). In a jazz session as in the mother-daughter dialogue, the solo performances "culminate in an ensemble performance" during which "the musicians mesh their solo efforts" (94). Placing the aural and improvisational structure of the mother-daughter dialogue within traditions of jazz and the blues, Eckstein explains that Morrison is adapting the musical forms that throughout African American history have enabled black people to voice traumatic experiences otherwise silenced. As in the chant of mother and daughters, the antiphonic structure enables the soloist to "probe into the abysses of painful personal experience," to tell of trauma, because of the security in knowing that the community of other speakers/musicians is there to bring him or her back to "rejoin the collective chorus." Morrison's deployment of antiphonic structures is "so firmly rooted in the African Diaspora that they establish a secure foundation for the exploration of suffering and pain" (279).

Cheryl Hall adds that, as in a jazz performance the audience's responses "influence the performance," so the prior experience that each reader brings to the text will shape the reading of the women's dialogue (95). I think that most readers would agree, though, that the mirroring repetitions of mother's and daughters' phrases is effective in creating an aesthetic space where a different kind of speech takes place, a flouting of difference in favor of the expression of fused and loving sameness.

Beloved does not, however, idealize the devotional intensity of the mother-daughter bond. The grotesque dimensions of the belated nursing connection constitute Morrison's critique of a more general tendency of mothers to "suppress or displace [the self] and put it someplace else—in the children," as she says in a *New York Times* interview upon the publication of *Beloved* (Rothstein). Like other concepts in *Beloved*, the danger of losing the self in the beloved is presented in embodied terms, as a literally consuming overproximity: as Sethe gives and gives, denying herself food to sustain Beloved's life (or rather Beloved's insatiable appetite), Beloved grows "basket-fat" and Sethe wastes away to nothing.

"You are mine" is of course what the slaveholders also said, and as in the larger social order, the inability to see the other as a separate subject and the appropriation of the other to one's own desires lead to violence. Christopher Peterson challenges the dichotomy of slavery and family often assumed by scholars of slavery. Quoting Hortense Spillers, he asks, "While it may be true that kinship has the potential to undermine the institution of slavery insofar as the recognition of slave kinship would affirm that one's offspring 'belong to a mother and father' and not to the slave master, what are we to make of this displacement of one set of property relations for another?" "What does the intersection of property and kinship suggest about the violence of kinship?" (Peterson 549, quoting Spillers 75; Peterson 550). Through the relationship between Sethe and Beloved, Morrison implies that violence is immanent in overclose family relations, too—wherever love slides over the line into possessive love.[11] Originally, the disregard of subjective limits—"You are

mine"—allowed Sethe to exercise life-or-death rights over the child she con-
ceived as "part of her" (163). Now a selfless maternal devotion on one side and
an infantile disregard for boundaries on the other enable Beloved to eat up
Sethe's life.

The Skewed Temporality of Trauma, Personal and Global

The maternal idyll that Sethe lives out with her lost baby Beloved occupies
the dislocated time of trauma. As Freud and Laplanche tell us, trauma typ-
ically has deferred effects: overwhelmed in the moment by the enormity of
what is happening, one responds with appropriate emotion only months or
years later, when a seemingly innocuous event recalls the traumatic occur-
rence.[12] In *Beloved*, the traumatic event that skews time is the infanticide.
When the dead baby reappears in the body of Beloved, Sethe gets to live out
a nursing fantasy that would have been appropriate in the moment before
the trauma of the baby's death, when the two girls were babies and Sethe was
breastfeeding both of them. The baby died too early, and the nursing comes
too late. We are in the deferred time of Freud's *Nachträglichkeit*.

But the warped temporality that haunts 124 Bluestone Road pertains to
more than the personal tragedy of Beloved's death. Before Beloved takes the
shape of a young girl, her amorphous spirit fills all the spaces of the house,
so that "there was no room for any other thing or body" (39). It is not only
Sethe's dead baby but also the past of slavery that haunts the house. The larger
collective dimension that always doubles the personal in *Beloved* is suggested
by Baby Suggs's response to the idea that the family could move to escape the
haunting: "Not a house in the country ain't packed to its rafters with some
dead Negro's grief" (5). From this perspective, Sethe's house is nothing special: temporal displacement affects the home of every African American, fill-
ing it with the grief of the past. Slavery, and in particular the Middle Passage,
is at the heart of the novel.

The Middle Passage is evoked by the monologue where Beloved speaks
not in the voice of Sethe's lost daughter but in the voice of a child on a slave
ship during the Middle Passage. This passage is particularly disorienting for
a reader. First, we have to give up the assumption that a single person, with
a singular name, embodies one identity. We have to accept the fact that Beloved, like the haunted house, encompasses more than the singular tragedy of
a particular family. In addition to being Sethe's dead daughter, she is, as the

generic name "Beloved" suggests, the embodiment of all the loved ones lost through slavery, and, more particularly, of all the daughters separated from their mothers by the Middle Passage and by slavery. "Morrison's triumph is to make her credible in all of these arenas, despite their mutual incompatibility," as Philip Weinstein observes (73).[13]

The voice of the child on the slave ship reaches across the centuries to speak to us through Beloved:

> I am always crouching   the man on my face is dead. . . . in the be-
> ginning the women are away from the men and the men are away from the
> women   storms rock us and mix the men into the women and the
> women into the men   that is when I begin to be on the back of
> the man   for a long time I see only his neck and his wide shoulders
> above me . . . he locks his eyes and dies on my face. (210–12)

Since Morrison does not identify these scattered perceptions as observations of life on a slave ship or tell how Beloved came to be there or give any coordinates of time and place, readers are baffled: we have no idea where we are. We experience a readerly version of the disorientation of the African captives who were thrown into the slave ships without explanation and suspended without boundaries in time and space. Contemporary historian of slavery Stephanie Smallwood suggests some of the reasons for the captives' disorientation. Because "Africans relied on the regular cycle of climatic events to locate themselves in time and space," and because the vast space of the Atlantic was outside their experience and knowledge, they experienced an "unparalleled displacement" on the ships. "Always in motion but seeming to never reach any destination, the ship plowed forward in time without ever getting anywhere, always seeming to be in the same place as the day before. It was as if time were standing still" (Smallwood 131, 132, 135).

The style of Beloved's monologue from the slave ship creates a linguistic facsimile of this temporal and spatial disorientation. The fragmented syntax and absence of punctuation robs the reader of known demarcations. And, perhaps in imitation of the captives' loss of a temporal order, the Middle Passage child speaks always in the present tense. In the above passage, events that occurred in the past are given the same temporal status as events in the present: "In the beginning the women are apart from the men"; each subsequent event is assigned the same tense: "storms rock us and mix the men into the women"; "he locks his eyes and dies on my face." There is no sense of a cause-and-effect sequence, no sense of a progression through time. The consistent present tense conflates past with present.

The second paragraph of the monologue explicitly describes this timeless present:

> All of it is now   it is always now   there will never be a time when
> I am not crouching and watching others who are crouching too   I
> am always crouching   The man on my face is dead . . . the men with-
> out skin bring us their morning water to drink   we have none. (210)

In conjunction with the Middle Passage, the dislocation of time—"it is now, it is always now"—means something different, something more complex, than does the sticking of time to the domestic spaces of 124 Bluestone Road. Early in the novel, Sethe says of the past: "Places, places are still there. If a house burns down, it's gone, but the place—the picture of it—stays. . . . the picture of what I did, or knew, or saw is still out there. Right in the place where it happened" (36). This description of a time that clings to place, because it is so baldly stated, seems to express only the individual pathology of Sethe. But when this spatialized time is attached to the Middle Passage, "the four-hundred-year holocaust that wrenched tens of millions of Africans from their Mother, their biological mothers as well as their Motherland, in a disorganized and unimaginably monstrous fashion" (Christian 364), when it is the numberless captive Africans who are "always crouching" in the slave ships, the past dislocated into the present expresses the ongoing trauma of a whole people. And the temporal dislocation means that this monumental tragedy is still here, in the timeless present of trauma, haunting the nation that made it happen.

By dint of hard work, a reader can pull together the scattered fragments of the Middle Passage child's monologue to compose a narrative. One hesitates to put into narrative order the language of the capture in Africa when the text's verbal disorder conveys so well the chaos of the scene of capture. Nonetheless, here is one interpretation. In Africa, the small child was with her mother, who was picking flowers when the slave-traders came. The smoke from the slave-traders' guns obscured the child's view of her mother, and when she saw her again, on the deck of a slave ship, she wore an iron ring (a shackle) around her neck. The small child notes the impossibly cramped conditions of the slave ship, registers the lack of food and water, and mentions the "men without skin" who violate her body, all in a matter-of-fact tone. Affect is reserved for her mother; her intense longing for her mother is expressed as a desire to see her mother smile at her, from across the crowd of piled-up bodies that separates them. Instead of smiling at her baby, the mother takes advantage of an unguarded moment when the sailors are throwing dead bodies in the water to jump into the water herself and drown. The child reacts emotionally not to the abduction into slavery nor to the horrendous overcrowding of the slave ship but to the mother's abandonment. "I drop the food and break into pieces she took my face away there is no one to want me to say me my name" (212). Without the mother, there is no face to reflect her existence ("she took my face away") or to recognize her (to call her by name) so she "break[s] into pieces," losing her self along with the mother. The loss of the mother leaves the child destitute of a self.

Morrison chooses to condense the multiple traumas of the Middle Passage and slavery in the figure of the child who, forcibly separated from her mother, also loses her self. Beloved and Florens, the slave daughter in Morrison's later novel *A Mercy*, each understands the determining event of her life to be the mother's abandonment. Thus Beloved reads Sethe's murder as abandonment: she relentlessly accuses Sethe of leaving her, never of killing her. Florens in *A Mercy* cannot make an adult life for herself, only repeating and reenacting the trauma of her mother's (seeming) rejection. Again and again, the child cannot understand the mother's gesture as an attempt at maternal care in a perverse system, but can read it only as desertion. The Middle Passage child's experience of maternal abandonment represents the Ur-trauma of slavery, to be repeated down the generations. "If there is an 'original' trauma in *Beloved* . . . it is the trauma of Middle Passage, which establishes a pattern of separation and desertion" (Morgenstern, "Mother's Milk" 113).

Sethe and Her Mother:
Perspectives from the Historical Archive
on Slave Mothering

There is yet another abandoned child in *Beloved*: Sethe herself. The terrible truth that Sethe cannot articulate, even to herself, is that her mother left her small child Sethe behind when she tried to escape from the plantation on which she was enslaved (203). More important even than this final maternal betrayal is the everyday abandonment the child Sethe experienced as a result of the conditions of slavery. The passages in which Sethe recalls her childhood on a rice plantation are few, but they are richly suggestive of the material conditions that deprived Sethe of her mother's presence. These passages also suggest that Morrison is at pains to ground Sethe's difficulties with mothering in a historical context, an aim that I extend here by citing the historical archive on actual slave mothers' practices. If psychoanalysis is the appropriate discipline to address Sethe's troubled relation to language and the traumatic belatedness of the nursing relation in *Beloved*, historical research can provide a material grounding for the disruption of maternal care, including the disruption of nursing cycles, in Sethe's own childhood.

In connecting the maternal neglect suffered by the child Sethe with the intensity of Sethe's determination to breastfeed her own babies, I am only following Morrison's lead; for Sethe's reverie, as she begins the retreat into the closed mother-daughter circle, associates the two.

> I'll tend her [Beloved] as no mother ever tended a child, a daughter. Nobody will ever get my milk no more except my own children. I never had to give it to nobody else . . . Nan had to nurse whitebabies and me too because Ma'am was in the rice. The little whitebabies got it first and I got what was left. Or none. There was no nursing milk to call my own. I know what it is to be without the milk that belongs to you; to have to fight and holler for it, and to have so little left . . . Beloved . . . She my daughter. The one I managed to have milk for and to get it to her even after they stole it. (200)

Sethe's reminiscences of having no mother's milk to call her own interweave with her insistence that she overcame all obstacles to get her milk to Beloved—and always will. It seems that Sethe's overmothering is her way of compensating for her own lack of a mother: her children will never have to suffer from maternal absence. "The milk would be there, and I would be there with it" (16).

Feminist archivists' work on slave mothering indicates that mother's milk was indeed a scarce resource on southern plantations. Nursing mothers were caught between two systems that made conflicting demands on their time: the systems of slave labor and infant nurturance. "Few could satisfy the demands made by the master on the one hand and their children on the other" (White 126). It is not difficult to guess whose demands went unanswered. Sethe's longing for a mother who was never there because her time was swallowed up by labor in the fields suggests that slave children experienced maternal abandonment not just in the traumatic moment of separation reflected in *Beloved* and *A Mercy*, but as a fact of daily life.

To a degree, histories of the period tell us, the desires of slaveholder and slave parent coincided: for different reasons both wanted to maintain the life and health of slave babies—the mother for the sake of her baby and the slaveholder for the sake of his future labor force. And the only safe way to nourish babies, in a time before pasteurization was invented, was to give them breast milk. So slaveholders had to make some time available for mothers to breastfeed. On smaller plantations mothers often took babies to the field, leaving them at the end of the row; when their babies cried, they could stop work and nurse them. This arrangement, one might imagine, could provide the opportunity for a system to develop from within the mother-child relationship, a temporal system that synchronized the child's hunger with the mother's need to work. But increasingly, as larger plantations supplanted smaller holdings, mothers were sent to the fields alone and a schedule of nursing was imposed from above. As former slave H. C. Bruce told a WPA interviewer, "During the crop season . . . sucklings were allowed to come to [their infants] three times a day between sun rise and sun set, for the purpose of nursing their babes, who were left in the care of an old woman" (qtd. in Schwartz, "At Noon" 246). The *Southern Cultivator* published "Rules of the Plantation" recommending that nursing mothers "visit their children morning, noon and evening until they are eight months old, and twice a day from thence until they are twelve months old." The *Farmer and Planter* specified that mothers should feed their infants only in the morning, before leaving for the field, and upon returning in the evening (Schwartz, "At Noon" 245, 249). Rather than a schedule emerging from within the mother-child dyad as an accommodation to the baby's needs, the schedule is motivated by the slavemasters' interests in keeping nursing mothers working as long as possible. "Women of childbearing age were in their prime as productive laborers, and neither the biological fact of motherhood, nor the traditional gendered construction of mothering applied to them as far as slaveholders were concerned" (Shaw 245).

There are of course no records of the distress that babies suffered from their mothers' unavailability to their cries. We have only numbers—in particular, the "extraordinary rates of slave infant mortality (twice that of whites in 1850). . . . Fewer than two out of three black children survived to the age of ten in the years between 1850 and 1860" (Jones 33–34). We can imagine—although this is pure speculation—that in the intervals of the required morning and evening feedings (or, on some estates, the morning, noon, and evening feedings), babies were in considerable physical distress from hunger. When they called, no one came. In such an environment, the baby gets no response to its signals and is left with nothing. Historical analogues begin to emerge for Sethe's memory that she had "to fight and holler for" "the milk that belonged to [her]" and that she was left with nothing—with "none," "no nursing milk to call my own" (200). Feelings of infantile deprivation carry over into her adult obsession with breastfeeding her own children.

Sethe's account of being left, along with other babies and small children, with the one-armed woman Nan also jibes with historical fact. Between feedings, slave babies were left either in their family's cabin—sometimes alone, sometimes with an older sibling—or in a "nursery" with all the other babies and small children under the care of a single slave, one who could no longer be productive in the fields because of age or disability (Shaw 243). Because there were so many children left in her care and because the overseeing woman was expected to perform tasks for her owners like cooking, sewing, or spinning, "adult supervision in the nurseries tended to be minimal" (Schwartz, "At Noon" 245). "There was a great chance the children would not receive close attention; they might even unavoidably be neglected" (Shaw 243). Because "many caregivers found it impossible to keep up with the large number of rambunctious children left to their supervision, especially when they had to cook, sew, or perform other chores in addition" (Schwartz, *Born* 87), they resorted to practices such as the collective feeding of all the small children at a trough. As former Virginia slave Nannie Williams described it, "Aunt Hannah" would "po' dat trough full of milk an' drag dem chillun up to it. Chillun slop up dat milk jus' like pigs" (Schwartz, "At Noon" 250).

Morrison expresses the incommensurability of Nan's resources to the overwhelming number of tasks she was expected to perform through synecdoche: Nan has only one arm. She cannot hold even the one small child Sethe in a full embrace, let alone the horde of children left to her care.

Sethe has not talked about (or consciously remembered) her experience with her mother, until Beloved asks if Sethe's mother ever combed her hair. Sethe explains:

> I didn't see her but a few times out in the fields and once when she was working indigo. By the time I woke up in the morning, she was in line. If the moon was bright they worked by its light. Sunday she slept like a stick. . . . She didn't even sleep in the same cabin most nights I remember. Too far from the line-up, I guess. (60–61)

From early morning to late at night, the mother's time belonged to the slaveholder. Being "in the line" early took precedence over time given to the child in the morning, precedence over proximity to the child even while both were sleeping (the mother slept in a cabin nearer the line-up). In fact, Sethe saw her mother "but a few times," and that was from a distance, while she was laboring "in the fields."

Contemporary archival research supports this description of maternal time. Once an infant was past the age of breastfeeding, the work schedule allowed no time for childcare. Slave parents exercised their ingenuity to provide nurturing to their children—but it was always a "struggle to secure time for their families" (Schwartz, *Bond* 4). More often than not, "the work re-

quirements that slaveholders and overseers imposed on them and their children . . . made it impossible for mothers to carry out or even to improvise
this personal maternal work" (Shaw 245). Slave women labored "eleven to
thirteen hours" of each day, excepting Sunday, for the master; their days'
work in the fields was supplemented by spinning, weaving, and sewing tasks
in the evenings; and that was followed by sewing and washing for their own
families. Ex-slave Will Sheets says that he saw his mother only at night when
she came to the cabin after work, and "den, us chilluns was too sleepy to
talk" (qtd. in Shaw 245–46); Tom Singleton reported that the adults "were
too busy to talk in de daytime, and at night us wuz so wiped out from hard
work (us) just went to sleep early and never talked" (Shaw 246).

Sethe recalls having only one sustained conversation with her mother:

> One thing she did do. She picked me up and carried me behind the smoke-
> house. . . . she opened up her dress front and lifted her breast and pointed
> under it. Right on her rib was a circle and a cross burnt right in the skin.
> She said, "This is your ma'am. This," and she pointed. "I am the only one
> got this mark now. The rest dead. If something happens to me and you
> can't tell me by my face, you can know me by this mark." . . . "Yes, Ma'am,"
> I said. "But how will you know me? How will you know me? Mark me,
> too," I said. (61)

It is a hallmark of Morrison's style that a single bodily irregularity or mutilation condenses a large amount of information about the character—as we
have seen in the case of Nan's amputated arm. The mother's mark is an exemplary instance of this economy. First, the "mark" is not just a mark, but
a brand, and the mother's breast shelters it: the breast intended for the nurturance of her child is dedicated instead to the signifier that marks her as the
master's property. Compressed in this alignment of breast and brand is the
information about slave mothering that I have been charting all along by jux-
taposing the text with the historical record: in the contest between the child's
need for nurturance and the master's need for field labor, the master wins.

The mother's urgent demand that Sethe learn to know her scar is surely
surprising and perhaps baffling to a contemporary reader used to the dailiness of mother-child interactions. The bizarre message unsettles our ordinary
understandings of what it means to be a mother—a deliberate unsettling, I
would say, meant to provoke readers to think through the effects of slavery
on mother and child. For why would it be so urgently important that Sethe
recognize her mother by her scar? The reason must be that Sethe has spent so
little time with her mother that she would not recognize her face should she

be killed. Recognition between mother and baby in a non-enslaved situation usually occurs first through face-to-face interaction: in games of facial mirroring or, later, peek-a-boo, the baby crows with the pleasure of recognizing the other and of having the other recognize it. In the slavery situation, the press of labor leaves so little time for the child to interact with the mother's face that she would not recognize it; and the desperate mother must improvise a sign for her child to "know her by."

Striving for mutuality, Sethe asks her mother to mark her too. Here the child initiates mother-daughter mirroring and joins in the mother's system of signs. But instead of reciprocal communication she receives a slap, which at the time Sethe "did not understand." Communication fails. After her mother is hung, Sethe does indeed look for a body with her mother's mark, but by the time the lynched bodies are cut down and piled up, "nobody could tell whether she had a circle and a cross or not—and I did look" (61). Communication fails again.

The key word in Sethe's one exchange with her mother is "know." The mother wants Sethe to "know" her body through the sign, and the child Sethe anxiously repeats the query, "But how will you know me? How will you know me?" The mother intends "know" to signify "recognize," but in context, the word "know" reverberates with the sadness of the slave child who does not and cannot know her mother, but only the mark of the master's possession. As Sethe tells Beloved, "I never knew my mother . . . but I saw her a couple of times" (118).

This historical situation of deprivation for both slave mother and slave daughter is condensed in yet another material object, the mother's hat. When in the final scene Sethe approaches the position of speaking subject by beginning to articulate and thus acknowledge her losses, she lists among them her mother's hat: she thinks about how she could "tell [Paul D] that . . . her ma'am had hurt her feelings and she couldn't find her hat anywhere" (272). The reader may well wonder, Why a hat? Why not "she couldn't find her *mother* anywhere"? The answer seems to be that Sethe could discern only the hat, not the face of the mother, in the distant fields.

> Of that place where she was born (Carolina maybe? or was it Louisiana?) [Sethe] remembered only song and dance. Not even her own mother, who was pointed out to her by the eight-year-old child who watched over the young ones—pointed out . . . among many backs turned away from her, stooping in a watery field. Patiently Sethe waited for this particular back to gain the row's end and stand. What she saw was a cloth hat as opposed to a straw one, singularity enough in that world of cooing women. (30)

Her mother's distance prevents Sethe from distinguishing anything more than her hat. Subsequently, among the things that the adult Sethe "did *not* remember" is "the face of the woman in a felt hat as she rose to stretch in the field" (98; italics mine). The unspoken regret here is that Sethe can remember only the hat, not the face. After her mother's hanging, Sethe lives for a while in denial: "For a long time I didn't believe it. I looked everywhere for that hat" (201). There is no maternal presence to miss, only the hat that already signified maternal distance. The mother's death but redoubles the mother's absence.

Sethe, Language, and the Middle Passage

Sethe's difficult relation with language also has a historical as well as a psychoanalytic dimension. Again in response to Beloved's relentless questioning, Sethe suddenly calls up a remote message that links her to the Middle Passage:

> [Sethe] was remembering something she had forgotten she knew. Something . . . that had seeped into a slit in her mind. . . . Nan was the one she knew best, who was around all day, who nursed babies, cooked, had one good arm and half of another. And who used different words. Words Sethe understood then but could neither recall nor repeat now. . . . What Nan told her she had forgotten, along with the language she told it in. The same language her ma'am spoke, and which would never come back. But the message—that . . . had been there all along . . . she was picking meaning out of a code she no longer understood. . . . Nan holding her with her good arm, waving the stump of the other in the air. "Telling you. I am telling you, small girl Sethe." And she did that. She told Sethe that her mother and Nan were together from the sea. Both were taken up many times by the crew. "She threw them all away but you. . . . The others from more whites she also threw away. Without names, she threw them. You she gave the name of the black man. She put her arms around him. The others she did not put her arms around. Never. Never. Telling you, I am telling you, small girl Sethe." (62)

The scene is from the slave ships—so we are back again at the Middle Passage. And Sethe hears the story of her own conception. Sethe has retrieved from memory her own primal scene, mediated by Nan's telling. It also constitutes a "message" from the mother; but that message is ambiguous. The mother embraced Sethe's father during intercourse, and she did not throw

Sethe away. But why? Because she liked? loved? desired? the black man? Because she liked? loved? Sethe? The mother's subjectivity remains hidden, but the enigmatic message is meant to serve as Sethe's consolation: the mother valued Sethe's father, and she valued Sethe enough to keep her alive.

Even more important than the content of the message is its difficult transmission, which deftly conveys the breach with Sethe's mother tongue. Nan "used different words. Words Sethe understood then but could neither recall nor repeat now." The maternal language is forgotten, and the loss is final: it "would never come back." Yet Sethe can "pick meaning out of a code she no longer understood."

The relation to language is quite unusual: Sethe can get a sense of the message's meaning, but she lacks any sense of the words. It seems that her relation to English is just the opposite: Sethe is literate (she can read the columns dividing the animal and human characteristics ascribed to her in Schoolteacher's notebooks), but that white racist American language is inadequate to her experience. She has the words, but she cannot use them to make sense of her experience. For in the symbolic register of American slavery, Sethe is a body only—a point Morrison stresses by means of the master's discourse of scars on her back. The African language has "meaning" relevant to her life, but she cannot access the words so she cannot use the language to articulate her experience. History supplies a material ground for Sethe's troubled relation to speech.

A reader is necessarily on a quest parallel to Sethe's—a quest to bring Sethe's relationship to her mother out of a repressed traumatic past. Sethe cannot translate the words of Nan's language; just so, there are gaps in the text where one would expect to find indications about how Sethe felt about her lost mother. Instead of such explanatory passages, we get a hat—a hat that bobs up every now and then, in relation to Sethe's childhood. But a hat is just a hat. As Sethe has to give meaning to words that no longer signify, a reader has to pick out meaning from a "code" that we cannot fully understand. The meaning is there, but it is not completely translated into words. Because the references to the hat are both unexplained and scattered throughout the text, a reader has to work hard: she has to remember and bring together the dispersed mentions of the hat. And then she has to interpret: Sethe's daily suffering from maternal distance is condensed in the hat. Excelling even the modernists' artful uses of objective correlatives, the hat effectively crystallizes a whole material and affective situation: maternal deprivation.

The reader's task parallels Sethe's in yet another way. Like Sethe, a reader must not only bring the unarticulated past into the present but integrate that past into the present. We can surmise—again using all our imaginative and interpretive forces—that in place of putting the feelings of loss attached to her absent mother into words, Sethe displaces loss onto the body. She over-compensates for never having the mother's breast ("no mother's milk to call my own") by ensuring that her breast will be ever-present to her children, with "milk enough for all." Her children will never suffer from maternal dis-tance—not for a moment. "My milk would be there, and I would be there with it," she says, counterfactually, as she sends the nursing baby off without her toward Ohio. We readers are left to make the connection for ourselves between the absent mother of Sethe's childhood and her excessive claim that she can provide her children with a constant, unfailing, unchanging maternal presence. Jill Matus makes a similar connection between Sethe's longing for a mother who would be present and protective and the excesses of her own mothering, adding a further inference about the intergenerational transmis-sion of a certain kind of mothering under slavery: "Through Sethe's emerging memories of her mother, Morrison suggests a genealogy of mothering under slavery that would logically produce the excesses and extreme forms of Sethe's maternal subjectivity" (111).[14]

Sethe's recall of Nan's story suggests yet another historical cause for the excesses of Sethe's mother-love. Along with her natal language, Sethe has lost connection to her original culture. We can now perhaps better understand the significance of Sethe's complaint to Paul D that she had no older woman to advise her about baby care. As a young mother, she had tried "to recol-lect what I'd seen back where I was before Sweet Home. How the women did there. Oh they knew all about it. How to make that thing you use to hang the babies in the trees . . . was a leaf thing too they gave em to chew on" (160). But Sethe cannot retrieve from her memory the maternal knowl-edge shared among the African slaves who came over the Atlantic with her mother. Hence, she lacks crucial information: "There wasn't no [woman] to talk to . . . who'd know when it was time to chew up a little something and give it to em. Is that what make the teeth come on out, or should you wait till the teeth came and then solid food?" (160). Sethe lacks a weaning narrative. Surely that loss of maternal guidance goes some way toward explaining why Sethe is stuck at the stage of breastfeeding. And of course the lack of a wean-ing narrative stands in for the larger absence of a cultural story about how to raise children. Divided from her cultural heritage by the rupture of the Mid-dle Passage, Sethe has to rely solely on her maternal body for cues about how to mother. Sethe's mothering is consequently unbalanced, focused on giving, giving, giving of herself to her children without asking for anything in return, in a one-sided version of maternity modeled on breastfeeding. Denied training in the social, linguistic, and communicative aspects of mothering, she is unable to pass on to her children an understanding of the uses and the limits of social and linguistic communication.

The Middle Passage has made messages from the maternal generation all but unreadable. Both the mother's message about the scar and Nan's message about Sethe's conception are enigmatic, withholding meaning even as they insist on the crucial importance of their address ("Telling you. I am telling you, small girl Sethe. . . . Telling you, I am telling you, small girl Sethe" [62]). The urgency combined with the ambiguity of the messages anticipates the enigmatic messages of Florens's mother to her daughter in *A Mercy*—messages that Florens desperately needs to hear but cannot receive. Subtly but effectively, Morrison adds the dimension of cultural loss to the devastating maternal losses of slave daughters caught in the wake of the Middle Passage.

The Middle Passage and the
Narrative Ethics of *Beloved*'s Epilogue

The overall structure of *Beloved*—the framing of the narrative between epigraph and epilogue—conveys some key information about the Middle Passage. We know from Morrison's interviews that the epigraph, "Sixty Million and more," constitutes her estimate of those who, having perished on the slave ships midway between a place in African history and a place in the history of American slavery, never made it into any text. Lost still, they remain stranded in the epigraph, outside the story, outside narrative temporality. Their human features are erased beneath a number: they are quantified in death, as they had been in life by a property system that measured wealth in terms of a body count. Morrison's "and more" indicates the residue left over, left out, unaccounted for by any text—like Beloved at the end.

After the narrative closure, after the resolution in which Sethe hesitantly enters the symbolic order of language and sociality—"Me? Me?" she says, tentatively claiming the subject position in response to Paul D's encouragement—the figure of Beloved wanders lost in a two-page epilogue, closed out of the narrative intended to encompass her along with the pain of the Middle Passage she embodies. Bookending the narrative proper, her position in the epilogue is symmetrical with that of the "Sixty Million and more" of Morrison's epigraph.

By moving these two evocations of those lost on the Middle Passage to positions outside narrative enclosure, Morrison uses structure to make two points: first, that the Middle Passage has been excluded from dominant histories; second, that the Middle Passage, despite her efforts to capture it in prose, remains "unspeakable," outside narrative still. A central project of *Beloved*, to put the unspeakable experiences of the Middle Passage into language, both succeeds and fails. It succeeds insofar as, despite the near-collapse of the telling into complete disintegration, the small child's monologue from the deck of the slave ships begins the "recovery of this nearly lost body of history and of the bodies lost to this history" (Dobbs 572). But it also fails. Its failure is itself eloquent: the collective trauma of those who experienced the horrors of the Middle Passage exceeds the resources of language and therefore exceeds attempts to contain it in narrative. Yet the unnarrativized sufferings of the Middle Passage linger on as ghostly reminders of what happened. Separate from the story yet present in the text, epigraph and epilogue express both that exclusion and that lingering.

Lacan's notion of language, too, rests on the assumption that language cannot be all-encompassing: there is something left over, left out of the symbolic order, something that cannot be captured within the symbolic register's logic of limit and differentiation—the real. The real is not the same as reality, which we perceive always through the categories of the symbolic. The real exists in the outside world—and also within each of us—but because it exceeds the logical categories through which we understand things, we cannot make sense of it. The notion of the real gives us a way to grasp what Toni Morrison is up to in the enigmatic prose of the epilogue.

The epilogue emphasizes Beloved's exclusion from the symbolic order.

> Everybody knew what she was called, but nobody anywhere knew her name
> . . . they couldn't remember or repeat a single thing she said, and began to
> believe that . . . she hadn't said anything at all. (274)

Each of Beloved's identities contributes a way of understanding this exclusion from language. As the preverbal child killed by Sethe, Beloved never entered into the symbolic order of language. As the motherless child speaking from the ship in the Middle Passage, she has no name ("nobody anywhere knew her name") because those lost at sea were nameless; they were entered into the slavers' logs only as part of a group number (Spillers). In Lacan's terms, the nameless person has no existence within a social/symbolic structure of interconnected subject positions because that kinship structure is determined by the Name of the Father and the interconnections among subject positions that it establishes.

So Beloved is "disremembered and unaccounted for" (274), for no organization of the symbolic—language, history, narrative, kinship—can en-compass her in her role as the Middle Passage dead. Beloved remains in the real—"this something faced with which all words cease and all categories fail" (Lacan, *Seminar* 2:164). Eluding language with its definitions and categories of meaning, the real is indeterminate. Morrison's description of Beloved's traces precisely captures this indeterminacy. Morrison evokes something just beyond the grasp of conscious knowledge—"the rustle of a skirt" half-heard in sleep that "hushes when they wake," the photograph of a close friend or relative that suddenly "shifts," so that "something more familiar than the dear face itself moves there," footprints by the river that "disappear again, as though nobody ever walked there" (275). All these half-glimpses of the lost Beloved convey the idea of something intermittent, fragmentary, ephemeral, something that eludes the categories of symbolic knowledge but is nonethe-less there; the text insists on the persisting but ungraspable existence of that which escapes symbolization.

Enigma functions as ethical imperative here. In the passage quoted above, the past tense initially locates the disappearing appearances of Beloved in the fictional world: "Everybody knew what she was called, but nobody anywhere knew her name." Then the past tense gives way to the present:

> Disremembered and unaccounted for, she cannot be lost because no one is looking for her, and even if they were, how can they call her if they don't know her name? Although she has claim, she is not claimed. (274)

This shift to present tense, James Phelan argues, "includes [Morrison's] con-temporary audience among those who are not looking for Beloved" ("Toward a Rhetorical" 719). We readers begin to be among those who would rather not remember the experiences that Beloved embodies. Beloved "has claim": claim on whom? The lack of specificity as well as the present tense leave open the possibility that Beloved has a claim on present-day readers. A claim for what? Attention? Recognition? "But she is not claimed": in reference to read-ers, what can this mean? Have we not throughout our reading been devoting attention to Beloved's story—as well as putting considerable effort into the struggle to understand it? The open-endedness of the claim seems to imply that something more is wanted. What would it mean to claim Beloved?[15]

The vagueness demands some ethical work on the part of the reader. What is her responsibility to the experiences embodied by Beloved? Beloved's claim on us might be a demand that we claim, or own, our responsibility for the suffering the nation as a whole inflicted through the Middle Passage. If Be-loved's exile from the narrative proper to an epilogue is a symptom of the

Middle Passage's exclusion from the collective history of the United States, her "claim" would be a demand for recognition and inclusion in history, story, and memory. [16]

The epilogue steadily erodes Beloved's presence, first noting her erasure from the community's memory, then her reduction to fading and evanescent traces, and finally, in the penultimate paragraph, her disappearance: "By and by all trace is gone, and what is forgotten is not only the footprints but the water too and what is down there" (275). Here the text obliquely recapitulates what Beloved represents: "the water" of the black Atlantic and "what is down there" under the sea, the remains of African captives lost in transit to the New World, the detritus of the Middle Passage. All these, represented by the figure of Beloved, are gone—erased from history and thus from the memory of the living.

Yet after this wipeout, there is a final paragraph consisting of one word: "Beloved." Here she is still, surviving all the moves of the previous paragraphs (and of American history) to erase her and the Middle Passage she embodies. Beloved and all she represents may be eliminated from the symbolic order, but here she stands, the real that escapes symbolic enclosure, returning from the repressions of history. Isolated on the page, "Beloved" is a fragment left unfinished, to go on echoing in the reader's mind and making her claim.

CHAPTER 2

Riffing on Love and
Playing with Narration in *Jazz*

Jazz (1992) plays with many varieties of love and, in the end, invites the reader to play too—to create her own love story. Narrative form in *Jazz* mirrors and expresses each of these different kinds of loving: both the narrative structure, with its open ending, and the various inventive uses of the narrator formally reflect the text's changing ideas of love. While the narrator begins her story by voicing a traditional Western notion of love that leads in a straight line from passion to the death of the beloved, she ends by embracing the idea of love as a continuing innovation. She changes because she learns from her characters, who ignore the predetermined story line of the narrator to make up their own idiosyncratic kinds of love. The narrator ends the novel by calling on the reader to take up the story she has just finished and make up her own version. Here the call-and-response pattern of African American oral and musical traditions, which subtly undergirds the dialogues between text and reader in many of Morrison's later works, becomes visible: the reader is called to create her riff on the theme just elaborated by the narrator, to take up the story and continue it. The open ending thus carries on and enacts a central lesson on love that the novel has been teaching its reader through more conventional means: love demands imagination on the part of the lover, a constant "making and remaking" of innovative ways to express love.

The narrative begins with a model of love as traumatic loss: the experience of losing their mothers pulls both Violet and Joe ever backward, toward reenactments of their tragic losses. If we follow the progression of love through the narrative, however, we can see that as the characters change, they enter into improbable new combinations with one another and create original forms of loving.

Joining the chorus of critics who have posited various theories about the identity of the narrator, I offer a reading of the narrator as the City itself; that reading has the advantage of bringing out the humor in Morrison's treatment of the narrator. When I claim that the narrator is the City, I do not mean that her voice is the collective voice of the City's inhabitants but rather that she is the material city—the city of concrete and brick, of sidewalks and streets and tall buildings. I argue that Morrison has imagined with some consistency the way the mind of a City might operate: the narrator's epistemology is based on the geometric logic of her city plan, which lays out the streets in straight lines for the citizens to follow and sets out avenues and streets that intersect in predictable ways. The narrator is complacent about the efficacy of her street plan to guide the steps of her citizens: "If you pay attention to the street plans, all laid out," you will thrive in the city (8).

As narrator, she has equal confidence in the predictability of her characters' trajectories, which she understands to be governed by the straight lines of the traditional love plot. Limited by an epistemology based on the linearity of her streets, the narrator thinks of a love story as a straight line from cause to effect, a straight line that in her mind quickly becomes the straight line of determinism. She narrates that her characters' loving in the present is determined by their past; and, adhering to the traditional Western love plot, she foretells that their loving will end in death. The characters, meanwhile, are busy innovating original forms of love—each different and each surprising, escaping any rigorous logic of cause and effect. In the end the narrator has to admit that she has missed understanding the characters altogether because she has left out "something rogue" (228). I posit that love is the "something rogue."

Central to the thematics of love is a structural mystery of *Jazz:* halfway through the story of Joe and Violet in the Harlem of the 1920s, the narrative makes a sudden unexplained drop into the 1880s, introducing the story of new characters—Golden Gray and Wild—before returning after fifty pages to the narrative of Joe and Violet. The narrative structure thus repeats the design of *Beloved*, where the tale of the present-day characters is inexplicably interrupted by a voice from the past, as a child from some generations earlier speaks from a slave ship on the Middle Passage. In neither novel is there an explanation, through plot or exposition, of this digression. It seems that narrative structure alone is suggesting the necessity of confronting the traumatic past of African American history.

The trajectory of love in the novel is upward. It begins with the narrator foreshadowing a predetermined future for doomed lovers and ends with these same characters evolving their own forms of love, original yet sustainable.

Love Determined by the Past

The novel begins with two models of love that are decidedly pessimistic. The first is the narrator's presentation of a master narrative of Western literary tradition: passionate love leads inevitably to death. The second yet more negative model of loving is lived out by the characters Joe and Violet: love in the present can only replicate earlier loves.

The first page of the novel suggests the narrator's allegiance to the plot of Western literary convention, in which passionate love leads inexorably to death. In the story she is about to tell (and we are about to read) Joe ends by shooting his girlfriend, Dorcas. The narrator reports, "He shot her just to keep the feeling going" (3). Sick and self-defeating as such a motive may seem, the desire "to keep the feeling going" is, according to at least one cultural critic, Denis de Rougemont, the motive force in all the great romances of Western literature. De Rougemont asserts that "what [the lover] loves is love and being in love" (43): the lover is attached not to the beloved so much as to his own feelings of love. And since love can be maintained at the height of intensity only when it is unfulfilled, "what [lovers] need is not one another's presence, but one another's absence" (43). Obstacles are what keep love going. And since death is the largest obstacle of all, imposing a separation that is absolute, "it is the one most suited to intensifying passion" (45).

According to de Rougemont, the desire to maintain the intensity of passion becomes a textual desire, the motor of the great love stories, driving the plot inevitably toward the death of the beloved. From the twelfth-century romance of Tristan and Iseult to the twentieth-century novel and film *The English Patient*, passionate love ends in death.

Then, still in the opening pages, the narrator repeats the schema of love-death as she predicts that yet another murder will end a second love story. Felice, a young woman who resembles the dead Dorcas, will at the end of the novel join Violet and Joe to complete a "scandalizing threesome" like the first triangle of Dorcas, Violet, and Joe. "What turned out different was who shot whom" (6). The narrator's heavy use of foreshadowing formally expresses the determinism of a view of love whose end can be predicted with certainty. In the novel no such death follows Felice's affiliation with Violet and Joe, which is beneficial for all three. The narrator, sticking to the standard Western plot, is dead wrong.

Yet even the narrator, despite her fixation on the love-death plot, does not remain stuck. In this text that is fundamentally optimistic about the multiple possibilities of love, the narrator too can change. In the end, she stops trying to make the love story she is telling conform to the traditional Western plot and makes up a narrative form that expresses a view of love as innovative, fluid, and open-ended—like African American art forms, like jazz.

In a different way, the loves of the protagonists Joe and Violet also replicate old scripts. Violet herself voices the principle of love as regression. Remarking that Joe was a poor substitute for Violet's first love object, the photograph of Golden Gray, and that, to Joe, she herself was a substitute for a prior ideal, Violet says, "From the very beginning I was a substitute and so was he" (97). According to this view, the beloved is only a surrogate for an earlier love. In the lives of Joe and Violet, the chain of substitutions goes back to their first love objects, their absent mothers. Violet's mother, unable to sustain life for herself and her children under the duress of extreme poverty, drowned herself in a well. Joe suspects that Wild, a voiceless woman who lives in the forest, is his mother, but she is elusive and evades all his efforts to make contact. When Joe and Violet become part of the Great Migration of the 1920s, moving from Virginia to the City in the North (unnamed but clearly evoking New York City), they supposedly leave their traumatic pasts behind. But a subtext of attachment to the lost mother distorts the loving of both Joe and Violet in the present.

Wild's absent presence obsessed Joe's youth; he tried in vain to track her down in the Virginia woods, tried in vain to get some sign of acknowledgment that he is her son. He leaves the South for the northern City explicitly to escape Wild's felt absence, that "ripe silence" (30). But underneath Joe's willed action, the maternal absence continues in force, becoming "the inside nothing he traveled with" (37). Dorcas, knowing "what that inside nothing was like . . . filled it for him" (38).

The subtext of Joe's lost love surges into the text when his memory of his youthful quest for his absent mother becomes fused with his search for Dorcas, who has left him for a younger man. The identification of past and present is reproduced formally, as the narrative cross-cuts between Joe's present-day hunt for Dorcas and the fourteen-year-old Joe's hunt for Wild in Virginia. Joe's memory closes in on the crucial moment when, looking for Wild among the stone formations on a hillside, he notices a "crevice" in the rock and "went into it on his behind until a floor stopped his slide . . . [in] a stone room where somebody cooked in oil" (183). Tracing in reverse the movement of birth, Joe backs into the "crevice" in the rock and falls into the womb of Wild's cave. It makes sense that Joe should track his mother all the way back to the (metaphorical) womb, since it was in the womb that he was last in contact with her.

The section ends with Joe's question—the crucial question of his youth—as he surveys the emptiness of Wild's cave: "But where is *she*?" (184; emphasis in the original). The next section begins, "There she is" (187). But now we are in the present, and "she" refers to Dorcas, whom Joe has just located. At the culminating moment of the hunt, the pronoun "she" conflates the two figures, formally reproducing the conflation of mother and lover in Joe's mind. He shoots Dorcas, unable to tolerate a maternal abandonment that happens again.

Violet's relation to maternal loss also distorts her present loving. Violet tries to sever her attachment to her dead mother through disidentification: "Her mother. She didn't want to be like that. Oh never like that" (97). But conscious intention apparently cannot reach deeper levels of identification. At the level of the body, Violet remains connected to her mother. She thinks repeatedly and obsessively about how cramped her mother's body must be in the "narrow well" where she threw herself to die—"a place so narrow, so dark" (104, 101); it is as if Violet feels the narrowness and darkness of the well in her own body. It is the body of the dead mother that she continues to identify with, a body "twisted into water much too small" (104). The "narrow well," "suck[ing] her sleep" (102), pulls her toward a reenactment of her mother's drowning.

Violet disidentifies with her mother by refusing to become a mother herself: "The important thing, the biggest thing Violet got out of [watching her mother's dispossession and destitution] was to never never have children" (102). That conscious rejection of being a mother like her mother does not, however, destroy maternal desire, which comes back as "a panting, unmanageable craving," leaving Violet "limp in its thrall" (108). Violet begins sleeping with a doll, and then she steals a baby; the text explicitly connects the delight Violet feels in holding the baby to what she lost to the darkness of the well (22). Then Violet falls in love with Dorcas, an inappropriate love object on several counts: she is the rival who stole Violet's husband, and she is dead. Violet has "whispered conversations with the corpse" (15) and sees in her "mama's dumpling girl" (109). The text calls Violet's feelings for Dorcas "crooked" (111). And "crooked" is an appropriate label for all Violet's twisted expressions of mother-love. Love for and identification with the abandoning mother, repressed and subject to the labyrinthine distortions of unconscious identification, reemerges in grotesque forms of loving: first a doll, then a stolen baby, finally a dead girl.

In this part of the novel, love can only repeat a traumatic script, dragging the characters back to reenact the original loss of mother-love. After this negative point of departure, Joe's and Violet's loving evolves into more creative modes.

The City as Narrator

In interviews, Morrison repeatedly emphasizes the centrality of the narrator to her conception of *Jazz*. "The process of trial and error by which the narrator revealed the plot was as important and exciting to me as telling the story" (Schappel 110). I would add the claim that the play of wit around the narrator of *Jazz* and her views on love constitute perhaps the most innovative, and certainly the most elaborate, variation on narrative form in Morrison's oeuvre. I make the case here that the narrator is the City.

As *Jazz* begins, the text unsettles all the accepted categories of narration, flummoxing a reader's expectations and issuing a challenge to him or her to participate in the fun of figuring out where that narrative voice is coming from. For the first four pages (3–6) the narrator speaks from a position embedded in the fictional world. Referring to the neighbors' guesses about the identity of the woman who tried to slash Dorcas's corpse, she says: "Like me, they knew who she was, who she had to be, because they knew that her husband, Joe Trace, was the one who shot the girl" (4). She does not speak from a privileged position of knowing all—she is not omniscient—but can only speculate on the doings of those around her: "I suspect that girl didn't need to straighten her hair" (5); "[the head singer in the band] must be his woman since why else would he let her insult his band" (5); "Whether she sent the boyfriend away or whether he quit her, I can't say" (5). What the narrator "knows" is guesswork, based like the neighbors' gossip on conjecture. Furthermore, this narrator speaks in the idiom of neighborhood gossip: "Sth, I know that woman" (3); "good luck and let me know" (5); "quiet as it's kept" (17). We recognize this kind of narrator from our prior reading as a first-person character narrator (a homodiegetic narrator) who is part of the narrated world and therefore has a necessarily partial view of it.

Then, on the fifth page, the narrator foils the convention: "When I look over strips of green grass lining the river, at church steeples, and into the cream-and-copper halls of apartment buildings, I'm strong" (7). Where is this narrator positioned? She must be looking down on the city from a vantage point above it in order to see everything from the river to the church steeples reaching into the sky; yet in order to look into the halls of apartment buildings she must be stationed on the street, looking into the buildings. This panoramic view is inaccessible to a first-person character narrator, whose knowledge is by definition restricted. A third-person omniscient narrator (a heterodiegetic narrator) could of course view everything everywhere at once;

but this cannot be an omniscient narrator, for as we have seen she says "I" and locates that "I" firmly in the fictional world; she has explicitly situated her partial knowledge on a level with that of her community. Flaunting the impossibility of the narrator's perspective, the text baffles the attempt to assign her to any traditional category of narration.[1]

Previous critics have responded to the impossibility of the narrator's position by proposing various ingenious interpretations. Paula Eckard identifies the narrator as jazz: "Jazz as narrator constructs the text" (18). Eusebio Rodrigues claims that the narrative voice belongs to Thunder Perfect Mind, the speaker of the Gnostic text that figures in Morrison's epigraph to the novel ("Experiencing *Jazz*" 748–49). Caroline Brown interprets the narrator as Morrison's rendering of the "self-conscious artist" through whom "the abstract and intangible process that is creativity becomes an active manifestation of love" (634). Veronique Lesoinne sees the narrative voice as "the voice of the whole African American community" (158). Richard Hardack views the narrator as "the sweet and sharp tooth of double-consciousness . . . she hungers for and feeds off . . . the split-consciousness of her characters" (463). Martha Cutter argues that "this voice can be read as that of language itself" (70). Caroline Rody invents a new category, "the first-person omniscient anonymous," to accommodate what she calls "the ghostlike presence, the here-but-not-here . . . quality" of this "narrating phantom" (622, 624).[2]

Morrison herself has said, "The voice is the voice of a talking book" (Carabi, "Nobel Laureate" 95). But the authoritative voice of the author is no guarantee of stable meaning; the narrator's shape-shifting and contradictory self-definitions throughout the novel cannot be contained in the trope of the talking book—seductive as that concept is, especially when at the conclusion, the book (or the narrator?) addresses the reader intimately and directly. What Caroline Brown says of *Jazz* as a whole is especially true of the narrator: "it [is] impossible to accept a single rendering of either its form or content" (639). Since no one interpretation can encompass all the narrator's multiple perspectives or explain the full range of her contradictions, the question of the narrator's identity remains open, calling on each new reader to contribute her own interpretation. That invitation forms part of the novel's call on the reader to "make up," or improvise, her own riff on the materials offered by the text. I respond to the challenge by offering a reading of the narrator as the City. Identifying the City as the narrator can explain some of her blind spots and provide a way of understanding why she is almost always wrong about the direction of the lives she narrates. And it brings out the humor in *Jazz*, especially the play of wit around the pretensions to absolute knowledge of any governing authority—whether it be a narrator who pretends to omniscience or a civil authority that claims a panoptic management of its people.[3]

To make the case that the narrator is the City, I take as a first example the passage from which I quote above, the passage that first demolishes the reader's assumption that the narrator is one of the neighborhood women.

> Daylight slants like a razor cutting the buildings in half. In the top half I see looking faces and it's not easy to tell which are people, which the work of the stonemasons. Below is shadow where any blasé thing takes place. . . . A city like this one makes me dream tall and feel in on things. Hep. It's the bright steel rocking above the shade below that does it. When I look over strips of green grass lining the river, at church steeples and into the cream-and-copper halls of apartment buildings, I'm strong. Alone, yes, but top-notch and indestructible. (7)

Although the narrator's perspective would seem to be impossible, her identity as City resolves the contradiction. For it makes sense that a City would know what is taking place on her streets as well as what is going on at her outermost borders. Her view is nonetheless partial, for of the interior life of the people in the apartments she can perceive only what can be seen from the streets (she sees only "into the halls"). And she does not seem to have much interest in the human occupants of the city. The people who look out of the windows are no more arresting to her gaze than the faces carved on the buildings' façades. Observing the play of light on all the buildings simultaneously, the narrator is focused on the general, the external, and the material. This lack of interest in the people of the City could turn out to be a serious liability for a narrator whose job includes conveying to the reader the inner lives of the characters.

It would seem to defeat my hypothesis that the narrator says, "A city like this one makes me dream tall": how can the city be both the subject "me," and the object that acts upon the subject, "a city"? My defense here would be that throughout the novel Morrison baffles the easy expectations of the reader—in order, presumably, to keep the reader working on the enigma of the narrator. Indeed, the narrator herself concedes that she "mak[es] sure no one knows all there is to know about me" (8).

If we posit the city as the narrator despite the misleading grammar, we can perceive the jokes embedded in her "dreaming tall." As she says, "It's the bright steel rocking above the shade that does it"—makes her dream tall. In other words, it's her tall gleaming buildings that make her feel tall—because she *is* tall; she is the height of the buildings that constitute her. A similar literalization is in play in her claim that looking over the city makes her feel "top-notch": since she *is* her skyscrapers, she is literally at the top. And, to follow the wordplay even further, some of New York City's buildings are indeed "notched" at the top. That is, some of the Art Deco skyscrapers built in the 1920s (notably the Barclay-Vesey Building and the New Yorker Hotel) have setbacks at the top, meaning that each level is cut a bit shorter than the one below it, creating the impression of stair-steps, or notches, at the top. Thus the narrator who is the City feels "top-notch and indestructible." As in most of the City's musings from which I quote, the text invites us to enjoy the wordplay—the punning, playful "signifying" that Morrison shares with classic African American narratives.[4]

The same impossibly comprehensive perspective governs other cityscapes. The narrator describes "sweetheart weather" coming to the city:

> Sweetheart weather, the prettiest day of the year. . . . On a day so pure and steady trees preened. . . . I could see Lenox widening itself, and men coming out of their shops to look at . . . a street that spread itself wider to hold the day. Disabled veterans in half uniform and half civilian . . . went to Father Divine's wagon and after they'd eaten they rolled cigarettes and settled down on the curb. . . . And the women tip-tapping their heels on the pavement tripped sometimes on the sidewalk cracks. . . . Young men on the rooftops changed their tune; spit and fiddled with the mouthpiece for a while and when they put it back in and blew out their cheeks it was just like the light of that day. . . . The young men with brass . . . on the rooftops. Some on 254 where there is no protective railing; another at 131, the one with the apple-green water tank, and somebody right next to it, 133, where lard cans of tomato plants are kept. . . . So from Lenox to St. Nicholas and across 135th Street, Lexington, from Convent to Eighth I could hear the men playing out their maple-sugar hearts. (195–97)

Here again, the narrator's view is more extensive than any character narrator could command. It includes both the general and the particular: all the women tripping down the sidewalk and also the specific veterans who gather around Father Divine's wagon. This view from street level is effortlessly combined with a panoramic view from above, as she looks down on all the rooftops where the young men play their trumpets. Who but a City could see everything, all the people at once and at the same time each individual? In addition to dramatizing the perspective of a city, the text also imagines how a city would think: in units of blocks and street numbers. Who but a

City would think to map out the perimeters of the music's sound in city blocks? "From Lenox to St. Nicholas and across 135th Street, Lexington, from Convent to Eighth I could hear the men playing." What narrator but a City would focus on the precise addresses in Harlem where the men played— "some on 254 where there is no protective railing; another at 131, the one with the apple-green tank, and somebody right next to it, 133, where lard cans of tomato plants are kept" (196).

My notion that the narrator is the City fits in with and enhances other critics' perceptions that the novel is structured like a jazz piece.[5] Roberta Rubenstein points out that the novel follows the same basic pattern of call-and-response as jazz. "Each of the ten sections of Morrison's novel concludes with an idea or phrase to which the opening words of the next section respond; . . . each 'response' opens into a new (narrative) direction" (154). A glance at the call-and-response sequence from the fourth section's concluding words to the opening words of the fifth section will show how distinctive the voice of the City is. Section 4 ends, "[Violet] noticed . . . that it was spring. In the City" (114). Section 5 begins, "And when spring comes to the City people notice . . ." (117)—the same words, in a different order with a different rhythm, to begin a new riff on the theme of spring's arrival. "And when spring comes to the City people notice one another in the road. . . . Going in and out, in and out the same door, they handle the handle; on trolleys and park benches they settle thighs on a seat in which hundreds have done it too" (117). Contrasting with Violet's inner-directed, personal musings on her life and on her intimate conversations with Alice, the narrator focuses on the external movements of the populace as a whole.

Then, apparently affected by the expansive spirit of spring, the narrator/ City brags a little, admiring herself for

> the range of what an artful City can do. What can beat bricks warming up to the sun? The return of awnings. The removal of blankets from horses' backs. Tar softens under the heel and the darkness under bridges changes from gloom to cooling shade. After a light rain, when the leaves have come, tree limbs are like wet fingers playing in woolly green hair. Motor cars become black jet boxes. . . . On sidewalks turned to satin figures move shoulder first, the crowns of their heads angled shields against the light buckshot that the raindrops are. The faces of children glimpsed at windows appear to be crying, but it is the glass pane dripping that makes it seem so. (118)

Again, there is the broad perspective (all the bridges, all the sidewalks). What is more striking is the focus of the narrator's description of spring: not, as in Chaucer's "Prologue" and other traditional poems on spring, a focus on the quickening of life in nature—the flowers, the birds—but rather a focus on how the streets are on the move again: the tar expands in the sun, the buildings sprout awnings, the bricks warm up to the sun, the motorcars shine like jet, and the sidewalks turn to satin. Compared with the vivid awakening of the streets, the people appear faceless and insignificant. They are merely "figures"—all the same, all moving shoulder first against the rain, less personalized than the street's trees, which wave "wet fingers playing in woolly green hair" (118). And unlike the streets, the humans are not participating in the new vitality of spring but fending off the weather.

The coda that ends this description sums up what is important to the narrator: "At springtime it's clearer than at [any] other time that citylife is streetlife" (119). The wordplay turns on a literalization, as "streetlife" takes on new meaning: the word does not refer to the human denizens of the street but to the macadam, the tar, the concrete: it is they that are lively, expanding and brightening in the spring warmth.

As Ralph Ellison writes, "True jazz is an art of individual assertion within and against the group. Each true jazz moment . . . springs from a contest in which each artist challenges all the rest; each solo flight, or improvisation, represents . . . a definition of his identity as individual [and] as member of the collectivity" (36). My hypothesis that the narrator is the City brings out the distinctive qualities of the narrator's solos, the idiosyncrasy of her voice. By contrast with Violet's introspective, contemplative tone in section 4, the narrator's riff is marked by the enthusiasms of the City for "what an artful city can do" with the materials at her command. Just as jazz fans begin to recognize the characteristic style of an instrumentalist in a jazz ensemble, we learn to recognize the peculiarities of the City's style that persist throughout the variations she plays on life in the City.

The Straight Line and the Swerve

What are the effects of having a City in the position of narrator? How does it affect the telling of this love story? The main effect is comedy, as the narrator misreads her characters and gets the plot wrong. But the comedy plays with some fundamental philosophical issues as well. And the narrator affords Morrison the opportunity to parody the presumption of any governing authority to a full knowledge of its citizenry.

As we have seen, the narrator has a panoptical view of the whole city. That leads her to the conviction that she knows everything, as well as sees everything, in the city. In particular, she believes that she knows the direction of her citizens' lives. How that affects her attitude as narrator toward her characters we will see.

The narrator's understanding of how to thrive in the city rests on her faith in the excellent spatial organization of her streets. "All you have to do is heed the design—the way it's laid out for you, considerate, mindful of where you want to go and what you might need tomorrow" (9). The city plan is so competent that it has anticipated the citizens' needs, so that knowledge of their future desires and needs lies compact within it. The comic elements of the City narrator's grandiosity derive from the precision with which Morrison grounds the narrator's complacency in the physical properties of a city. A city is constituted by a grid of streets laid out precisely to be predictable. That is, the addresses follow a numerical sequence and are grouped together in a more or less regular order of rectangular blocks. We might say this of any city; but New York City, which is clearly the city in *Jazz*, is known for and proud of its geometrical regularity, its logical organization of avenues and numbered streets. The city-narrator's imagination is then constrained by this geometry, so that she assumes that the citizens follow the straight-ahead paths marked out for them.

It is the assurance of a totalizing civil authority that Morrison mocks through the narrator's pretension to certain knowledge about her citizens' destinations. For the city-narrator's calculations leave out the factor of human ingenuity. As Michel de Certeau reminds us in *The Practice of Everyday Life*, institutions may impose a governing structure on those who must exist within them, but within these structures individuals make a space for their own self-invented practices. For example, a civic authority—city planner, city council, urbanist—does indeed lay out a spatial system to direct the movements of walkers in the city. "A spatial order organizes an ensemble of possibilities (e.g., by a place in which one can move) and interdictions (e.g., by a wall that prevents one from going further), then the walker actualizes some of these possibilities. . . . But he also . . . invents others, since the crossing, drifting away, or improvisation of walking privilege, transform or abandon spatial elements" (98). Walking in the city insinuates "surreptitious creativities" into the machinery of surveillance and composes the actual conditions of city life, escaping the eye of a panoptic administration. "Spatial practices in fact secretly structure the determining conditions of social life" (96).

Such a capacity for individual initiative escapes the narrator. Joe "thinks he is free . . . free to do something wild," but he is deluded:

Take my word for it, he is bound to the track. It pulls him like a needle through the groove of a Bluebird record. Round and round about the town. That's the way the City spins you. Makes you do what it wants, go where the laid-out roads say to. All the while letting you think you're free. . . . You can't get off the track a City lays for you. (120)[6]

Since the City is also the narrator, "the track a City lays for you" carries a double meaning: it is not only the immutable track organized for him by the street grid that Joe the pedestrian must follow, but also the "track" of the plot to which Joe the character is bound. In the narrow range of possibilities the city-narrator can imagine, the characters' directions in life are laid out in simple, straight lines like the straight lines of the streets: no swerving.[7]

As a pedestrian is bound to the path prescribed for him by a city that has anticipated his every need, so the character's destiny is certain: the pull of the ending draws him ineluctably toward his death. Combining the two in one voice enables Morrison to parody both the presumption of governing bodies that claim to know their citizens' ways (and to know what is best for all of them) and the predictability of the traditional plotline from love to death.

The narrator's teleological thinking becomes especially prominent once Felice enters the picture, toward the end of the novel. The narrator stresses Felice's resemblance to Dorcas: with "four marcelled waves" on each side of her head, Felice appears to be a "true-as-life Dorcas" as she climbs the steps of Violet's apartment building for the first time (197). "She is climbing the steps now, heading for Violent" (198). In a not-so-subtle intimation of the violence to come, the narrator shifts the spelling of Violet's name to "Violent." As she has predicted from the opening pages, the doings of the "scandalizing three-some" will surely end in death (6). Her logic is linear: if love led to death in the past, then, given the same configuration of characters, love must lead to death again. The narrator is wrong. There is no death; rather, Felice, Joe, and Violet make up a new, sustaining kind of family love.

The narrator's deterministic view of love—the past determines the present, the standard plot determines the end of lovers—contrasts with the actual lives of the characters, who are busy devising their own innovative forms of love. Like the pedestrians who take their own unpredictable paths within the spatial order laid down by the city, the characters take their own unpredict- able swerves from the straight-ahead story the narrator is trying to tell. Love impels them in all sorts of unforeseen directions.

Toward the end of *Jazz* the narrator's confidence in the straight line be- tween past and present, between cause and effect, is shaken when she realizes that she hasn't understood the characters at all—because she has left "something rogue" out of her calculations. The "something rogue" is, I posit, love: like Epicurus's "swerve" in the order of things, in his canonical debate against the determinism of Democritus, love is unpredictable, rests on the random encounter, allows for chance and choice in human life.[8] In the end, the narrator is persuaded not only to leave behind the straight line of linear reasoning and take the unpredictability of love into account but to join the characters in improvising new forms of love.

The last section of this chapter explores the novel's treatment of love as improvisation. First, it is necessary to think through the implications of a swerve in the narrative structure.

"A Little Archaeological Exploration":
Golden Gray, the Ancestors, and Love as Absence

After following the experiences of Violet and Joe along the present-day timeline of the 1920s, a reader experiences a sudden unexplained dip into the past to learn about new characters in a new plot set in the 1880s; then, after some fifty pages, the text returns to the horizontal line of the present. What is this narrative swerve doing in and to the narrative line? How does it function in the narrative of Joe and Violet? What impact can such a tale, told outside the ken of Joe and Violet, have on their ways of loving?

Morrison provides a hint about what she is up to in an interview with Salman Rushdie. Referring to *Beloved* and *Jazz*, Rushdie asks, "Is this an alternative history of America?" Morrison answers, "In a way it's a little archaeological exploration. . . . [I] want to do this sort of archaeology about the history of black people in the United States" (Rushdie 61). Freud uses the same metaphor when he describes the psychoanalytic method in his and Breuer's early *Studies in Hysteria* (1895). He theorizes that the hysterical symptom of the patient was produced by a traumatic event now beyond the reach of conscious memory. Picturing the unconscious as a field of memories "stratified concentrically round the pathogenic nucleus," he describes encouraging the patient to dig down from "the superficial strata" where the memories are more easily accessible "into the depths" (293), finally arriving at—that is, bringing into consciousness—the buried trauma. At that point, what is important is that the patient feel the full force of the traumatic event—something he was not able to do in the moment because the memory was immediately repressed and thus unavailable to the normal processes for discharge. "If the reaction is

suppressed, the affect remains attached to the memory" (8). It goes on working subterraneously, "like a foreign body, . . . [like] an agent that is still at
work" (6), busy creating symptoms. The cure for a hysterical symptom, then,
is to make the repressed memory conscious and especially to express the affect attached to it—to "abreact" it (6).

The metaphor of archaeological excavation common to Morrison and
Freud points to a shared faith in the psychological benefits of uncovering and
reanimating the hurt at the source of present-day dysfunction.

The plot of the interpolated historical episode can be quickly told. Growing up in Baltimore with his white mother, Vera Louise, and her slave/servant
True Belle, Golden Gray thought he was white. At the age of eighteen,
Golden Gray finds out that he is the son of a black man. Vera Louise tells
him that she was exiled from her Georgia plantation home by her father
when he discovered she was pregnant with a black man's child—that is, with
Golden Gray. Golden Gray leaves home to return to his mother's hometown
in Georgia to find his father—whether to kill him or embrace him, Golden
Gray is not sure. Indeed, he is the very figure of ambivalence, in particular racial ambivalence. Passing through a wood, he startles a naked pregnant black
woman, who is Wild, the putative mother of Joe Trace. Turning to run, the
naked woman bumps into a tree and is knocked unconscious. Golden Gray
lifts her into his carriage and finds his way to his black father's house.

Golden Gray struggles against his newly discovered black identity throughout the episode. Disavowing his own blackness, he projects it onto Wild and
then, in the carriage, tries to maintain the color line by keeping a distance between his body and the unconscious Wild's, all the while "holding his breath
against infection or something. Something that might touch or penetrate
him" (144). Yet he is also obscurely attracted to Wild, who reminds him of
"his first and major love," the black servant True Belle who brought him up
(150).[9]

Finally, we arrive at (what I regard as) the central point of the historical
interlude, as Golden Gray, on the way to his father's house, expresses his loss
of the father through a metaphor:

> he was crying. . . . Only now, he thought, . . . do I feel his absence: the
> place where he should have been and was not. Before, I thought everybody
> was one-armed, like me. Now I feel the surgery. The crunch of bone when
> it is sundered, the sliced flesh and the tubes of blood cut through, shocking
> the bloodrun and disturbing the nerves. They dangle and writhe. Singing
> pain. (158–59)

The metaphor of the severed arm speaks not only to the pain of separation but also to the paradoxical feelings of connection with the disconnected parent. The lost parent is a phantom limb that continues to exist in ghostly presence ever after the amputation—absent, yet felt as a palpable presence. Morrison enhances the concrete presence of loss through the lament that continues Golden Gray's metaphor:

> this part of me that does not know me, has never touched me . . . . This gone-away hand that never helped me over the stile, or guided me past the dragons, pulled me up from the ditch into which I stumbled. Stroked my hair, fed me food; took the far end of the load to make it easier for me to carry. (158–59)

The text gives body to absence by imagining in physical detail all the help and protection the arm/father would have extended to his son.

In Freud's account of recapturing the repressed memory of the traumatic event, the point is not just to retrieve the memory but to express the emotion still unconsciously attached to it, "allowing the strangulated affect to find a way out through speech" (Freud and Breuer 17). The outpouring of Golden Gray's suffering exceeds what we usually think of as mourning: his pain is fresh-blown, felt with the intensity of the original severance from the parent, as the immediacy of the corporeal imagery—shattered bone, severed flesh, cut veins, dangling nerves—suggests. What is more, Golden Gray recognizes that this is the ultimate purpose of his journey: "I am not going [on this journey] to be healed, or to find the arm that was removed from me. I am going to freshen the pain, point it, so we both know what it is for" (158). The aim is ultimately to "freshen the pain" or, as Freud puts it, not just to recall the traumatic memory but to "arouse its accompanying affect . . . and put the affect into words" (6). In Freud, that "abreaction" is the key to healing.

In a 1993 interview with Angels Carabi, Morrison refers to her motivation in writing *Beloved*; since she had recently (in 1992) published *Jazz*, the novel that accompanies *Beloved* in the trilogy, I think we can regard her comments as relevant to both novels. In the early African American folklore and tales, she says, there is little mention of the Middle Passage—and by extension, little mention of the subjective sufferings of slavery in general:

> I understand that omission, because to dwell on it would perhaps paralyze you to the point of not being able to . . . survive daily experience. It was too painful to remember, yet I had the impression that it was something that needed to be thought about by . . . Afro-Americans. With *Beloved*, I

am trying to insert this memory that was unbearable and unspeakable into
the literature. . . . It was a silence within the race. So it's a kind of healing
experience. There are certain things that are repressed because they are unthinkable and the only way to come free of that is to go back and deal with
them. (Carabi, "Toni Morrison's *Beloved*" 105)

Morrison thus shares with Freud a faith in the potential healing that comes
from opening up and processing traumatic memories of the past. But unlike
the buried individual trauma that Freud is looking for, Morrison excavates
toward the collective historical traumas of African Americans.

The Golden Gray interlude functions like the speech of Beloved when
her voice inexplicably becomes the voice of a child several generations back,
yearning from a slave ship on the Middle Passage for her lost mother. The
two interludes are structurally parallel intrusions on a present-day chronological sequence by an Ur-trauma of African American history, the breakup
of the mother-child unit.[10] In Morrison's work on slavery from *Beloved* to
A Mercy, the multiple injuries of slavery crystallize in the figure of the child
forcibly separated from the parent. The separation from the parent creates
a wound that never heals in the child: like a phantom limb, the parent is
severed and lost but continues to be present to the child as a felt absence.
As Roberta Rubenstein eloquently expresses it: "What Morison calls the 'absence of love' I would term *loss*, because individuals experience it not merely
as absence—something missing—but as a lack that continues to occupy a
palpable emotional space: the *presence* of absence" (150; italics in the original).
Thus Golden Gray's outpouring of grief for the lost parent represents the processing and catharsis of a repeated historical trauma.[11]

What about the "freeing" that Morrison says will follow on the effort to
"go back and deal with" repressed historical memory? As we shall see, Violet
and Joe, against all logic of cause and effect, seem to feel the effects of Golden
Gray's catharsis. But more immediately, Golden Gray's overflow of powerful
feelings produces an unexpected moment of grace, or mercy. The narrator
wishes him well:

> I have to be a shadow who wishes [Golden Gray] well, like the smiles
> of the dead left over from their lives. . . . I want him to stand next to a
> well, . . . and while standing there in shapely light, . . . his mind soaked and
> sodden with sorrow, or dry and brittle with the hopelessness that comes
> from knowing too little and feeling too much . . . from down in [the well],
> where the light does not reach, a collection of leftover smiles stirs, some
> brief benevolent love rises from the darkness. . . . There is no reason to stay

but he does. For the safety at first, then for the company. Then for him-self—with a kind of confident, enabling, serene power that flicks like a ra-zor and then hides. But he has felt it now . . . he will remember it, and if he remembers it he can recall it. That is to say, he has it as his disposal. (161)

If Golden Gray's journey to find his father represents in miniature the move-ment of the novel as a whole—the same drive back into the past and down into memory—the well is an even more condensed version of the same form. A well is a container for that which is deep down; and a well motivates a plunge into the depths, a lowering of the bucket to bring up what is con-cealed below. Indeed, the novel with the Golden Gray episode inside it and the well inside the Golden Gray episode constitute a fractal structure, or in mathematical terms a self-similar structure, or in more homely analogy the nested structure of inset Russian dolls: each part repeats in reduced size the form of the whole.

The surprise is that what emerges from the depths of the well is not the pain of the past but "a collection of leftover smiles." Rather than enjoining the living to carry forward into their own lives the intergenerational pain of loss, the ancestors send Golden Gray the blessing of their smiles. Picking up the other meaning of "well," the ancestors wish him well: "some brief benev-olent love rises from the darkness." Perhaps the combination of "a collection" of smiles with the image of water suggests that this collectivity includes ances-tors from the waters of the Atlantic and the Middle Passage.

Perhaps, indeed, Morrison is going back beyond the slave ships of the Middle Passage to draw on African traditions that associate spirits of the dead (as well as other spiritual beings) with water. Discussing *Beloved* in the same Carabi interview, she mentions "the African conviction" that the spirits of young people who "die uneasily . . . come out of the water" to be reincar-nated as family members. And she affirms the larger African belief that "the water is interesting, but also a dangerous and a haunted place because spirits dwell in it" (Carabi, "Toni Morrison's *Beloved*"107). Wells also figure in Afri-can spiritual traditions. For example, among the Yoruba of Nigeria, a well in the compound of one of the chiefs "is said to be the actual water into which [the goddess] Oshun transformed herself . . . the well has many curative properties" (Wyndham 60). The blessings that flow onto Golden Gray from the well may then come from African as well as African American ancestral spirits.[12]

The passage closes with the evocation of a healthy kind of remembering: Golden Gray senses from the well "a kind of confident, enabling, serene power that flicks like a razor and then hides. But he has felt it now . . . he will remember it, and if he remembers it he can recall it. That is to say, he has it as his disposal" (161). Like Freud, Morrison draws careful distinctions between different kinds of memory. Having "abreacted" the full measure of sorrow for the lost parent, Golden Gray is poised to experience a different kind of memory. He will be able to "remember" this moment; indeed, he will be able to "recall" it—to call it up on demand. Morrison thus differentiates voluntary memory from the involuntary "reminiscences" that in both Freud's and Morrison's work plague trauma survivors (like Sethe in *Beloved*), intruding fragmentary, dismembered images on the traumatized. Golden Gray, having abreacted the anguish of losing a loved one, will now have the voluntary kind of memory "at his disposal." Memory itself is healed.

Who are these characters, Wild and Golden Gray? And *where* are they? Once their scene is over, both vanish—although, as we have seen, traces of Wild continue to haunt Joe's narrative. Wild and Golden Gray have a double status. On the one hand, they are corporeal beings. Wild is enormously pregnant, and she gives birth to a baby. And Golden Gray is manifestly an embodied human being working out the dilemmas of his interracial birth. But Wild is also Beloved from the novel of that name. As Morrison herself says in interviews, Wild is naked and pregnant like Beloved at the end of *Beloved*, and the date of 1888 when she appears to Golden Gray jibes with Beloved's dates. Morrison is quite explicit: "Wild is a kind of Beloved. The dates are the same. . . . The woman they call Wild . . . could be Sethe's daughter, Beloved . . . who runs away, ending up in Virginia, which is right next to Ohio" (Carabi, "Nobel Laureate"96). (See Martha Cutter for a full listing of the textual details that connect Wild with Beloved [66–67].)[13] If Wild is Beloved, or even "a kind of Beloved," then on one level she represents slavery. For in *Beloved*, Beloved embodies all the children left motherless by the separations of slavery, including the Middle Passage. And Golden Gray too has a mythic dimension: in his person, he embodies what W. E. B. Dubois was the first to call the color line, the line of strict demarcation between black and white. It is the color line that his white mother trespassed when she slept with a black man, it is the color line that deprived him of his black father, and it is the problematic of the color line that he has to work through. He *is* the color line incarnate, for it runs right through his body.[14] At the innermost core of what Morrison calls her archaeological dig into African American history are these two emblematic figures that represent the social injustices at the origins of African American identity: slavery and the color line.

Loving as Improvisation

In the final part of the novel, love surprises everyone—and especially the narrator—by shifting from a regressive force that binds the characters to old relational patterns to a creative force that inspires the characters to devise new
and invigorating forms of connection.

At the end, the narrator has to recant her determinism, recant the straight
line between cause and effect, past and present. She acknowledges that she
had thought that the past determined the present absolutely—that "flesh,
pinioned by misery, hangs on to it with pleasure. Hangs on to wells and a
boy's golden hair" (228). She refers here to the traumatic elements of Violet's
past—the site of her mother's drowning, the well, and the photograph of
Golden Gray, Violet's first and forever unattainable love object. That is, the
narrator used to believe that people are transfixed by trauma and doomed
to repeat it: "I was sure one would kill the other. . . . That the past was an
abused record with no choice but to repeat itself at the crack and no power
on earth could lift the arm that held the needle" (220). Yet no one dies. The
narrator says goodbye to the teleology that makes death the inevitable conclusion of the love story she is telling—and in doing so abandons her loyalty
to the Western plot of love that ends in death.

She is still telling a love story, though: what kind of story replaces the linear Western plot? I will argue that the love-death plot is replaced by a loving
that imitates the improvisational forms of African American art, notably jazz.
Noting that her characters are slipping out from under the narrative line she
has imposed on them, the narrator identifies what she has left out. "Something is missing there. Something rogue. Something else you have to figure
in before you can figure it out" (228). I think that the "something rogue"
is love. Like Epicurus's "swerve," love emerges from a chance encounter, an
entirely unpredictable "collision" of two people; and its trajectory thereafter
is unpredictable. Will it last? Will it fail? Will the two human atoms cling to
each other or will another swerve carry them apart? A logic of cause and effect
fails to predict. As the characters enact it, love springs up in the most unlikely
places, forming the most unexpected combinations of people; and those part-
nerships in turn re-create love in innovative new forms.

Throughout *Jazz*, love takes surprising turns. For example, Violet finds
that she is "falling in love" with Dorcas, who would traditionally be her hated
rival (15). And Violet, the woman who slashed Dorcas's corpse, becomes
the trusted intimate friend of Alice, the aunt who cared for and loved Dorcas. Timorous and defended against all other possible relationships, Alice is

unpredictably open, honest, and forceful with Violet, "the only visitor she looked forward to" (83).[15] Surprisingly, again, it is the repressed Alice who, in the space of this friendship, adumbrates a view of love that Violet can take away with her and use. Violet is wondering aloud what to do about the husband who betrayed her with Dorcas. Alice responds, "You got anything left to you to love, anything at all, do it." When Violet objects, "You saying take it? Don't fight?" Alice responds, "Nobody's asking you to take it. I'm sayin' make it, make it!" (112–13). Alice suggests that love is creative, something you "make" or, as I would read it, "make up" out of the materials available to you ("anything left to you to love").

In the end, Violet seems to have taken in Alice's words and made them her own, for she says to Felice, "What's the world for if you can't make it up the way you want it?" (208). If Violet is riffing on Alice's words, Morrison is riffing on Woolf's *Mrs. Dalloway*. Mrs. Dalloway's way of loving is to throw her imagination into the world she perceives around her—into "what she loved; life; London; this moment of June." Her loving is a continual process of "making it up, building it round one, tumbling it, creating it every moment afresh" (Woolf, *Mrs. Dalloway* 4). The allusion to "making it up" in *Mrs. Dalloway* enriches *Jazz*'s theme of love as improvisation, as a spontaneous, original re-creation out of what is given—in this case, literary tradition. Love is like jazz itself in Caroline Brown's description, taking "the familiar and fixed and mak[ing] it novel, distinct" (631). Alice's idea of love (enhanced and enriched by Woolf's) is the view of love that in *Jazz* replaces the Western script of love-death. Or, in the musical metaphors that structure *Jazz*, love is not a record that plays the same love song over and over but an art of improvisation like jazz, forever creating new variations on the old theme.

Thus, against the heavy foreshadowing of the narrator's deterministic view that Felice, Joe, and Violet were doomed by the past to repeat it, Felice doesn't fall in love with Joe and Violet doesn't kill her. Instead, Felice comes to love the couple Joe and Violet in her own way and for her own reasons—"making up" her own version of family love. Violet's directness, honesty, and way of looking at things aslant help Felice shape her ambitions for herself; and she admires Joe's affection for his wife, the way he "touches her. Sometimes on the head. Sometimes just a pat on her shoulder" when he walks past her (207). And Joe and Violet come to love each other in ways that one would never have predicted from their troubled pasts and their mutual alienation and anger. Gradually, imperceptibly, in the process of doing everyday things together in the city—nothing dramatic—each comes to be "inward toward the other"; and they share a "whispering, old-time love" (228). As they lie together under the blue blanket, Joe sees through the window "darkness taking the shape of . . . a bird with a blade of red on the wing. Meanwhile Violet rests her hand on his chest as though it were the sunlit rim of a well and down there somebody is gathering gifts . . . to distribute to them all" (225). Red-winged blackbirds always heralded Joe's mother's unseen presence; and of course the well is the site of Violet's mother's suicide. The signs of Joe's and Violet's lost mothers that used to suck them down into despair or trigger their twisted reenactments of maternal trauma come back now transformed into distanced aesthetic forms. Joe and Violet are at peace with these memories.

What has healed them? Beyond Alice's wisdom on love as a creative force and Joe's pleasure in the new family structure formed with Violet and Felice, the text doesn't provide explanations for Violet's and Joe's recovery. The narrative structure alone, wherein the healing of Violet's and Joe's pathological loving follows hard upon the interpolation of the Golden Gray episode, implies that somehow the full expression of the ancestor's grief—Golden Gray's abreaction of his sorrow for the lost parent—has healed memory for Violet and Joe, too. This process remains mysterious in psychological terms, for neither Violet nor Joe has gone through a therapeutic process of recalling and reliving the pain of losing their parents. But Morrison has been urging us, through the interruption of the present by the Golden Gray episode from the past, to think in historical, not psychological, terms. Perhaps the text's structural message is that since the emotional twists and torsions of present-day African American individuals like Joe and Violet originate in traumas in the ancestral past, a confrontation with the ancestors' pain is necessary to heal the loving of the descendants. That seems to be what Morrison implies when, in the Carabi interview cited above, she says, "There are certain things that are repressed because they are unthinkable and the only way to come free of that is to go back to them and deal with them" ("Toni Morrison's *Beloved*" 105).

The narrator becomes innovative, too, improvising an original song of love to her reader. How could a city whose ways of thinking are as rigidly linear as her street plan become thus changeable, flexible, creative? I think the answer lies in the tautology that if the narrator is the City, the City is a narrator. The narrator has learned and changed through her practice, through the narrational practice of following the lives of her characters.

For example, Violet, Joe, and Felice are making up their own original love story, so the narrator has to acknowledge that she was wrong. "I saw the three of them, Felice, Joe and Violet, and they looked to me like a mirror image of Dorcas, Joe and Violet" (221). The spatial logic of the City equated the triangle of Felice, Joe, and Violet with the fatal triangle of Dorcas, Joe, and Violet and assumed a straight line between past and present: "I was sure one would kill the other" (221, 220).

The original acts of her characters cause her to call into question her old way of thinking: she had thought, she says, that "my space, my view was the only one" (220). Then she elaborates the flaws in "my view"—which is the view from the vantage of a city: "I was watching the streets, thrilled by the buildings pressing and pressed by stone; so glad to be looking out and in on things I dismissed what went on in heart-pockets closed to me" (220–21). The perspective of a city foregrounds the buildings and the streets, the elements that compose her being (that is only "natural"). And when she looks at people, she sees them only from a vantage point outside—"looking out" on their doings on the streets, or "looking . . . in" through doors and windows: "I watched them through windows and doors" (220).

We have been privy to the narrator's streetwise way of understanding people all along, for she has bragged about its efficacy from time to time: "The best thing to find out what's going on is to watch how people maneuver themselves in the streets. What sidewalk preachers stop them in their tracks? Do they walk right through the boys kicking cans along the sidewalk or holler at them to quit?" (72). When the narrator claims, "I know Joe," she describes only what she divines from Joe's actions on the street (119). (In an interpolated first-person narrative, Joe tells his story in a very different mode that encompasses the complex feelings the narrator didn't see.) Now, the narrator realizes that her vision ("my space, my view") was so narrowly focused on the external elements of her cityscape that "I missed the people altogether" (220). She saw nothing at all of the "heart-pockets closed to me" (221), nothing at all of their intimate feelings.

Meanwhile, she realizes, the characters were "busy being original, complicated, changeable" (220)—their actions not predetermined by the linear plotline of love leading to death but riffing, like jazz performers, on the old melody of love, "chang[ing] it, complicat[ing]" it, making up their own variations on love.

Inspired by her characters, the narrator now does the same, addressing her own song of love to the reader:

I have loved only you, surrendered my whole self reckless to you and nobody else. . . . I want you to love me back and show it to me. . . . I love the way you hold me, how close you let me be to you. I like your fingers on and on, lifting, turning. I have watched your face for a long time now, and missed your eyes when you went away from me. (229)

This love song is a triumph of innovation, for it reaches across the impassible barrier between a narrator who is part of a disembodied text, made up of abstract marks on a page, and the flesh-and-blood reader to address the body of the reader directly and demand a physical, corporeal communion.

And then, in another improvisational turn, she invites the reader to love her back:

> If I were able I'd say it. Say make me, remake me. You are free to do it and
> I am free to let you because look, look. Look where your hands are. Now.
> (229)

The narrator takes up Alice's rendition of love as an act of the imagination—"I'm sayin make it, make it" (113)—and improvises her own riff on that theme—"make me, remake me"—inviting the reader to love her in a particular way. Adopting the call-and-response pattern from jazz, where one instrumentalist challenges the next to respond to the musical phrase he has just performed, the narrator calls on the reader to "remake," or signify on, the narrator's performance of the whole novel.

As love has changed over the course of the novel from a regressive force that pulls the characters back into reenactments of past traumatic loves to a force that frees the characters to make up new, freely chosen scenarios, the narrator has moved from believing in the straight line, the single direction toward a predetermined end, to an embrace of the innovative, the spontaneous, the unforeseen. That move encompasses a shift from Western literary tradition to African American oral tradition: in place of the old Western story where love leads ineluctably to the closure of death, the narrator adopts both the call-and-response pattern of African American art forms and the open ending of African American oral tradition. The ending remains open on the assumption that the next teller will take up and retell the story in her own way—as the narrator calls on the reader to do "now."

CHAPTER 3

Displacement—Political, Psychic, and Textual—in *Paradise*

The central event of *Paradise* (1998) is the massacre of the women in the Convent by the men of Ruby. There is an explanation for this violence, but it seems inadequate: the men are trying to get rid of what they see as the disorderly sexual excesses of the women who live in the deserted Convent eighteen miles away because they believe that the women's display of uninhibited female licentiousness threatens the disciplined order of their community. Since the excesses of the Convent women pose no real threat to Ruby, and since these excesses are largely the products of the Ruby men's fantasies, the overt reasons for the massacre seem incommensurable with the virulence of the men's murderous rage. The murders do make a kind of sense, though, if we understand them to be motivated by a logic of displacement.

I want to offer displacement as a conceptual tool for working out the complex and irrational couplings of politics and psychology, of race and gender, that lead up to the massacre. Displacement has two different meanings, which accord with two intertwining dimensions of *Paradise*, the political and the psychological. At the political level, displacement means the process whereby someone is forced out of their home country by circumstances that make it impossible to remain, forced to relocate in an alien land. In its psychic sense, displacement refers to the unconscious process whereby the emotional energy attached to one object is transferred in its entirety onto another object.

Displacement in the political sense characterized the lives of the community's founding fathers, who in 1890 migrated from the American South to Oklahoma and then were forced to wander again by the citizens of Fairly, Oklahoma, who refused them entry into their all-black community. That rejection, and the displacement that followed, do not remain in the background of the story, as facts of a dim history, but rather arouse intense feelings of shame in the present-day (1973) leaders of Ruby. The community was forced, after World War II, to dislocate again, so they have also experienced anew the earlier generation's loss of place.

Perhaps the most frequently voiced complaint about *Paradise* is that the text continually baffles reader understanding. More than in any other Morrison novel, the burden of making meaning shifts from writer to reader. Philip Page views the heavy demands the text places on the reader's interpretive processes as part of the novel's thematics of interpretation: the characters are all engaged in interpreting one another's utterances and actions as well as the meaning of the words inscribed on the Oven. The text thus offers a model for reader participation in making the text's meaning and endorses a multiplicity of interpretations ("Furrowing" 638–39). Page's analysis is multifaceted and persuasive, but I think there is yet more to be said about the specific ways that the reader's experience of the text reflects the characters' experiences. All the characters—in the Convent as well as in Ruby—have been displaced geographically. I will argue that a reader undergoes a parallel displacement when the text moves abruptly from familiar territory into a new fictional world with no signposts to tell a reader where she is or who the new characters are or why they are doing what they are doing. This exile into an unknown world happens not just at the beginning of *Paradise* but intermittently throughout. If we come to see the structural displacement the reader suffers as a reflection of the characters' geographical displacement, we can perhaps understand the repeated bafflement of the reader as a formal enactment of the characters' disorientation, as they try but fail to make sense of a new place.

I will argue that displacement in its psychic sense is at work in the massacre of the Convent women. Displacement is a primitive unconscious mechanism; together with condensation, displacement governs the operations of unconscious thought, as Freud outlined in his *Project for a Scientific Psychology* (1895) and *The Interpretation of Dreams* (1900). The fact that the intensity of the emotional charge attached to one object can be fully displaced onto a different object shows that energy in the unconscious is free, unbound, as opposed to the energy bound within structural confines that characterizes conscious thought. Displacement functions as a process of substitution: "There is something you cannot bear to think about or remember, so you think about, or remember, something else" (Jacqueline Rose 42). When you cannot master an experience or bear its memory, you transfer the whole load of anxiety or fear from that thing to something else. And then you cannot stop thinking about that other thing. Displacement, originally characterized by the extreme motility of unconscious processes, leads to an arrest of mental mobility, as the subject clings rigidly to the substitute object (see Rose 42–43).

It is clear from early in the text that displacement is the default mechanism for dealing with problems or conflicts in Ruby. When "a mother was knocked down the stairs by her cold-eyed daughter," when "four damaged infants were born in one family," when "daughters refused to get out of bed," when "brides disappeared on their honeymoons," the men who govern Ruby dislocate the cause of the trouble from Ruby to the Convent: "the one thing that connected all these catastrophes was in the Convent. And in the Convent were those women" (11). As J. Brooks Bouson helpfully points out, all the individuals from Ruby who went to the Convent for help when their shameful actions put them outside the rigid rules governing behavior in Ruby—Arnette, Sweetie, Menus, K. D., and Deacon—end up projecting their own shame onto the Convent women (*Quiet* 202–4). The Convent is constructed as a place of unbounded license so that it can serve as dumping ground for all the disorderly behaviors plaguing Ruby. The text is explicit about these displacements; they require no commentary. Much more subtle (and thus more interesting) are the two strategies of displacement that this chapter will be examining.

As a first approach, I argue that the men of Ruby displace their anxieties about their own wives' out-of-bounds behaviors onto the Convent women. The men of Ruby exert absolute patriarchal control over all aspects of their citizens' lives. But their power necessarily rests on their women's willingness to conform to the rules imposed on them. As the virtuous wives of Ruby covertly enact various forms of feminine *jouissance* that exceed the precise limits on feminine behavior they are meant to observe, the men's amorphous anxiety about their own women builds, and at the same time they construct wilder and wilder fantasies about the Convent women's sexual and reproductive practices. The men displace anxiety about their own women's transgressions onto the Convent women and punish jouissance in the Other to avoid confronting female jouissance at home.

Widening the interpretive lens to take in the history of Ruby, we can perceive a second and more fundamental displacement at work in the Convent massacre. The founding fathers of the Ruby community were doubly displaced when, in fleeing the violence and poverty of the racist South, they were forbidden entrance into the all-black town of Fairly, Oklahoma. Although Fairly was an all-black community, the deep black skin color of the migrating group was too dark for the light-skinned citizens of Fairly to tolerate. I will show that the shame attached to this racial insult remains alive in the descendants of the Old Fathers; it is revived and felt as if it were their own. My second hypothesis is, then, that the shame attached to race is displaced onto gender, onto the shame of womanhood, and wiped out there, at the displaced locus of the Convent. The nexus of race, gender, and shame is fundamental to the history and the group psychology of Ruby. More generally, Morrison's shrewd political and psychological analysis exposes the ways that the mechanism of displacement defends patriarchal privilege against confronting its own vulnerabilities.

The Men and the Women of Ruby:
Morrison's Critique of Patriarchy

The notion of psychic displacement not only offers a way to understand the seemingly arbitrary murders of the Convent women. It also opens a view of gender politics in *Paradise* that is perhaps more fruitful than the standard contrast in the scholarship between the men of Ruby and the women of the Convent. Critics and readers who understand this gender binary as the basic structure of the novel tend to find *Paradise* schematic and static. Thus, among the early reviewers Brooke Allen claims that the novel's "male-female dichotomy" of Ruby men versus Convent women is "a cliché, and Morrison plays it too heavily" (6); and Michiko Kakutani claims that *Paradise* is "a heavy-handed, schematic piece of writing," "a contrived, formulaic book that mechanically pits men against women" (that is, the men of Ruby against the women of the Convent ["Worthy Women"]). However, a focus on gender relations between the men of Ruby and the women of Ruby opens up a snarl of entangled elements of race and gender, politics and psychology, history and present-day anxieties that, far from remaining static and fixed within opposing categories, move and mix with one another.

The men of Ruby establish a strict binary between their own virtuous and obedient women and the unruly, out-of-bounds women of the Convent. Such a binary enables displacement: all the bad or questionable aspects of one's own women can be displaced in their entirety onto the sinful group of Other women. But some behaviors of the good wives of Ruby threaten the absoluteness of this binary: they indulge in practices that exceed the limits and restraints of "good women" as defined by the Ruby patriarchy. These practices arouse persistent vague anxieties in the men, which they deal with not by confronting their own women but by displacing anxiety about female transgression onto the Convent women. *Paradise* is the one novel among

Morrison's works that does not accord love a central place; gendered power relations take the place of love—as if to say that relations of domination squeeze out love.

Writing on displaced individuals such as those who move to Israel, Jacqueline Rose asks a question that is relevant to *Paradise*: Does displacement in its political sense—the forced exodus from one's native land—lead to a fluidity of psychic boundaries corresponding to one's physical mobility, as some contemporary theorists (Braidotti, Friedman) argue, or does the movement of bodies into a new territory not rather provoke a freezing of mental agility, with "thought fastening on and seizing its ground" (50)? It is the second response to displacement—the fixity of thought tenaciously gripping its new ground—that best characterizes the mode of governance in Ruby. The grandsons and heirs of the original patriarchs, the twins Steward and Deacon, enforce stasis, an absolute adherence to the example of the forefathers. Patterns of living that were perhaps necessary in the perilous days of the founding continue two and three generations later because of their sanctity, not because they are relevant to changing conditions. The public symbol of the originators' social ethic is the Oven and the words engraved on it by the founder of Haven, Zechariah: "[Beware] the Furrow of His Brow." Steward and Deacon will tolerate no new interpretation of these words, despite the desire for a new interpretation—and thus for change—on the part of the younger generation.

Deacon and Steward keep the citizens of Ruby faithful to the patriarchal patterns of the past by imposing absolute control. Having built the town, they know and so believe they can control all its spaces. Thus Deacon makes a point of patrolling, in his imposing black Cadillac, every inch of Ruby's collective spaces on his way to work each morning (113–15):

> As Deek drove north on Central, it and the side streets seemed to him as satisfactory as ever. Quiet white and yellow houses full of industry; and in them were elegant black women at useful tasks; orderly cupboards, minus surfeit or miserliness; linen laundered and ironed to perfection; good meat seasoned and ready for roasting. It was a view he would be damned if . . . the idleness of the young would disturb. (111)

Deek imagines that his knowledge of every inch of the town he built extends to its interiors. Each cupboard contains precisely the correct quantity of goods—neither lack nor excess—according to Deek's idea of the proper measure. The women, like their goods, are contained within ordered domestic spaces, their activities limited by the domestic norm of usefulness to their families: full of "industry," the women are busy at "useful tasks," which extend to perfectly ironed sheets and meat seasoned and roasted just so. Focalized through Deacon's eyes, everything in these "quiet yellow and white houses" is balanced and proportional, uniformly "orderly."

The rule of the patriarchal figures is all-encompassing. Yet their power rests on the women's domestic labor and thus on the women's compliance with the limits imposed from above. Ruby's caryatids, the women hold up the overarching patriarchal edifice and guarantee its stability. This dependency on the women's willingness to conform to the men's expectations means that there is always an invisible chink of vulnerability at the base of the patriarchal structure: What if the virtuous women abandoned conformity?

A shift in focalization presents a contending view of the "quiet yellow and white houses" complacently viewed by Deacon. When Dovey, Steward's wife, earlier walked up the same Central Avenue driven by Deacon—the women of Ruby walk, the men drive, emphasizing in everyday practice the distribution of power in Ruby—what she saw is quite different from the domestic order perceived by Deacon:

> Dovey walked slowly down Central Avenue. . . . Dovey turned left into St. Matthew Street. The moon's light glittered white fences gone slant in an effort to hold back chrysanthemums, foxglove, sunflowers, cosmos, daylilies, while mint and silver king pressed through the spaces at the bottom of the slats. (88–89)

This profusion, Dovey thinks, is a result of the Ruby women competing and cooperating with one another over a ten-year period to produce more and more flowers.

In the patriarchal leaders' binary imaginings, female desire has run wild in the Convent but is subdued into domestic activity within the houses of Ruby. The flowers present a subtle but nonetheless resistant expression of female desire—not safely compartmentalized in the outside space of the Convent, but overrunning the boundaries of Ruby's own yards and streets.

The proliferation of flowers is "driven by desire, not necessity" (90). Naming the women's motivating energy "desire," Morrison explicitly calls attention to the flowers' function as a metonymy for female desire. The flowers do not obey limits: in the passage quoted above they have massed in such quantity that they have warped the fences, pushing them outward; and they escape the fences marking off private property by pressing through any little gap: "mint and silver king pressed through the spaces at the bottom of the slats."

In their anarchic abundance the flowers embody a female desire that refuses containment and disobeys the patriarchal notion of just and proper measure articulated by Deacon.

Indeed, the men of Ruby seem to have an inkling of the threat to their order expressed by the flowers' profusion:

> Finally, front yards were given over completely to flowers for no good reason except there was time in which to do it. The habit, the interest in cultivating plants that could not be eaten, spread, and so did the ground surrendered to it. [It] became so frenetic a land grab, husbands complained of neglect and the disappointingly small harvest of radishes, or the too short rows of collards, beets. (89)

The flowers have no use value. They flout Deacon's ideal of women producing only for use within the household. The cultivation of "plants that could not be eaten" "spreads" past all containment, wiping out the vegetable gardens that would serve family need.

Dovey muses that the abundance of the flowers has attracted new species of butterflies:

> Iris, phlox, rose and peonies took up . . . so much space new butterflies journeyed miles to brood in Ruby. . . . The red bands drinking from sumac competed with the newly arrived creams and whites that loved jewel flowers and nasturtiums. Giant orange wings covered in black lace hovered in pansies and violets. (90)

The butterflies contribute to the beauty of the flowers, multiplying the aesthetic pleasures of the women; but they are useless to domestic need. They are associated with female desire through words that suggest the allure of the feminine: they wear "black lace" and they are attracted to "jewel" flowers. Their modes of reproduction suggest something surreptitious, eluding the public eye: "Their chrysalises hung in secret . . . clumps and chains of eggs. Hiding. Until spring" (90). There is only a whisper here of the theme of rampant disordered female reproduction that will later inform the men's obsessions about the Convent women. The dominant impression conveyed by the superabundance of flowers and butterflies is excess—excess associated with the Ruby women's desires.

There is a more explicit connection between the butterflies and female desire: a sudden influx of butterflies announces the arrival of a stranger who becomes the object of Dovey's desire.

that first time . . . there was a sign. She had been upstairs, . . . lean[ing] forward [out of the window] to see what was left of the garden. . . . But-terflies. A trembling highway of persimmon-colored wings cut across the green treetops forever—then vanished. Later, as she sat in a rocker under these trees, he came by. She had never seen him before and did not recog-nize any local family in his features. . . . this man was walking straight and quickly, . . . using this yard as a shortcut to someplace else. (90–91)

Like the flowers and the butterflies, the stranger disregards boundaries, cut-ting through Dovey's yard.

As time goes by, Dovey begins to spend more and more time in the little house in town, where she can be available should her Friend pass by. On the present occasion Dovey has insisted, against her husband Steward's wishes, on remaining in town. "[Steward] was headed out to the ranch . . . in Stew-ard's mind it was home"—and he wants his wife to come with him. But "the little house they kept on St. Matthew Street—a foreclosure the twins never resold—was becoming more and more home to Dovey" (88). Repetition with variation makes the point: "home" is by patriarchal definition where the wife makes a home for the husband and shares his bed. To Dovey, on the contrary, the house on St. Matthew Street is "becoming home" because she can enjoy the company of her women friends and of the Friend.

Dovey is, however, not an unfaithful wife—that is, not unfaithful as it is defined in the heterosexual contract. The pleasure she derives from her meet-ings with the other man (or spirit?) is not sexual; it is rather the pleasure of talking. And talking in a particular way. Upon their first meeting, Dovey doesn't mention the stranger's trespassing on her property, but instead goes on and on about butterflies: "I saw some butterflies a while back . . . Orangy red, they were. Just as bright. Never saw that color before. Like what we used to call coral" (91). Dovey is herself surprised by the quality of the speech that comes out of her mouth: Dovey "wondered . . . what on earth she was talking about and would have stuttered to a polite close . . . except he looked so interested in what she was describing" (91); "She was babbling, she knew, but he seemed to be listening earnestly, carefully to every word" (92). Out of a desire that overflows patriarchal roles, Dovey conjures up not an ideal lover but an ideal listener.

As in the case of the women's proliferating flowers, Dovey's speech is not for use but for pleasure—serving not the needs of family and community but the woman's own satisfaction. The stream of words running on and on is of a piece with the overabundance of flowers and butterflies: it is out of bounds, exceeding the proper measure. In its excess, this purposeless female productivity begins to suggest jouissance.

In Lacan's lexicon, excess is the hallmark of jouissance. While desire exists within the parameters of social law, jouissance exceeds the limits of social rule and custom. To participate in jouissance is to override the restraints imposed by civilization on erotic and aggressive drives, to pursue an unlimited intensity of experience that goes beyond social norms, beyond pleasure, beyond self-interest, even beyond self-preservation. Because the patriarchy represented in *Paradise* is so fixated on the proper measure and the proper boundaries for female behavior, Lacan's concept of jouissance offers a relevant analytic tool, enabling us to see the subtle ways that the Ruby women's excesses defy patriarchal definitions of limit and measure and thus resist patriarchal control.

In *Seminar XX*, Lacan states, "*Jouissance ne sert à rien*": that is, "Jouissance is what serves no purpose" (3); or, translated differently, "Jouissance is useless" (Evans 12). When Dovey is enjoying the flow of words streaming from her mouth, her speech is useless. Words lose their instrumentality as communicators of meaning. "Babbling," Dovey is indulging in the pleasures of the mouth as it forms syllables, the pleasures of the voice as it makes sounds, and the pleasures of putting one word next to another without regard for sense.[1] That excess takes Dovey out of her gender identity as patriarchal woman, whose words and acts are meant to serve domestic purposes: instead of "serious business," Dovey thinks, she is speaking "nonsense" (92). Her "babble" also takes her out of a gendered silence: although we often see the wives Dovey and Soane thinking about and analyzing their husbands, we rarely see them talking to Deacon and Steward; we can assume that silence more often than words serves the purpose of signifying wifely obedience.

Lacan describes a specifically feminine form of jouissance marked by self-sufficiency: "the jouissance of the woman is in herself and is not connected to the Other" (Lacan, *Le Séminaire X: L'Angoisse*, 1963; qtd. in Neroni 221). While feminine jouissance may be sexual, it could also be a mystical experience, as in the rapture of Saint Theresa (*S XX* 76), or inspired by solitude in nature. The key point is that feminine jouissance does not require an other; it is self-generated and self-fulfilling.

The self-sufficiency of feminine jouissance is especially problematic for a social order governed, as Ruby is, by the principle of male dominance. The pleasures of Ruby's women are contingent on what they themselves produce and what they enjoy by themselves, or in the company of other women. For these out-of-bounds pleasures, they don't need men. (Dovey's male friend would seem to be the exception, except that he seems less a man than a spirit summoned up by Dovey's desire.) Since the women's enjoyments are independent of men, they also exceed the men's comprehension.

They can and do, however, feel obscurely threatened—troubled by something in their women they cannot put their finger on. They are rightly disturbed by the "fat, overwrought yards" where flowers multiply past all "reason" and "necessity" (90). The flowers crowd out and displace the vegetables, as the feminine enjoyment of useless beauty takes them away from their utilitarian duties as domestic providers. And, as we can see from Deacon's reliance on that domestic order, the patriarchy depends on women accepting and acting out the roles the men ordain for them.

Deacon, despite his complacent inventory of the orderly domestic spaces of Ruby, feels increasingly worried by something awry in his own wife, Soane. Yet, he thinks, "there was nothing in her behavior he could fault. She was as beautiful as it was possible for a good woman to be; she kept a good home and did good works everywhere" (112–13). Because Deacon is unable to perceive his wife apart from the abstract gender codes that define a "good woman," his understanding of her as a person is necessarily limited. So he is left with only vague intimations of trouble in place of comprehension: "He was increasingly uneasy about Soane. Nothing he could put his fingernail under, just a steady sense of losing ground" (112). The one concrete behavior that Deacon can find to pin his anxiety to is the one area where Soane is excessive: her sorrow for her two sons killed in the war exceeds Deacon's idea of the proper measure for mourning. He thinks, "The residue of that loss seemed to be accumulating in a way he could not control" (112). What Deacon cannot comprehend, he cannot control. The quiet forms of feminine excess I have been describing escape patriarchal control because they are outside standard patriarchal definitions of female sin and so outside the reach of the men's understanding and control.

But, you may ask, what's the big deal about a few extra flowers? What makes the men's anxiety intense and painful enough to require displacement? Women out of control raise the specter of female sexuality out of control. *Paradise* is, after all, Morrison's critique of patriarchy. And at the base of patriarchy is the control of female sexuality.[2] It seems that Morrison's aim is to strip away the inessentials of patriarchy to get back to its founding principles. As Engels tells us, the origin of monogamous marriage is the desire of the man to guarantee the transmission of his property to his son; the only way to do that is to gain control of the woman's sexuality. "In order to guarantee the fidelity of the wife, that is, the paternity of the children, the woman is placed in the man's absolute power" (737). In Ruby, the patriarchal leaders have "absolute power" over the intimate pairings of their citizens—or, in Patricia's blunt language, they determine "who fucks who" (217). The aim, as in Engels's myth, is control over reproduction—but not for the purpose of guaranteeing the legitimate transmission of private property. What are the town fathers aiming for?

Only marriages among scions of the founding families are countenanced in Ruby. And if some young woman is without a mate, her male relatives can give her away to a widower, as long as the widower carries the blood of one of the founding families. Ostensibly, the patriarchal figures' absolute control over reproduction is meant to guarantee the racial purity of the citizens. The founding families are distinguished by their deep blue-black color; only children who have that deep color are honored as the offspring of two of the original lines. All other pairings and births are dealt with by exile or internal ostracism. As Ana Maria Fraile-Marcos sums up this racial dimension of patriarchal control over female sexuality, "The control over 'race' becomes intrinsically linked to the control over women as the ultimate producers of generations" (16). While agreeing with Fraile-Marcos's concise statement, I would go further—to make the case that the aim of the patriarchal figures (at least according to Patricia's genealogical history) extends beyond guaranteeing the transmission of racial purity, into a kind of phantasmatic dimension of loyalty to the Founding Fathers.

Patricia, the town's schoolteacher, is also the town's "self-appointed historian" (Davidson 362). Consulting family trees and listening to stories of the founding passed down to her students from their families, she uncovers the existence of individuals written out of the town patriarchs' official story of Ruby's origins. Her counterhistory, by including "messy" details of persons and events obliterated from official history, undermines the heroic saga of the Founding Fathers, the nine families who founded Ruby.[3] Patricia puzzles over some aspects of the Ruby families' genealogy. "No one ever dies in Ruby": that is the town's claim, and Patricia questions how that can be true. Suddenly, in a flash she understands: "Did [Deacon and Steward] really believe that no one died in Ruby? Suddenly Pat thought she knew all of it. Unadulterated and unadulteried 8-rock blood held its magic as long as it resided in Ruby. That was their recipe . . . For Immortality" (217). Here are the pieces of the genealogical puzzle that Pat evidently puts together to understand "all of it": "unadulterated," "unadulteried," "immortality." But the text (characteristically) withholds what Patricia sees; her narrative ends a few lines later. Readers are left with enigma, which like all the enigmas in *Paradise* is meant to elicit the reader's participation in co-creating the text.

Here is my attempt to do so. Women must be kept "unadulteried"—faithful to their husbands—in order to avoid "adulterat[ing]" the gene pool. That bestows "immortality"—on whom? Characteristically, the text does not say. I speculate that "immortality"—"nobody ever dies in Ruby"—refers to the original patriarchs, who do not die because their descendants carry forward their "unadulterated" genes. But how could that be construed as immortality? I think the idea is that the reproduction of the line is so closely monitored by the patriarchal leaders that the original genes of the forefathers are transmitted intact, transferred to new bodies which carry them on. It is not just the laws and social codes of the Old Fathers that must be preserved intact, but the flesh and blood of the Old Fathers as well. The Old Fathers are to be given new embodiment in younger generations through the transmission of unadulterated genes. In this sense the patriarchal figures are "immortal." This is the parodic extreme of the ordinary paternal wish that the son carry on the father, embodying his values and ambitions. It takes to the logical extreme the desire to find in one's children a replication of the same. The young are meant to be not just offspring but clones of the Old Fathers.

I think that is what the claim of "Immortality" means. Richard Misner, trying to understand the leaders of Ruby, wonders why they constantly drum stories of the Founding Fathers into the ears of the younger generation. It is "as though, rather than children, they wanted duplicates" (161). Whether or not Misner means the word "duplicates" literally, in the context of the rigidly controlled patriarchal program of coupling among the first families of Ruby, his words take on the meaning of biological "duplicates." (This elaborate eugenics project is not going well: the constant incest and inbreeding meant to keep the gene pool undiluted have so weakened the offspring that they cannot thrive: witness the four defective babies born to Sweetie, kept barely alive by her and her mother-in-law's constant ministrations; one of them, Save-Marie, dies in the end.) With the report on the institutionalized appropriation and dispensation of young female bodies to older male relatives and with the implication that the patriarchy is trying to clone itself, the representation of the patriarchal figures' control over female sexuality becomes so extreme that parable becomes parody, and Morrison's myth of patriarchy acquires the bite of satire.

Patricia follows up her enigmatic musings on "unadulteried" and "immortality" with the thought, "In that case, . . . everything that worries them must come from women" (217). Glossing Pat's phrase, James Mellard claims that "'everything that worries them' . . . comes, however, not from all women. It comes only from the women of the Convent" ("The Jews" 359). On the contrary, I believe that "everything that worries them" comes from their own women. For the threat to Ruby from the Convent women is almost purely imaginary. Until the Convent becomes a dumping ground for the men's displaced anxieties, "most folks said" the Convent women were "helpful. . . . Early reports were of kindness and very good food" (11). Harmless, even helpful and benign, the Convent women have neither the means nor the motivation to bring harm to Ruby.

It is rather the women of Ruby who have the power to damage the patriarchy. As condensed in Pat's pairing of "adulterated" with "adulteried," it is the Ruby women's sexuality slipping out from under the tight behavioral codes imposed by the men that could result in "adultery" and introduce an admixture of foreign genes, hence "adulteration," into the gene pool. The Ruby women have the potential to make a mockery of the town fathers' careful management of reproduction to produce heirs who mirror them exactly. Jouissance, which is oblivious to social rule and custom, threatens to slip over from the harmless overabundance of flowers and butterflies to the lawless sexual excess it usually signifies.

It is telling that when the men meet to plan the attack on the Convent (or rather to whip themselves up to the pitch of irrational rage necessary for the extermination), they project not just loose sexuality onto the Convent women but, more frequently, disorderly reproduction: "What in God's name little babies doing out there? . . . Whatever it is, it ain't natural. . . . [Arnette] thinks they kept her baby and told her it was stillborn" (275). Thus aberrant sexual practices are paired with aberrant reproduction: "Kissing on themselves. Babies hid away" (276). (Fantasies of freaky reproductive practices extend even to the hens in the Convent garden: one of the Ruby men, "peering out [the door of the Convent], sees an old hen, . . . cherished, he supposes, for delivering freaks—double, triple yolks in outsize and misshapen shells" [5].) What the men fear, what they are trying to rub out by exterminating the Convent women, is not so much transgressive female sexuality as its results: female reproduction running wild.

"Everything that worries them must come from women" (217). Steward sleepless because he cannot keep Dovey in her rightful place in her husband's bed (100), Deacon obscurely worried about his wife Soane's alleged excess of mourning, the men who grumble about the flowers crowding out their vegetables—these represent a generalized male malaise about some of the Ruby wives' excesses. The women's willingness to indulge in enjoyments outside patriarchal norms and domestic containments—even though so far these enjoyments produce only flowers and butterflies and a superfluity of babble—makes the men vaguely nervous. For no matter what specific practices it engenders, feminine jouissance exceeds the limits of social rule and restraint.

The Other's Jouissance:
The Convent Women at the Wedding Reception

The men's accumulating vague worries about women find an outlet in displacement. When the Convent women come to the reception celebrating Arnette Fleetwood's marriage to K. D., they perform an unrestrained exhibition of female jouissance that provides the Ruby men with a convenient site for the displacement of anxiety about their own women.

A wedding celebrates the legal enclosure of sex, with its unruly impulses, into the closed space of the marriage unit. Female jouissance is tamed and enclosed within the role of good wife and the rule of monogamy. "In a legally sanctioned marriage ceremony, the law codifies enjoyment [jouissance] and thereby contains the danger that it represents to the social order" (McGowan, *End* 115). The marriage being celebrated represents an especially explicit containment of unruly sexuality. The wedding recalls K. D.'s roving passion from his four-year sexual obsession with Gigi, one of the Convent dwellers, and reroutes it into proper channels: he, the nephew of Deacon and Steward Morgan, must marry Arnette, the daughter of another founding family of Ruby. Thus the wedding reception celebrates not just the union of two leading families but also the tightness of patriarchal control over who sleeps with whom in Ruby.

The wedding ceremony itself has not gone well because of the odd behavior of the two ministers who officiated. Now, at the wedding reception, unease reigns and people begin to calm down only as the singing of a hymn begins. The solemnity is interrupted by the arrival of the Convent women—four of them in Mavis's Cadillac:

> They piled out of the car looking like go-go girls: pink shorts, skimpy tops, see-through skirts; painted eyes, no lipstick; obviously no underwear, no stockings. Jezebel's storehouse raided to decorate arms, earlobes, necks, ankles, and even a nostril. (156–57)

Then they turn the boom box in the Cadillac up high, interrupting the hymn:

Inside, outside and on down the road the beat and the heat were ruthless.
. . . The Convent girls are dancing; throwing their arms over their heads,
they do this and that and then the other. They grin and yip but look at
no one. Just their own rocking bodies. . . . One of them, with amazing
hair, asks [a small girl] can she borrow a bike. Then another. They ride the
bikes down Central Avenue with no regard for what the breeze does to their
long flowered skirts or how pumping pedals plumped their breasts. One
coasts with her ankles on the handlebars. Another rides the handlebars with
Brood on the seat behind her. One, in the world's shortest pink shorts, is
seated on a bench, arms wrapped around herself. She looks drunk. Are they
all? (157–58)

The mark of feminine jouissance that distinguishes the women's behavior
from that of any rowdy group is self-sufficiency. Each dances alone, needing
no male partner. They derive full enjoyment from "just their own rocking
bodies"; "they look at no one," needing nothing from any outside other. As
in Lacan's notion, feminine jouissance is self-generating and self-contained.
And as celebrants of female excess they of course have no regard for the social
order; they act as if oblivious to its rules for proper behavior. Everything they
do is in excess of the norm.

But wait. Who is describing this? We might take the third-person narrative perspective for omniscience, for focalization by an objective extradiegetic
narrator. But if we look more closely, the description appears to be not objective but tinged by moral outrage. This is not the omniscient discourse of
a faceless narrator but free-indirect discourse, filtered through the focalization of the group. The site of focalization is the townspeople—but not all the
townspeople, as the later responses of Anna and Kate to the scene make clear.
The narrative perspective is that of the collective disciplinary consciousness of
the Ruby men. Morrison is experimenting in *Paradise* with the thinking of
groups, and narrative form reflects that interest.

We can find out something about the kinds of thinking involved in displacement by paying attention to the way the men perceive the Convent
women. Whereas the jouissance of Ruby's women is hard to pin down, involving as it does flowers and butterflies and spectral kindred spirits, the
Convent women's blatant jouissance provides a site for displacement, a
seemingly legitimate place to discharge anxiety over women out of order.
But displacement creates its own misperceptions: the Convent women are
depicted with a broad brush that, in the effort to paint them all as uniformly
shameless, misrepresents. For example, in the first sentence of the passage,

they all seem to be wearing pink shorts; yet later, when they are on the bi-
cycle, the breeze lifts all "their long flowered skirts." All of them "obviously
[are wearing] no underwear": obvious to whom? Who could say this with
authority? Who would be able to ascertain that this is true, and true of all
four women? They all exhibit themselves shamelessly on bicycles, enjoying
the display of "plumping breasts" and lifting skirts. But this last bit of gen-
eralizing is exposed as false because one of them is not riding a bike but "is
seated on a bench, arms wrapped around herself." (Again, the stamp of feminine jouissance is self-sufficiency.) The patriarchal gaze universalizes, making
the women into a generic group marked with the stamp of "Jezebel," whose
"storehouse" has been raided "to decorate arms, earlobes, necks, ankles." This
last formulation generalizes so completely that the separate female bodies appear to agglomerate into a single collective body with multiple shamelessly
decorated limbs.

The details of this description come from the focalizing group's perception. But through the inadvertent contradictions of their description, the implied author insinuates that this perspective is warped. Narrative form makes
the point that universalizing—the attribution of identical qualities to all
members of a group—distorts reality.

And the implied reader, prepared by the novel's previous dedication of a
chapter to the subjective experience of each Convent woman in turn, knows
how unique is the subjectivity of each. It is true that Gigi seems to enjoy scandalizing the bourgeois and flaunting her body provocatively to tease out men's
responses. But here Gigi's attitude is generalized to the whole group, and we
know from previous chapters that the others are not wild sexual women but
rather waifs and strays, sad lost girls who emerge from separate histories of
abandonment, battery, and sexual abuse to find refuge in the Convent. So
the implied reader is equipped, from the chapters she has already read, to be
aware of the contradictions in this passage and, perhaps, to perceive the folly
of a universalizing perspective.

I would argue that the tendency to universalize, to make every member of
a group the same, belongs to the process of displacement. Displacement relies
on a binary structure. In displacement, the full charge of emotion attached to
A (the original object of attachment) is shifted to B (the substitute object). In
the present case, the whole weight of opprobrium that could be attached to
the excesses of Ruby's own women is shoved off and piled onto the excesses
of the Convent women. For this operation to work, the full measure of the
quality that occasions the opprobrium—here, feminine jouissance or, as the
men would call it, female licentiousness—has to be transferred from A to B.

What the binary operation of displacement excludes is the possibility that a little bit of jouissance dwells within women in both groups.

The text itself gives us a hint of the displacement going on here: Anna, whose residence outside Ruby for much of her adult life gives her a somewhat detached perspective on events, comes close to identifying the social dynamic at work: "Whatever else, thought Anna, the Convent women had saved the day. Nothing like other folks' sins for distraction" (159). The textual cue nudges the reader toward an understanding that a process of substitution is at work: the "sins," or jouissance, of the other group offer a welcome shift of focus from the community's own problems.

Having displaced their anxiety about feminine jouissance onto the site of the Other, the men can deal with it there—by exiling the offending females or, if their presence is still perceived as close enough to contaminate the home group, by trying to exterminate feminine jouissance altogether at the site of the Other. Displacement enables the men to continue believing in the existence of total patriarchal control over their own docile and accepting women. As in any displacement, however, the solution does not touch the original source of anxiety, here the quiet jouissance of Ruby's own women; the initial problem remains intact. Binary thinking underpins displacement, and both are shown by Morrison to be primitive processes that distort reality, prevent actual solutions, and lead to violence that misses the mark altogether.

Shame and Displacement:
A Second Hypothesis

Brooks Bouson's *Quiet as It's Kept* is a comprehensive and insightful study of shame as it functions in Morrison's novels, including *Paradise*. But I think that linking shame to displacement can open up yet another dimension of the way shame works in the novel. Following the thematics of shame will lead us to see that at the most fundamental level of the novel, political displacement and psychic displacement intersect.

Some peculiarities of narrative structure point the way toward this junction. Chapter 1 is called "Ruby," and it develops two aspects of Ruby: the fury of Ruby, expressed in the deadly attack on the Convent; and the history of the community, from its early displacements as it tried but failed to find a home to the founding of Haven and then of Ruby. These two elements are placed side by side, but there is no indication of a connection between them. The structural juxtaposition poses a puzzle: What is the connection between the slaughter of the women and the history of Ruby?

Chapter 1 withholds all information about the individuals committing the massacre we witness: we do not know their names, their situations, their motives. Yet the text reveals in minute detail the collective history that the two nameless, faceless leaders hold in their "powerful memories"—as if the story of the ancestors was the primary and fundamental thing to know about these two men. Geographical displacement is front and center in what they remember in "the controlling [story] told to them by their grandfather" (13):

> On the journey from Mississippi and two Louisiana parishes to Oklahoma, the one hundred and fifty-eight freedmen were unwelcome on each grain of soil from Yazoo to Fort Smith. Turned away by rich Choctaw and poor whites, chased by yard dogs, jeered at by camp prostitutes and their children, they were nevertheless unprepared for the aggressive discouragement they received from Negro towns already being built. (13)

The ancestors are not only denied a place but shamed by the lowest of the low: Indians and poor whites turn them away, prostitutes "jeer" at them, and the very dogs bark their contempt. But the worst insult, we are told, comes from the Negro towns that close them out. So from the first, shaming and geographical displacement go hand in hand.

This ancestral story of roaming and being denied a place is repeated five times in scraps interspersed among present-day events (13–14, 95–99, 109, 189, 194–95), indicating that the ancestral past is ever-present in the daily doings of Ruby's citizens. The worst shaming occurred at Fairly, Oklahoma, the goal of their migration from the South: the black citizens of Fairly refused to let them join the community, so the forefathers were forced into a yet more painful displacement. Yet it is only on the fifth rendition of the historical drama, late in the novel (194–95), that the fundamental reason for their rejection is revealed: race. The text keeps the worst shaming quiet, as if in response to the community's embarrassment over it.[4]

The lighter-skinned inhabitants of Fairly turned them away because of their deep black color:

> It had not struck them before that [color] was of consequence, serious consequence, to Negroes themselves. Serious enough that their daughters would be shunned as brides; their sons chosen last; that colored men would be embarrassed to be seen socially with their sisters. The sign of racial purity they had taken for granted had become a stain. (194)

They feel the shame of racial stain, of an inferiority stamped onto their skin where everyone can see it. This is the shame usually conveyed by the white gaze of contempt, but now, in an inconceivable betrayal, it is the black gaze that shames them for their color. The passage works out all the ramifications of this racial shaming: their daughters will be shamed, their sons shamed, their sisters shamed—and by black people like them, "men like them in all ways but one" (189): their color. The subjects of shame are the men: the women are not regarded as subjects who are shamed but referred to as "their" daughters and "their" sisters; and the boys are not boys but "their sons." It is only the men who are full subjects, and it is the manhood of the men that is shamed, because their definition of masculinity depends on their ability to protect their womenfolk (and ancillary children), and this they are unable to do. The refusal of entry at Fairly condemns them to an arduous further displacement and wandering, charged now with the animus of shame.

"Everything anybody wanted to know about the citizens of Haven or Ruby lay in the ramifications of that one rebuff out of many" (189). This key sentence insists that "everything" about this group can be traced to the Disallowing. I propose that we take this statement seriously and include in the category of "everything" the present-day massacre of the Convent women. The men of Ruby took the hit of Otherness at the level of race, but rather than acting out against the perpetrators (the colorist men of Fairly), they displace the shame they feel onto the Otherness of women—onto the shameful looseness of female sexuality (they imagine) in the Convent women. They displace the shame of race onto gender and deal with it there, with guns.

One might well object that the shaming took place in 1890, to a generation of men no longer alive in 1973, the year of the Convent massacre. Shouldn't the shame then be "over and done with?" as Patricia, rethinking history, asks. "Oh, no," she answers, and the text persuades us to say the same.

For the shame of that original displacement lives on intact in the mind of the Ruby leader, Steward, and presumably in the mind of his twin brother leader, Deacon. I say "mind" rather than "memory" advisedly, because when Steward is by himself, his stream of consciousness follows patterns we would expect to find in the Old Fathers. That is, rather than wander along paths of association drawn from his own experience, Steward's ruminations follow the traces of the Old Fathers' narratives (153–54). I have argued that Morrison's parody of patriarchy extends to making fun of the patriarchal impulse to reproduce the same—"my" son reflects "me"—by taking that impulse to its logical extreme, in rules on sexual coupling designed to reproduce the Old Fathers in the sons and grandsons. In Steward, filial piety takes a similar form, with Steward repeating the old fathers' patterns exactly not just at the level of governing—requiring, for example, that the citizens adhere to the precise sense of the words Zechariah carved onto the Oven—but also in the ungoverned movements of his mind. It is as if respect demands that he keep the forefather alive by reproducing him as completely as he can, down to the smallest mental activity.

Here is Steward's daydreaming:

> After leaving Fairly, Oklahoma, . . . Big Papa and Big Daddy and all seventy-nine were . . . on foot and completely lost. . . . And angry. . . . The pregnant women needed more and more rest, Drum Blackhorse's wife, Celeste, his grandmother, Miss Mindy; and Beck, his own mother, were all with child. It was the shame of seeing one's pregnant wife or sister or daughter refused shelter that had rocked them, and changed them for all time. The humiliation did more than rankle; it threatened to crack open their bones. (95)

This is history told in terms of intimate feeling: the dismissal from Fairly leaves the forefathers feeling shame and the impotent anger produced by shame. Intensely, they feel a humiliation that "threaten[s] to crack open their bones" (95). Shame, as shame theorists like Helen Lewis tell us, so overwhelms the subject that it disorganizes the personality, leaving the self without the means to speak or think, producing more shame (Lewis 19; qtd. in Bouson, *Quiet* 10). The whole wandering group of ancestors feels this shame, as the deep black color they had prided themselves on becomes a "stain"; racial shame threatens to undermine the ground of their collective identity.

The grandfathers' sufferings become Steward's own sufferings:

> Steward remembered every detail of the story his father and grandfather told, and had no trouble imagining the shame for himself. Dovey, for instance, before each miscarriage . . . looking inward, always inward at the baby inside her. How would he have felt if some highfalutin men in collars and good shoes had told her, "Get away from here," and he, Steward, couldn't do a thing about it? (95–96)

Steward doesn't just empathize with the old fathers. Through identification, he feels the shame of his grandfathers "for himself." What he cannot bear is his own shame. His manhood is based on the masculinity defined by his forebears, resting primarily on the man's ability to protect his woman. Fully engulfed in the impotence of not being able to protect the ancestral pregnant women "Celeste and Miss Mindy and Beck," who blur into his own wife, Dovey, Steward experiences the "helplessness" to which his forefathers were reduced by the Disallowing. The grandfathers' shame becomes Steward's shame, deeply felt and leading to rage: "The thought of that level of helplessness made him want to shoot somebody" (96).

The geographical displacement of the ancestors, who after their expulsion from Fairly wander "lost" and "angry," results finally in a psychic displacement of shame and rage from race to gender. Steward does shoot—not the men of Fairly who shamed his color through his grandfathers, but all the women in the Convent. For the men have seen enough and manufactured enough fantasies about the Convent women that they have convinced themselves that these loose women embody the shame of womanhood. Racial shame is displaced onto the shame of womanhood and wiped out there, in the "lewd" female bodies they destroy.

To support this premise, I note that in writing *The Bluest Eye* Morrison was already alive to the mechanism of black men displacing race shame onto gender. Cholly displaces the shame he feels under the gaze of the white men who humiliate him onto Darlene, his fellow victim in the forced sexual intercourse his white tormentors demand they perform. "He cultivated his hatred of Darlene. Never did he once consider directing his hatred toward the hunters. Such an emotion would have destroyed him. They were big, white, armed men. He was small, black, helpless . . . hating them would have consumed him, burned him up like a piece of soft coal." So "he hated the one who had created the situation, the one who bore witness to his failure, his impotence" (150–51). Cholly's race shame—his impotence compared to the big white men, his necessary subservience to their sexual orders—is displaced onto the woman, where the shame of race becomes sexual shame; and Cholly's rage against their tormentors turns on her as the embodiment of shameful female sexuality.

In *Paradise*, as in *The Bluest Eye*, Toni Morrison uncovers a mechanism of displacement that extends well beyond the world of the African American communities she portrays, to other cultures organized by male dominance. For example, the indigenous peoples of Mexico displaced the shame of having lost control of their land to the invading Spanish onto the sexual guilt of La Malinche, who was blamed for being Cortés's mistress and for having given birth to mestizos, to mixed-race children. La Malinche was taxed with the betrayal of her people, a betrayal that could well have been laid at the feet of the warriors who failed to protect that people; the shame of male impotence was displaced onto woman's sexual shame. La Malinche was (and continues to be) reviled as "la Chingada," shamed by her own unwilling participation in rape.[5]

In turn-of-the-century Vienna, Freud's theoretical work bears the mark of displacement: Freud, according to Sander Gilman, dealt with the anti-Semitism that infused the medical science of his time by displacing traits attributed to the Jew onto his theoretical model of woman.[6] That displacement freed him from anxiety about the limitations of the Jewish mind and body (his own mind and body) and enabled him to constitute an identity as the race-neutral figure of male scientist (Gilman 37). As in *Paradise*, shame about race is displaced onto gender. Two different strands of psychic displacement thus propel the Ruby men's extermination of the Convent women. The anxiety aroused in the patriarchal figures by their own women's quiet displays of jouissance is displaced onto the female bodies at the Convent. And the original race shame created by the ancestors' ejection from Fairly is displaced onto the shame of womanhood.

Dislocating the Reader

Mirroring the geographical displacement of the characters, the reader experiences again and again a radical displacement. *Paradise* begins and ends in ambiguity. We do not know where we are as we begin the novel. And the ending leaves us wondering, too, unable to interpret events that escape our everyday understanding of the distinctions between life and death. More disconcerting, displacement, in the sense of losing a familiar narrative world and being forced to enter into a new and unknown territory, is a recurring experience for the reader as she makes her way through the novel. The confusion we feel at losing familiar ground and being forced to set off in a new direction does have a signifying function, though: our disorientation mirrors the disorientation of the characters, every one of whom has been displaced and had to struggle to get his or her bearings in an unfamiliar world.

The novel opens, "They shoot the white girl first. With the rest they can take their time. No need to hurry out here" (3). For the next few pages, we observe nameless men killing nameless women, in an unspecified place and time. We can make the argument that the violence of the opening, hitting us before we have a symbolic structure within which to understand and contextualize it, captures the shock of real violence. That is, it captures the way violence, unforeseen and inexplicable, breaks in upon the victim seemingly out of nowhere.

It is also true, as Stephanie Li has argued, that in the novel's first sentence violence accompanies the use of racial appellation ("white girl"), as if to say that representing someone as raced is already a violence to that person's subjectivity. Summarizing Dana Nelson's work on race, Li says, "The racial identification of another is an inherently violent act because it severs individuals from the infinite possibilities of identity. Racialized subjects are circumscribed by the dictates of prejudice and stereotype" (Li 46). In the rest of *Paradise*, Morrison avoids racialized language, trying "to carve away the accretions of deceit, blindness, ignorance, paralysis, and sheer malevolence embedded in raced language" (Morrison, "Home" 7). However, we do not know all this as we enter *Paradise*. We have no idea where we are or who is shooting whom, or why. We can tolerate this indeterminacy at the beginning of a text, even though it makes unusual demands on us because it goes on for eight pages, because we expect to know nothing about the fictional world when we enter a novel; and we expect, if we are good and patient readers, to learn in time where we are, and with whom.

This first chapter, "Ruby," eventually gives us enough information about the history of Ruby to enable us to find our way into the fictional universe of Ruby. However, just as we find our footing in the narrative world, that world is pulled out from under us and we are thrown into new and baffling textual territory.

Chapter 2, called "Mavis," begins, "The neighbors seemed pleased when the babies died" (21). Again, we are confronted with an unfamiliar narrative world that, devoid of known characters and of indications of time and space, baffles the reader's desire for meaning. We can say again, as we said about the first sentence of chapter 1, that the textual blow of sudden death, unprepared and unexplained, replicates the shock and the meaninglessness of a traumatic event. It thus reflects, at the level of the reader, Mavis's inability to understand the death of her babies or grasp the unthinkable truth that she has herself caused their death. We have entered the world of "Mavis," as the chapter is entitled, and so, as we enter into her focalization, we share in the character Mavis's confusion. For Mavis is herself displaced, even in the heart of her family. As mother and housekeeper, she is ineffectual, perhaps because she is often beaten by her husband (she has been to the local hospital fifteen times, only four of which visits were to bear children). From inside her mental fog she perceives the dirt in the house but doesn't know what to do about it (she is "not sure whether to scrape the potato chip crumbs from the seams of the [couch] or tuck them further in" [21]). And she perceives the actions of her husband and children as proof of a conspiracy to further batter and torture her (26). Her incompetence as a mother is crowned by her letting the twin babies die; as she admits to herself, she is "too rattle-minded to open a car's window so babies could breathe" (37). When she makes her escape from her home (which is where?; we are never located geographically), she doesn't make it to her destination, California, but becomes disoriented and ends up running out of gas in Oklahoma, dislocated again, in the middle of a "billion miles of not one thing" (37). After a long walk she finds herself at the Convent, where the bizarre states of the woman with all-white eyes (Connie) and the aged woman whose body radiates light (Mother) must make her feel displaced again—although the warm kitchen of the Convent makes her feel "safe," at last (41).

Thus the text's estrangement of the reader in the first part of the chapter mirrors Mavis's estrangement first in her own domestic world and subsequently in her travels into unknown territory. Each one of the four young women who wander into the Convent is similarly displaced, all (with the exception of Gigi) homeless as a result of abandonment or betrayal. Mavis's disorientation, together with the formal devices that reflect and reinforce it, is representative of all the displaced Convent dwellers' experience.

The narrative puts the reader through a different kind of uprooting at the end of the chapter called "Patricia" and focalized by Patricia. After reading through Patricia's careful study of the Ruby families' genealogies, we read that Patricia burns the documents we have been reading and studying. I want first to speculate on the effect of this burning on the reader and, second, to argue that the burning becomes a synecdoche, or enactment in miniature, of the reader's repeated experience of being displaced from the textual reality she or he has been carefully constructing.

Through the many long pages of the "Patricia" chapter the reader has been studying facts: Patricia inscribes genealogical facts—who married whom, who bore whom—and that is a relief from the ambiguity surrounding the events of prior chapters. As Lucille Fultz says, "The reader may . . . accept the accuracy of Patricia's ordered and labored 'research' . . . because it may provide some relief from the densely verbal morass of the earlier chapters" (88). Because one can do the work of interpreting effectively—connecting one element to another to make sequential hypotheses about the material as one reads—one's sense of readerly competence is restored. And "the reader can reconsider, reorder, and reevaluate her/his understanding of the other parts of *Paradise*" (Fultz 88), to begin to make sense of the whole text. Patricia's burning of the documents dumbfounds the reader. If Patricia is so unbalanced and self-destructive—perhaps she is even mad—that she burns her life's work, her account is probably not credible. And one's sense of mastering the text is misplaced. A reader feels displaced from the ground of certain knowledge when Patricia's authoritative history of Ruby goes up in smoke.

The chapter's structure reverses the usual function of a surprise ending: usually, a surprise ending imparts some new information that shifts a reader's perspective and enables a sudden understanding of all that has gone before (as in Morrison's *Love*, whose narrative structure I discuss in chapter 4). Here, on the contrary, the surprise at the end represents an undoing of knowledge—both at the level of the storyworld, where Patricia's history of Ruby is destroyed, and at the level of reader response, as the reader experiences the basis of her knowledge unraveling. The burning of the text also serves as an apt metaphor for the reader's repeated experience of interpreting *Paradise*: we are displaced again and again, as the ground of our understanding is pulled out from under our feet.

We may take another suggestive episode of *Paradise* as a figure for what the implied author is aiming at. After the massacre at the Convent (that is, quite late in the novel), Anna Flood and Richard Misner go to the Convent garden. Both sense an opening, a "window" or a "door"—into what? (305). "He . . . felt it beckon toward another place—neither life nor death—but there, just yonder, shaping thoughts he did not know he had" (307). As Linda Krumholz says of this passage, "Morrison indicates the presence of spiritual meaning and mysteries without trying to 'nail down' their significance; she . . . opens windows onto new visions, while also demonstrating the limits of human vision" ("Reading" 31). I would agree that here, in the last part of the novel, which introduces many spiritual mysteries—like "stepping in" to another's body to reverse his dying—ambiguity seems fitting, a sign of respect for a metaphysical reality that is beyond human thought.[7] Neither Anna nor Richard goes through the door or even looks through the window into that "other place." They pause in not-knowing, letting go of old certainties—the difference between life and death, for instance—but they refrain from replacing the old knowledge with anything concrete. Their vision simply keeps the door open. I think that the implied author wants to open the door for the reader to a new way of thinking—and *to keep it open*. Anna and Richard model an ideal reader response to Morrison's frequent erasures of the reader's hard-fought-for insights and knowledge; having to tolerate enigmas that are resolved only later or not at all trains a reader to remain open to new possibilities without "nailing down" any of them, without closing down on a singular meaning.

It seems that *Paradise* endorses ambiguity as a good in itself. Thus the female characters of Ruby with whom one is most inclined to sympathize tend to embrace ambiguity and a fluidity of meaning (Krumholz, "Reading" 25). Of the words carved onto the Oven, Dovey says, "'Furrow of His Brow' alone was enough for any age or generation. Specifying it, particularizing it, nailing its meaning down, was futile" (93). Dovey's words about a text in the fictional world offer a synecdoche for the reader's relation to the larger text of *Paradise* itself (Page, "Furrowing" 639). The reader is encouraged to abandon the effort to find a singular truth and to welcome in its place a multiplicity of possible meanings, or to remain open to some new revelation that may or may not come.

On the political level of the novel, this makes sense: the embrace of ambiguity is an antidote to the patriarchal mode of authoritarian thinking that yields absolute certainty—an absolute certainty that we have seen lead to the annihilation of five human lives.[8] Resisting the tyranny of the single truth, enigma leads to a democracy of interpreters. In the storyworld, each character interprets the text of the Oven differently; just so, the enigmas of *Paradise* open the text to a multiplicity of readers' interpretations, each one valid.

And Morrison evidently intends this egalitarian relation of interpreters to extend to her own relationship with the reader. In interviews about *Paradise* she indicates that at certain places of textual undecidability, such as the parallax at the end, Morrison "want[s] the reader to decide for his or her self" what she "want[s]"—the women alive, or the women dead ("Interview with Toni Morrison"; qtd. in Page, "Furrowing" 638). Are the women alive again at the end? Are they dead? There is evidence for both, but the two states are mutually exclusive. The responsibility to choose meaning shifts from author to reader ("Interview with Toni Morrison").[9]

If my analysis of reader displacement as a formal mirroring of the characters' geographical displacement does not make the hard work of reading *Paradise* easy or alleviate a reader's frustration at working through an enigma only to find a new enigma blocking the road to understanding, it does argue for the formal coherence of *Paradise*. A reader's confusion at being displaced into unknown fictional territory or at having the ground of her interpretation whisked out from under her formally reflects the characters' troubles as they are dislocated, time after time.

CHAPTER 4

Love's Time and the Reader

Ethical Effects of *Nachträglichkeit* (Afterwardsness) in *Love*

In Morrison's *Beloved, Jazz*, and *Paradise*, disruptions of chronological narrative sequence reflect the dislocations of African American history—Middle Passage, the journey north from the post-Reconstruction South, the Great Migration—together with the psychic upheavals that accompany them. The disruptions of chronological sequence in *Beloved*, for example, formally reflect the emotional and psychological disturbances that accompanied the displacements of the Middle Passage, which severed the enslaved Africans from their land, their culture, their ancestors, and their past.

In *Love* (2003), the characters' severance from their past is a personal, not a world-historical event, an individual rather than a collective trauma. Yet in one respect at least, Heed's and Christine's experience parallels the experience of the captive Africans on the slave ships: as a result of an early traumatic separation from the love that had been the ground of their childhood development, Heed and Christine lose connection with their past and its rich field of potentials and are consequently disoriented with regard to their present and future. The events that disrupt their temporal order are themselves a violation of chronology: Heed's marriage at eleven to her twelve-year-old playmate Christine's grandfather, the successful black entrepreneur Bill Cosey; and, hidden behind that marriage, the earlier intrusion of adult sexuality into the childhood world through Cosey's molestation of Heed. From the moment Heed is catapulted untimely into the world of adult sexuality and marriage, Heed and Christine lose the ability to order their lives fruitfully in relation to time's passage.

Narrative displacements reflect the protagonists' temporal disorientation, so that the time of the reading is itself discontinuous: we witness the effects—

the long wasting of Heed's and Christine's lives—before we uncover its cause, the premature marriage, nearly two-thirds into the novel; and we are privy to the beginning of things—to the deep love between Christine and Heed when they were young girls—only at the end of the novel, after 182 pages of witnessing the two women's bitter enmity. The ending not only overthrows our expectations of narrative sequence but reveals that the text has misled the reader regarding the most basic question one can ask about a novel: What is this story about? At the end, the new information about the characters' past—about the events that caused the whole sequence the reader has just processed—makes the reader reconstruct everything that has come before: the story centers not on the wanderings of male desire, as we had been led to believe, but on the mutual love of little girls.

The structuring of *Love* around a time lag in the reader's relation to systems of meaning suggests a new perspective on Freud's model of *Nachträglichkeit* (variously translated as afterwardsness, deferred action, après-coup, and belatedness)—and new ways of using that temporal paradigm to illuminate reader response to the asymmetries of nonlinear narrative structures like Morrison's.[1] This complex temporal structure, which Freud recognized in many of his hysterical patients, is composed of (at least) two scenes widely separated in time: in the first scene a child is exposed to some action on the part of an adult—usually a sexual act of some kind—that the child does not have the requisite knowledge or psychosexual development to understand. Years later, after the child has passed puberty and entered the world of adult sexuality, a second incident occurs that through some superficial resemblance reminds the individual of the first scene, and he or she reacts with the emotional and cognitive responses that would have been appropriate to the first scene.

Jean Laplanche, the contemporary theorist responsible for elaborating Freud's *nachträglich* model, often cites the example of "Emma" from Freud's *Project for a Scientific Psychology* (Freud 411–16; Laplanche 38–43). At the age of eight, Emma goes into a shop to buy candy, and the shopkeeper gropes her through her clothes while grinning; Emma, not yet inducted into the world of adult sexuality, does not understand what he is doing and so has little or no emotional response. Several years later, after passing puberty, the now-adolescent Emma goes into a clothing shop, sees two shop clerks laughing together, feels attracted to one, is assailed by overwhelming feelings of sexual excitation and horror, rushes out of the shop, and develops a phobia against shopping. It was apparently trivial details of the second encounter—the shop assistants' laughter and the focus on clothing—that triggered the memory of the candy shopkeeper's grin and his touching Emma through her clothing. Only now, after the advent of puberty, does Emma have the knowledge and the psychosexual development necessary to comprehend the meaning of the initial incident: it was a sexual assault. Her extreme emotional disturbance would have been appropriate to the first scene, but it was impossible for her to experience it then; now, when she has the information requisite for understanding, she grasps the meaning of the first scene and responds, but her response is inappropriate to the present moment. In this paradigm of the missed encounter, the readiness of the subject always fails to coincide with the offerings of the moment: she comes to the event either "too early" or "too late."

Psychoanalytic theorists have tended to focus on the trauma that triggers *Nachträglichkeit* and to emphasize the effects of trauma on the delayed functioning of memory—and indeed a focus on trauma would be relevant to *Love,* whose protagonists' lives are so clearly maimed by early trauma. But the feature of the Laplanche/Freud paradigm more relevant to my purpose here—to an analysis of the reader responses evoked by *Love's* narrative structure—is the paradigm's strange temporality.[2]

The distinctive feature of *Nachträglichkeit* is that it structures a dialectic of meaning. On the one hand, meaning is projected backward from the present onto the past, as the subject realizes what the first scene signified; on the other hand, the content of the first scene is projected forward from the past to fill, inappropriately, the present scene. In *Love,* the reader's belated discovery of the beginning of things when she nears the end of the novel similarly inaugurates a movement of meaning in two directions. Discovering belatedly the original scene of the young girls' love for each other induces the reader to go back over the earlier text and understand it differently. But there is also a cognitive movement in the opposite direction: the intimate knowledge the reader has gained from the earlier text about the effects of the women's forced separation—the barren waste of their entire subsequent lives—informs and intensifies the reader's response to the "second scene" of the women's revelatory dialogue.

I contend that Morrison also uses the narrative structure of too early/too late, the discontinuity between readerly spheres of not-knowing and knowing, for rhetorical and pedagogical purposes: first, through the main body of the novel, to engage readers' preconceptions about the nature of love and who qualifies to be a lover, and then, in the last chapter, to force a reflection on and perhaps a reevaluation of those assumptions. Morrison repeatedly remarks on how important it is to her to engage the reader in the co-creation of her novels: she always leaves "places and spaces" for the reader to fill in, she says ("Rootedness" 341); and in the essay "Home" she specifies the kind of information that she (sometimes) wants the reader to supply. She wants her prose to invite and "expose the reader's own politics" ("Home" 7).

It is specifically the "politics" of a reader's assumptions about love and power that *Love* calls into play. Like *Paradise*, *Love* is a critique of patriarchy. But whereas *Paradise*'s technique, approaching the mode of broad satire, exaggerates the characteristic features of patriarchy in the fictional world of the novel, *Love* targets primarily the patriarchal values of its readers and does so by subtle formal means. Morrison deploys all the tricks of her narrative art—implied author, surprise ending, two narrative voices between whom the charge of unreliability shifts unpredictably—first to lure out a reader's preconceptions about love and then to provoke her to reexamine them. In particular, the surprise ending makes a reader turn around on her own reading to ask just how far her assumptions about the relative value of women and men, about the primacy of male desire in a love relationship, and about the normativity of heterosexual romantic love have biased her reading of the first 182 pages of the novel.

Broken Time:
The Disrupted Temporality of Heed and Christine

Morrison represents the effects of trauma as a temporal disorder. The traumatic rupture of Heed's childhood friendship with Christine, which followed upon her premature marriage to Christine's grandfather, disabled both girls' ability to respond appropriately to the offerings of time: like Freud's Emma, they always come too early or too late to life's events. The paradigmatic scene of temporal incongruity in *Love*—the prototype for all succeeding moments of temporal misfit—is Heed's description of her honeymoon:

> Every day for three days they shopped, [her husband] letting her buy anything she wanted, including Parisian Night lipstick, . . . high-heeled shoes, . . . and fishnet hose. Only in the evening was she alone, for a few hours while he visited friends, tended to business. None of which Heed minded, because she had coloring books, picture magazines, paper dolls to cut out and clothe. (128)

This scene comes as a shock to the reader, who through the first 127 pages of text has been led to assume that Heed's marriage was age-appropriate—that it was, indeed, all that a romantic marriage between two loving adults could be (62). The conflation of honeymoon with paper dolls and coloring books emphasizes the temporal contradiction condensed in the figure of the child bride.

A lack of temporal congruity characterizes all the stages of Heed's subsequent life—and, to a lesser extent, the stages of Christine's life as well. At the simplest level, Heed and Christine are consistently out of phase with the biological time of their bodies—for example, with the stages of their reproductive cycles. As we learn from flashbacks, Heed ostensibly became pregnant, but the pregnancy lasted for eleven months—and then proved false; Christine developed a desire to have a child "too late"—in the moment when she saw the remains of her seventh abortion vanishing down the toilet bowl. Now in their sixties and thus well past menopause, "both women regularly bought and wore sanitary napkins, and threw them in the trash completely unstained" (119–20). Morrison insists on the radical nature of the two women's temporal dysfunction by disabling their relation to the most basic level of human temporality, that of the body.

At a second level, the women's disrupted relation to temporality includes a cognitive misalignment with events. And here the parallel with the *nachträglich* structure becomes instructive. What changed to make Emma react violently to the harmless second scene, Freud says and Laplanche repeats several times, is that the now-adolescent girl had "a new understanding," "new ideas . . . ideas allowing her to understand what a sexual assault is" (Freud, *Project* 413; Laplanche 40): the difference between the "too early" scene and the "too late" scene is a difference in knowledge. In the sense of not being able to grasp the underlying meaning of what is happening to them, I would argue, Heed and Christine remain in the "too early" phase for most of their lives—for the length of the fifty years represented in the main body of the text. That is, Heed and Christine lack the conceptual tools that would enable them to understand their situation. From the time that Heed is untimely jolted into the world of sexuality and marriage up until the present, when the women are in their sixties, she and Christine occupy a world of patriarchal meanings that precludes their understanding of what the loss of their friendship means to them; they can see each other only as rivals.[3] In the fictional present they are rivals still, locked in a struggle over which one of them is the "sweet Cosey-child" that Bill Cosey's makeshift will designates as heir to his property. For the thirty years since Cosey's death, the women have been fixated on that question. At the very end of the novel, they recapture the discourse of their girlhood, a world of meanings that enables them to value their love for each other and gives them a perspective from which to comprehend their oppression. But it is too late.

The occasion of their reconciliation is a mortal injury that Heed sustains in a fall: the accident jogs her and Christine out of their fifty-year-old enmity, so they are able to retrieve their eleven-year-old selves. The text introduces the extraordinary temporality of this scene by signaling an abrogation of chronological time: "The future is disintegrating along with the past" (184).

The women's dialogue is *nachträglich*, "afterward," inappropriate to its moment in time, in several ways. They take up their dialogue exactly as it was when it was broken off some fifty years before, in the idiom of eleven-year-olds complete with a secret language, a kind of pig Latin based on the suffix "idagay," arcane exclamations like "Hey, Celestial!"—a prepubescent epithet of admiration and congratulation—and childhood jokes. The scene represents a fold in time, as the women's eleven-year-old selves are superimposed on their sixty-year-old selves. Their "special language" conveys the quality and texture of their intimacy and makes us aware of the magnitude of their early loss.

The renewal of their mutually enriching dialogue promises a new beginning. Retrieving the potentials inherent in their childhood love can now generate movement into a creative future. Continuity is reestablished, past, present, and future reconnected in a potentially creative collaboration. But alas, this new birth is out of synchrony with the inexorable passage of chronological time. Heed is not an eleven-year-old child but a woman in her sixties who is about to die from the fall she has just suffered. There *is* no future. What should be a new beginning is truncated to the few minutes before Heed dies: (re)birth and death collapse into each other, obliterating the temporal spread between. It is too late.

The Freudian model of *Nachträglichkeit* clarifies the odd temporality of Christine's and Heed's final dialogue. In the *nachträglich* temporal structure, the arrow of time moves simultaneously in two directions. And that is the structure here. On the one hand, the prepubescent past of the characters projects its content, together with its language and values, into the present scene, so that Christine and Heed enact the past in the present; on the other hand, it is the temporal location of the women in the here and now of their sixties that enables them to project meaning backward onto the past and see the whole sweep of their lives differently. Time is presented not as a linear sequence but as a dialectic that produces new meanings.

The sentence that I take to be the leitmotif of their revised reading of the past sums up both their recognition of the wrong turn their lives took and the cause of that disastrous deviation: "We could have been living our lives hand in hand instead of looking for Big Daddy everywhere" (189).[4] The phrase "hand in hand" evokes the gesture of little girls walking together and so implies movement down a path, from childhood into a future evoked by "our lives." The phrase "could have been living our lives" suggests that the women have not been doing so, that having lost the thread of life, they have been circling fruitlessly somewhere outside life's temporal progression. The sentence also indicates the cause of their disorientation: "looking for Big Daddy everywhere." It is the forced entry into patriarchy and premature sexuality that put them off course, that made their attention swerve from the thing that mattered (their friendship) to the only thing that seemed to matter—what the man wanted. But now, recentered in their friendship, reflecting on the past from the regained perspective of the pre-heterosexual world, they can see the enormity of Bill Cosey's actions and name them, accurately, as a crime—as a theft of childhood, and more: "He took all my childhood away from me, girl," Heed says (194).

Yet the reconciliation of the women raises questions about the deferred actions of the plot. First, why is the understanding of the original situation deferred for fifty years? My answer would be that once the premature marriage thrust both little girls into the world of patriarchal heterosexuality, they became locked into a system of meaning that robbed girlfriend love of value and made the only love that signifies the love of a man. According to this worldview, the man is the central figure of importance, and the woman's task is to capture his favor, or his support, or, in the romance plot, his love. While Bill Cosey was alive, all the women—May (Christine's mother), Christine, and Heed—revolved endlessly around the enigma of the man's desire, each claiming the place of the beloved: "Each had been displaced by another; each had a unique claim on Cosey's affection; each had either 'saved' him from some disaster or relieved him of an impending one" (98). The singular "each," "each," "each" sketches the isolation of each woman estranged from the others by their competition for the only subject of importance, the man.

And a second question inevitably arises: Bill Cosey died thirty years before the present moment, and the women have been living together in the Cosey house for over twenty years: why did they not rediscover each other and renew their childhood love before? Counting only the twenty years they have been living together under one roof, that makes 7,300 days of missed encounters. Again, Morrison expands the time frame to make a point, to illustrate the force of patriarchal discourse: after Cosey's death, Heed and Christine remain preoccupied with the signifiers of capitalist patriarchy, with the terms that the Law of the Father endows with meaning: inheritance, property, legitimacy. Repeatedly, Heed and Christine identify their positions within a patriarchal domestic order—Heed insisting redundantly that she is Bill Cosey's lawful wedded wife and Christine going to law to establish, again redundantly, that she is "the last, the only, blood relative of William Cosey"—and hence the "sweet Cosey child" his will designates as heir (95). (L's disclosure at the end of *Love* that the will is a fake emphasizes the futility of their lifelong obsession.)

Within the patriarchal order, Christine and Heed can see each other only as rivals—first for the man's favor, then for the man's estate.[5] It is only from a retrospective vantage point in a changed frame of reference that Heed and Christine can perceive the real relations of power that prevented their living full lives. The text's disjunctive temporal schema exaggerates the schism between the two worlds of meaning—the heterosexual patriarchal world and the world of female friendship—in order to show that the patriarchal imaginary closes off all alternative spheres of meaning.

Reading Belatedly

The complexity of reader response to the final chapter's surprises depends on a narrative structure analogous to *Nachträglichkeit*. In the first structural moment of *Nachträglichkeit*, coming "too early" to experience means inhabiting a world of signifiers without the key to their meanings; the second structural moment involves comprehending the meaning after the fact. There is a similar split in *Love* between experiencing (during the "first scene" of the reading) and knowing (in the "second scene," comprised of the final chapter). That is, we read the first 182 pages of *Love* in ignorance of the original love between Heed and Christine and the mode of its destruction, so we read without grasping the underlying significance of events; like the child in the Freudian paradigm, we perceive only the surface of things. It is only the "second scene," the final chapter, that opens up the meaning of all that has gone before. Parallel to Emma's sudden realization, "So that was sex!" is the reader's retroactive enlightenment: "So that was what all that meant!"[6]

Of course, a surprise ending always "causes us substantially to revise our previous configuration," "to reconfigure our understanding" of the prior text (Phelan, "Narrative as Rhetoric" 344). But I would claim for Morrison's structure a more complex effect on the reader—a double movement of enhanced comprehension. As in the *nachträglich* structure, the arrow of meaning moves not only from present to past (the movement of retrospective "reconfiguration of understanding") but also from past to present. On the one hand, as a result of discovering the women's childhood love for each other, the reader understands for the first time the reasons for the long emptiness of the women's lives that she or he has been witnessing through the main body of the text. On the other hand, because the reader has experienced the prior text, he or she knows as she arrives at the final revelatory pages all the manifold painful *effects* of the cause that is now revealed. Because the information about the love that Christine and Heed lost reaches the reader afterward, after the reader has become acquainted with the two women's pitifully narrow and unripened lives, because he or she knows in advance all the crippling effects of the interruption of their love and their development, the revolution in the reader's understanding carries with it a revolution of affect. The surprise of discovering the women's childhood love and its traumatic loss intensifies the affect that floods the reader as she or he "gets" the meaning of all the textually prior episodes at once. The realization that "they were just little girls" (*Love* 136) evokes compassion—a compassion absent when we saw them as greedy, mean-spirited old women—and, because it opens up a perspective on the whole sweep of their lives from girlhood to death, horror at the recognition of lives wasted. As in the *nachträglich* temporal structure, it is not only meaning that relays from present to past and back again from past to present, but affect too. The textual displacement of information leads the reader to experience strong feelings about the waste of a whole life's time as the women themselves do—belatedly.

I am not arguing, however, as recent literary critics of trauma narratives have argued, that the novel's formal structure produces in its readers a linguistic simulacrum of the characters' traumatized state. Unlike Greg Forter, for example, who sees in Faulkner's *Absalom! Absalom!* the deployment of a *nachträglich* structure of withheld signification that "transmits a form of psychic disequilibrium 'directly' to the reader" and thus makes the reader experience a version of the trauma she or he is reading about (35),[7] I will argue that afterwardsness, or *Nachträglichkeit*, functions quite differently for the reader than it does for the characters. Heed and Christine live *nachträglich*, chronically out of phase with the time of their lives, because of the trauma that stunted their lives. By contrast, the *nachträglich* temporal structure that *Love* imposes on its reader—coming to the beginning of things at the end, coming to the meaning of the text after the fact of reading it—has, I will argue, a pedagogical purpose: to make the reader aware of the extent of her own mental and emotional subjection to patriarchal systems of meaning and value. Morrison accomplishes this ethical effect by presenting two distinct narrative frames of signification. When the reader moves into the final chapter, she moves into a new moral universe, into a discourse governed by entirely different values and understandings from those that pervade the first 182 pages.

By means of what narrative techniques does Morrison keep the two narrative spheres of meaning separate and distinct?

Love's Dual Narration

There are two narrators in *Love*; they approach the Cosey story from quite different angles. Although literary convention primes readers to privilege the seemingly objective heterodiegetic narrator over the first-person character narrator named L, I will argue that the third-person narrative apparatus, including the narrator and the focalizing characters whose minds he opens to us, is biased toward the interests of the man and permeated by patriarchal assumptions about human relations. The character narrator L, who initially seems less reliable, interpolates glimpses of a different love story throughout the body of the novel and becomes the voice of truth and authority in the novel's concluding pages.

Readers puzzled about the veracity of a narrator's account are instructed by narrative theorists to look to the structural features of a text that reveal the implied author's norms and values, to such markers of the implied author's organizing vision as book and chapter divisions; the sequence of events and handling of time; the perspective structure (Nünning, "Deconstructing" 112–13). These provide the standard against which to measure a narrator's reliability: if the narrator's statements "are consistent with the [overall] patterns of the text, the narrator is reliable; if inconsistent, unreliable" (Phelan, *Living* 42). If the reader of *Love* looks to the structuring features of *Love*—the chapter divisions, the perspective structure—she or he will find traces of an implied author who seemingly backs the male-biased values of the third-person narrative and thus guarantees its reliability: the chapter titles point to the importance of the patriarchal figure, Bill Cosey; the contrast between the two narrators' styles moves a reader to trust the third-person narrator's neutrality. Morrison, through structural features that seemingly endorse patriarchal norms, masquerades as an implied author whose belief system supports the values dominating the third-person narrative: the aggrandizement of the man and a corresponding trivialization of the women and their interests. Morrison's larger project, however, is to expose the male-centered norms of love stories that usually go unchallenged and to disturb the complacency with which readers habitually accept them.[8] She uses the literary convention of the heterodiegetic narrator's objectivity to play upon, draw out, and expose the reader's participation in male-preferential conventions and codes.

The book title and chapter titles direct a reader's attention to the man as the central figure of this love story—as of other love stories. The signifier *Love*, because it is a title, floats free of context, available to any and all of a reader's associations to the word—which will of course differ from reader to reader. But in a culture governed by compulsory heterosexuality, the single word "Love" is likely to summon up associations with romantic love and the romantic couple. Both classic Hollywood cinema and the traditional court-ship novel move inexorably toward the consummation of true love in a final image of man and woman united—an image, as Raymond Bellour puts it, of "the final reconciliation of desire and the law" (12). The other free-standing structural indicators, the chapter headings, indicate the importance of the man, Bill Cosey, to this love story. They read: Portrait; Friend; Stranger; Benefactor; Lover; Husband; Guardian; Father; Phantom. With the exception of the first and last headings, these titles name masculine roles, for the most part traditional roles of men in relation to loved (or subordinate) others. The chapter titles thus affirm literary tradition by focusing on the man: in the genres of the courtship novel and its popular-culture cousin, the romance, a female protagonist may be the focalizing subject, but the center of interest is the enigmatic desire of the man. While the man enacts a complicated dance of "approach and deferral," attraction and retreat, the woman's chief activity is the "interpretation and reinterpretation" of his ambivalent behavior (Boone 81; Radway 139, 151). This is as true in the ancestral text of romance, *Jane Eyre*, where the enigma of Rochester's desire is enough to sustain both Jane and her reader through some 150 pages, as it is in the contemporary offshoot of the courtship/romance tradition, *Bridget Jones's Diary*, where the diary form charts the moment-by-moment fluctuations of hope and despair inspired in Bridget by Daniel Cleaver's contradictory signals (15–52). If "getting" a man confers legitimacy and full personhood on a woman, then it is only "natural" to spend one's time speculating on the direction of his desire. The logic of romance supports male dominance by making the man's choice of a woman into the central event of a woman's life.[9]

If the book and chapter titles of *Love* indicate that the implied author is following convention by directing the reader to pay attention to the man, the first and lengthiest part of the narrative confirms the expectations thus aroused: it supplies several heterosexual romances, including the gratify-ingly torrid sexual affair between Romen and Junior; and speculation about the object(s) of Bill Cosey's desire occupies the several characters who circle around him, eternally trying and failing to read his desire. Thus, literary convention reinforces cultural convention to lull the reader into accepting a male-centered heterosexual model of love. It then comes as a surprise when the final chapter names the relationship between little girls as true love and deplores the intervention of heterosexual sexuality that destroyed it.

Morrison's perspective structure also makes it easy for the reader to slide into an uncritical acceptance of patriarchal norms. The reader is offered two different perspectives on events—one from a third-person narrator who dips into the minds of several focalizing characters, and one from the first-person narrator L, who used to be the cook in the Cosey family hotel. Throughout the novel, L's monologues interrupt the dominant third-person narrative. The two narrative modes are clearly differentiated by the use of italics for L's voice and the use of roman type for the heterodiegetic narrator and the internal focalizers within his narrative. From our prior reading experience, we import into the text the habit of extending virtually unlimited credit to a heterodiegetic narrator: as Jonathan Culler remarks, "the basic convention of literature is that narrative sentences not produced by characters are true" (Culler, "Omniscience" 27). For example, when we read the first sentence of Austen's *Emma*—"Emma Woodhouse, handsome, clever, and rich, with a comfortable home and happy disposition, seemed to unite some of the best blessings of existence; and had lived nearly twenty-one years in the world with very little to distress or vex her" (Austen 1)—we are not inclined to doubt the narrator's words or to object that Emma may well have been twenty-five and not at all handsome (Culler, "Omniscience" 26–27). The presumption of the heterodiegetic narrator's truthfulness is fundamental to the experience of reading. Consider, for example, the first sentence that the third-person voice utters in *Love*: "The day she walked the streets of Silk, a chafing wind kept the temperature low and the sun was helpless to move outdoor thermometers more than a few degrees above freezing" (13). On the other hand, a character narrator like L has by definition a subjective view of events: her understanding is necessarily limited by her partial view. We would expect that her vision, like that of all subjects, would be skewed by the angle from which she sees the world.

In *Love,* the narrative positions initially appear to follow these conventions; but ultimately we come to see that they are reversed. L, the first-person character narrator, who speaks in a meandering, personal, idiosyncratic style that defamiliarizes the reader, provides rare glimpses of the Cosey women's true story and ends up being the authoritative guide to the storyworld. The third-person narrative, on the other hand, frames the story of Cosey and his women in ways that enhance the stature of Bill Cosey and protect him from blame while subtly or not so subtly derogating the women. It is only in the novel's final chapter that we realize how misleading the entire third-person narrative frame has been.

Morrison uses the beginning of the third-person account to engage our assumptions about the reliability and objectivity of this frame; these assumptions carry over to much of the third-person internal focalization that follows, as perspective shifts among six character focalizers. Nevertheless, Morrison cannot legitimately be accused of clumsy or unethical manipulation of her audience. By highlighting differences of interpretation and judgment among the focalizers without clearly taking sides, Morrison signals her audience not to take any of the internal focalizers as authoritative. But it is just as important that she does not clearly undermine any of the focalizers, thereby leaving us to activate our own conventional expectations about love stories.

After a prologue delivered by L in an idiom both eccentric and fanciful, the heterodiegetic narrator's voice that opens chapter 1 is reassuring. Following his opening sentence, quoted above, his second sentence gives the panoramic view of the fictional world from "the classical position of a narrator-focalizer" common to the beginning of realist novels (Rimmon-Kennan 78): "Tiles of ice had formed at the shoreline and, inland, the thrown-together houses on Monarch Street whined like puppies" (13). When the omniscient view first gives way to the limited focalization of a character, Sandler, the convention of an introductory exposition voiced by bystander witnesses adds to the reader's sense of being in familiar and trustworthy narrative territory. Vida and Sandler, who know the Cosey history because they worked for Bill Cosey, fill in the background history of the two Cosey women we are about to meet, and we have no reason to doubt the basic event structure of that history. However, Vida and Sandler differ in their assessment of Bill Cosey: Vida admires Cosey unconditionally, while Sandler, who "knew his habits" (40), is more skeptical. Although Sandler's greater knowledge is a signal that his assessment is more accurate, his skepticism does not extend to telling us what Cosey's "habits" were or to criticizing him. Instead, Sandler suspends judgment: "The more Sandler learned about the man, the less he knew"; "he was still of two minds about Cosey" (44, 45). So Sandler's apparent skepticism merely inoculates us against a broader skepticism about the accuracy of the whole account. And his continual musings on the compelling mystery of Cosey's motivations and desires reinforce Vida's picture of Bill Cosey as the fascinating central figure of the story: "Mr. Cosey was royal . . . all the rest—Heed, Vida, May, waiters, cleaners—were court personnel fighting for the prince's smile" (37).

These two seemingly reliable expositors omit a key fact that would influence our judgment of Bill Cosey and Heed: Heed's age when Cosey married her. We do not learn about the premature marriage till the striking scene of the bride coloring and cutting out paper dolls on page 128, some two-thirds through the novel. (A very few hints of the bride's age precede this revelation, but they are mystified, cloaked in ambiguity: for instance, in her wedding picture Heed is "a tiny bride, . . . swamped by the oversize wedding gown falling from her shoulders" [60]; since the text repeatedly draws attention to her diminutive size in the present, when she is in her sixties, readers do not readily connect her size to her age.) In *Love*, we have a set of characters—Heed, Christine, Vida, Sandler—who constantly mull over events of the past, yet for the first 127 pages not one of them remembers that Heed was a child when Cosey married her—let alone some other historical facts, like Cosey's buying the eleven-year-old bride from her parents. Despite the seeming diversity of its multiple voices, the third-person narrative frame as a whole is unbalanced, skewed toward the interests of the man: it protects him from blame and shifts perspective just enough to present his actions in a positive light.

In addition to luring into the open the reader's preconceptions about the relative importance of male and female characters to a love story, Morrison's narrative structure may be mimicking, and thus obliquely critiquing, a gender dynamic of African American life in which loyalty to the race prohibits the disclosure of black male abuse of black women. Historically, as Johnnetta Cole and Beverly Guy-Sheftall demonstrate (79–94), complaints of sexual harassment and sexism have been suppressed by an African American community reluctant to provide the white oppressors with ammunition to further undermine black men. Such a taboo holds among the African American community in *Love*, where Bill Cosey's success as a world-class hotelier is necessary to the community's self-esteem and hope. Cosey has achieved financial success in a world that systemically deprives black men of the patriarchal position, and that provides everyone with race pride. He is a "race man," one whose "aggressive demonstration of [his] superiority . . . establishe[s] race pride" (Carby, *Race* 4). Bound by race pride to the outstanding accomplishments of the "great man," no one in the community speaks out against his sexual appropriation of a child.

As Mary Paniccia Carden says in a related argument (132), Morrison may also be critiquing the doctrine of racial uplift, which treats the achievements of the successful black man as a means sufficient in itself to "pull up," by force of example, the disadvantaged African American masses. Thus everyone in

Bill Cosey's community—"cannery workers and fishing families, . . . house-maids, laundresses, fruit pickers" (41–42)—is enchanted by the spectacle of Cosey's success, "proud of his finesse, his money, the example he set that goaded them into thinking that with patience and savvy, they could do it too" (40). But they do *not* "do it too." Bill Cosey's success is after all exclusive, a silent truth embodied by his barring all working-class members of his community from entry into his luxury hotel. As Cosey progresses, they remain closed out—stuck in poverty and lack. The logic of racial uplift, as exposed by *Love*, is based on a strict hierarchy, requiring the continuation of a disadvantaged black majority that can be led by the "Talented Tenth" (Du Bois 139), the few "exceptional" black men of privilege.[10]

Nonetheless, the members of the community "looked on him with adoring eyes, spoke of him with forgiving smiles" (40). The black community feels "forgiving," indulgent toward Cosey's various displays of power, including sexual power: the community does not criticize Cosey for his sexual exploitation of a child, nor did they try to prevent it. The narrative structure imitates their reticence: the multiple focalizing characters, along with the third-person narrator, suppress for nearly two-thirds of the novel the information that Heed was a child bride as well as other instances of Cosey's sexual exploitation of women and children. These events surface only in the truth-telling final chapter. The third-person narrative's withholding of damaging evidence against the race man, together with the absence of criticism from the community, perhaps constitute Morrison's critique of a loyalty ethic in which "Black women have a duty to the race while Black men are allowed to have a duty only to themselves" (Hammonds 8), an ethic in which race always trumps gender and black women suffer.[11] (Criticism of that ethic surfaces explicitly when Christine, as a member of a 1960s black nationalist group, notes that the group leader failed to admonish—"let alone punish or expel"—a group member who raped a fellow worker, a seventeen-year-old student volunteer [166]. See Cole and Guy-Sheftall for an account of sexism within the Civil Rights movement.)

The third-person narrative protects Bill Cosey from blame through yet another omission: his race politics are never mentioned. But May, his daughter-in-law and the manager of his hotel, acts out the dubious racial politics on which Cosey's prosperity is founded. Initially May is just an avid supporter of segregation (80). As the Civil Rights movement gains momentum, however, she becomes increasingly terrified—not of white reprisals, as a casual reader noting the reference to Emmett Till's death might think (81)—but of the Civil Rights marchers themselves. She sees the peaceful protestors as "waves of Blacks crashing through quiet neighborhoods," as "the Revolution," an angry proletarian mob out to destroy the African American aristocracy represented by Cosey and his family (81, 82). The mad extremes to which her paranoia drives her divert a reader's attention from connecting her politics to those of her father-in-law. But Bill Cosey too must fear the end of racial inequality: it is the Jim Crow laws that enable his success, that make his hotel unique as the one establishment where African Americans can walk in the front door rather than the kitchen door, dine on fine china and crystal, and dance to the music of the best African American musicians, who like the hotel for the same reason the guests do—they are treated to comfort with respect (34, 41, 102). The success of the Civil Rights movement, the securing of equal rights for blacks, will spell the demise of Cosey's Hotel and Resort by opening other posh hotels and establishments to African Americans. The heterodiegetic narrator and the various perspectives that he opens to us shield Bill Cosey from blame by deflecting his racial politics onto his daughter-in-law, where they can be dismissed as the delusions of a crazy woman.

The effect of these omissions is that very little in the narration supplied by the shifting internal focalization of the first eight chapters contravenes the depiction of Bill Cosey as a great man undone by the petty women surrounding him—"a commanding, beautiful man surrendering to feuding women, letting them ruin all he had built," in Vida's words (36). In the absence of the historical cause of the trouble between the women—Cosey's taking the child Heed as his wife—the women's "feuding" is presented as inherent to their gender: it is just women's nature to squabble, scheme against one another, and fight over a man. There is nothing to disturb the dominant perspective that foregrounds Bill Cosey's interests and treats the women as mere impediments to Bill Cosey's success and self-expression.

Nothing, that is, but the interpolated monologues of L, which occasionally offer a corrective to the dominant account. The credibility of L's narratives, however, is marred by the eccentricity of their content and delivery. For example, L opens the novel with a monologue whose first sentence is: "The women's legs are spread wide open, so I hum" (3). The reference to women's licentiousness remains obscure. And what use does a reader have for a narrator who hums? or who is habitually silent ("I shut up altogether," she says [3])? There is no voice of authority here.[12] Rather than easing our entry into the narrative proper by providing background information, as we might hope from a prologue, L provides extraneous information about supernatural figures (the "Police-heads") that she subsequently dismisses as "trash: just another story," admits to making things up, and announces that her narration is driven by a personal need for a story—any story—rather than by a desire to inscribe the truth of the events she has witnessed (10). At the start, L seems to disqualify herself as a reliable narrator.

Mariangela Palladino, basing her opinion of L's reliability largely on this introductory monologue, takes L to be an unreliable narrator throughout (341). She judges L's narrative to be "heavily informed by a patriarchal perspective" (345). I claim, on the contrary, that despite the opacities of her style, L is a reliable narrator, "humming" the real story of Heed and Christine in the background as a counterpoint to the dominant third-person narrative, which, as I have argued, is imbued with patriarchal views. L's narrative interpolations throughout the text give us glimpses of the true history of the Cosey family. For example, she says, "It was marrying Heed that laid the brickwork for ruination. See, he chose a girl already spoken for. Not promised to anyone by her parents. That trash gave her up like they would a puppy. No. The way I see it, she belonged to Christine and Christine belonged to her" (104–5). L's explanation of the source of the Cosey family's destruction—Cosey's improper marriage to Heed—contests the dominant third-person narrative of a great man brought down by the petty viciousness of quarreling women. And she here offers a glimpse of a competing story of love—one that honors the love between little girls and gives priority to girlfriends' rights to an enduring relationship. On the premature marriage and its effects on Christine and Heed, she says, "Pity. They were just little girls. In a year they would be bleeding. . . . They had no business in that business" (136–37). Condensed into these few words are three elements crucial to the repressed story: a vision of Heed and Christine as the little girls they were when Heed was forced into marriage; a reference to the incontrovertible evidence of the body—a prepubescent body—that Heed was still a child, too young to marry; and a recognition of the "business" nature of the marriage, an oblique reference to Cosey's purchase of Heed from her parents. Against Palladino's contention that L is an unreliable narrator, her narrative warped by her "veneration and devotion to the hierarchy of patriarchy" (347), I claim that L's condensed accounts of the premature marriage are accurate. And while Palladino claims that "L celebrates patriarchy and condemns female emancipation" (347), I understand L's remarks quoted above to deplore the abuse of patriarchal power that transforms a child into a wife and to show that L's sympathies lie with the women. Her "pity" is entirely appropriate to the actuality of the women's past lives.[13]

Because L's pronouncements about the little girls' losses are brief, condensed to the point of obscurity, and delivered in an idiosyncratic idiom that puzzles more than it clarifies, her allusions to Heed's and Christine's early love for each other and the tragedy of its loss remain enigmatic and ambiguous, hence less persuasive than the seemingly neutral presentation of the third-person narrator and the minds he opens to us. However, if we attend to the substance of L's intermittent monologues, we can see that their contextualization of the women's lives consistently challenges the bias that tilts the third-person narrative toward patriarchal values.[14]

Since Christine and Heed are the other two focalizers who, with Vida and Sandler, give us information about the Cosey past, one would think their deep friendship would be part of their extended memories. But Heed and Christine are no less than the other characters firmly enclosed in the meaning world of patriarchy: there is no space in the storyworld dominated by the third-person narrative for a love story that predates entry into the heterosexual patriarchal world. Occasionally, when Heed or Christine is focalizing, the aborted beginnings of an alternative tale graze the narrative surface. Through the time-honored phrase "once upon a time," a story driven by a different desire intermittently tries to introduce itself: "Once a little girl wandered too far," "Once there was a little girl with white bows" (78, 95). And isolated scenes from the girls' first meeting and subsequent separation float into Heed's and Christine's consciousness, growing more insistent as the text nears its conclusion. While the reader is processing a complicated surface story of heterosexual desire, with its numerous subplots, he or she intermittently glimpses a different love story whose signifiers are no sooner there than withdrawn—"something just out of reach, like a shell snatched away by a wave" (27)—in a textual imitation of the repressed but persistent motions of unconscious desire.[15] In the discourse governed by the conventions of patriarchal heterosexuality, the story of love between girlfriends cannot get itself told: its beginnings are truncated and suppressed. Or it might be that readers trained in the romantic love tropes of mainstream culture are slow to pick up on these fleeting signifiers because we participate in the cultural tendency to dismiss little girls—as well as women in their sixties—as invalid subjects of a love story.

It is true that in the course of her ruminations Christine perceives and articulates some dynamics of male power that the other focalizing characters gladly overlook. Listing her three dwelling places—Cosey's hotel, the posh boarding school where she was sent, and Manila's whorehouse—she says, "All three floated in sexual tension and resentment; all three insisted on confinement; in all three status was money. And all were organized around the pressing needs of men" (92). Christine sees through superficial differences of propriety and class status to pinpoint the governing mechanism of all three establishments: male desire, backed by male money. And, closer to home, she understands Bill Cosey's economy of commensurability. Imagining a scenario in which Heed burns her in her bed, Christine wonders whether her grandfather would "look finally at the charred flesh of his own flesh and settle that also as though it were a guest's bounced check or a no-show musician or a quarrel with a salesman who had shortchanged an order of Scotch whiskey?" (135). Megan Sweeney comments on this fantasy: "[Christine reasons that] in Cosey's economy of justice, her charred flesh would represent a generic quantity of harm that could be compensated like one would compensate for an insufficient check or supply of whiskey" ("Something Rogue" 451). Christine grasps the nature of her grandfather's capitalist thinking, in which everything becomes an object of exchange and women's bodies are commodities, quantified in the same way as a bottle of whiskey.[16]

Thus, the third-person narration is by no means uniform or monolithic: the use of shifting internal focalization enables Morrison to smuggle a critique of patriarchal systems into a narrative that by and large colludes with male-dominant values. Even in the case of Christine, though, patriarchal habits of thinking and feeling persist despite her keen perception of her social world's structuring mechanisms. Thus, despite her recognition that it is powerful men who control events in her world, and despite her anger with her grandfather, it is not him she blames for breaking up the friendship with Heed so much as Heed: "the real betrayal . . . lay at the feet of [Heed]" (133). And it is Heed, she thinks, who is scheming "some new way to rob her future just as she had ripped off her past" (24)—as if it were Heed rather than Cosey who robbed her of her childhood and adolescence and disordered her life's time.[17] Rather than pitying both herself and Heed as victims of Cosey's predations, Christine's rage targets Heed—that "high-heeled snake," "the meanest thing on the coast" (24), "the snake" (165), the "insane viper" (167). Despite the perspicacity of her insight into the gendered power relations that govern her various worlds, Christine's focalization is skewed by the values of the patriarchal worldview in which she remains invested.

It is, however, Heed's perspective that delivers the story most warped toward patriarchal understandings—most skewed toward the idealization of the powerful man and the perception of all women as rivals. As Morrison says in interviews, *Love* is as much about how women buy into their own oppression as it is about the patriarchal system that oppresses them (O'Connor).[18]

It is also Heed's focalization that most powerfully deploys cultural myth to

capture and reinforce readers' preconceptions about love and to secure readers' investments in the patriarchal vision of the novel's first eight chapters. As
Ansgar Nünning reminds us, meaning is produced not by textual signs alone
but by the interaction of textual cues with the "world-model or conceptual
information previously existing in the mind of the individual reader" ("Unreliable" 66). Heed reads her own life through a cultural myth so fundamental
to the ideology of social mobility that sustains capitalist culture that references to it may pass virtually unnoticed, influencing readers unawares: the
story of Cinderella. In the Cinderella story pattern, the woman moves from
abject poverty to wealth and class status as a result of the prince's choosing
her from among all women. The climactic moment of Heed's life story is the
moment of Cosey's choice: "[Bill Cosey] had picked her out of all he could
have chosen. Knowing she had no schooling, no abilities, no proper raising, he chose her anyway" (72). Like the prince in the fairy tale recognizing
Cinderella's merit beneath her rags, Cosey in this rendition sees beneath the
demeaning trappings of poverty—"no schooling, . . . no proper raising"—to
recognize Heed's true worth and to "choose" her for herself. Describing her
wedding to Junior, Heed explains, "Bill Cosey was very marriage-ing, you
know. A lot of women wanted to be in my slippers" (61). "Slippers" flags the
Cinderella story explicitly—as does an earlier reference to Bill Cosey as "the
prince" (37). The Cinderella tale is founded on the rivalry among women—
the internecine warfare between Cinderella and her stepsisters. Heed likewise
understands her relations with all women as a competition for the one place
that hinges on the prince's choice. "She had fought them all, won, and was
still winning. Her bank account was fatter than ever" (73). As her words show,
Heed also embraces the Cinderella theme of marriage as economic salvation
(127). But, as in the Cinderella fantasy, the economic drive toward upward
mobility is cloaked in the seductive language of romantic love. Her father,
Heed says, recognized her relationship with Cosey as "a true romance" and
so gave his blessing to the marriage; and, with a line straight out of *Jane Eyre*'s
final chapter, Heed describes her marriage as "almost thirty years of perfect
bliss" (62).

The Cinderella marriage plot has to be the principal capitalist myth for
women—the feminine equivalent of the Horatio Alger rise from rags to
riches (Kolbenschlag 71). The ever-new cinematic versions of *Pride and Prejudice*—a particularly witty derivative of the Cinderella story—produced by
Hollywood and London, as well as the never-ending stream of contemporary
remakes of *Cinderella* itself, such as *Ever After*, *Maid in Manhattan*, and *The
Cinderella Story*, testify to the ongoing currency of the Cinderella paradigm

in contemporary consumer capitalism. Cosey's entrepreneurial story draws on the corresponding masculinist model of social mobility, the individualist myth of the man who raises himself, through his sole and solitary efforts, to a position of wealth and status—a myth racially inflected in Bill Cosey's case by his success in overcoming a social and economic system designed to prevent black men from occupying the position of patriarchal figure.

Designating the paths to economic success appropriate to each gender, these two myths permeate the cultural unconscious, forming part of the "general cultural text" that readers bring to their reading (Culler, *Structuralist Poetics* 140). The details that recall these myths, scattered throughout the third-person narration but clustering particularly within the narrative focalized by Heed, infiltrate our understanding of the relations between male and female characters in a manner similar to the workings of the cultural unconscious itself. They lead us to accept the relative power positions of Heed and Cosey as given: Cosey is deservedly powerful because his superior intelligence, talent, and determination enable him to overcome obstacles and succeed; marriage to Cosey saved Heed from a life of bitter poverty.

The Conclusion:
A Different Love Story

With chapter 9, we break into a different world of meanings and values—a discursive world, I argue, that challenges the reader to confront the degree to which his or her assumptions about love and lovers are hostage to prevailing cultural conventions. Several technical narrative devices announce the shift from a patriarchal discursive world to an alternative discourse of love: the chapter title, the absence of quotation marks and speech tags, and the new authority granted to L as narrator.

The final chapter's title is "Phantom": it appears to the reader to refer to Bill Cosey and thus to continue the text's deployment of chapter headings to emphasize the centrality of the patriarchal figure—for Bill Cosey's ghost has been the "phantom" presiding over the world of sexual intrigue depicted in preceding chapters. Through Junior, the young woman whom Heed hires as a kind of live-in secretary, Cosey's ghost continues to participate in the sexual activities of the living. His spirit infuses Junior with sexual desire, encouraging her to "enjoy herself in front of him" clad in Cosey's own underwear (119). His whispered encouragements—"Sweet tits," "Take it," "Why not?" (116)—incite Junior to the ever more daring and outrageous feats of sexual bravura with Romen that take up much of the first eight chapters. As the novel switches out of the sexual and heterosexual world into the alternative love world of the final chapter, however, Bill Cosey's ghost vanishes (Junior cannot find him anywhere), displaced by the ghost of L. (We discover only now that she is dead.) The smell of baking bread permeates the Cosey hotel where Heed's reconciliation with Christine takes place, signifying the cook L's ghostly presence and enveloping the two women as they rediscover their lost childhood love. L is the tutelary spirit of the recovered world of girl-friend love. The title "Phantom" thus replays in miniature Morrison's overall game of misleading the reader—providing a signifier that invites the reader to invest in one set of meanings only to overthrow the whole implied signi-fying chain and show the reader that the word meant something else entirely. The final chapter as a whole performs this overthrow of prior meanings and brings the reader to see that, as in this instance, her misinterpretation of the text's significance was at least in part the result of her own prior investment in a patriarchal signifying system.[19]

As the dialogue of reconciliation between Christine and Heed begins, the text announces the advent of a new discursive dispensation in two ways. First, the coordinates of time and space on which the fictional world has been resting are withdrawn—"The future is disintegrating along with the past. The landscape beyond this room is without color. Just a bleak ridge of stone" (184)—opening up a new narrative space in which past and present, child-hood and age, coexist and unite. Second, the absence of quotation marks around the spoken words of Heed and Christine indicates the disappearance of the third-person narrator, along with the narrative apparatus of shifting in-ternal focalization. There is no evidence of a narrating agency at all, not even the minimal indication of speech through quotation marks and speech tags (he said, she said). We are left with the alternating speeches of Christine and Heed on the page, as if unmediated by any narrating agency—as if the reader were privy to their dialogue directly. And because the marks of attribution are absent, it becomes difficult to discern which of them is speaking; what we perceive is a dual voice that speaks truth after the lifelong patriarchal spell is broken.[20]

As the patriarchal imaginary dissolves, the real power relations between Heed and Bill Cosey come into view. The Cinderella economics of marital mobility gives way to a different economic model for marriage: slavery. The father who was said to have smiled on Cosey's courtship and marriage as "a true romance" (62) turns out to have been smiling because he had just pock-eted two hundred dollars in exchange for his eleven-year-old daughter, Heed (77, 193). Cosey bought the pleasures of a slaveowner: the absolute power over another human being, the license to subject her to his sexual whims. And Heed was reduced, like the slave narrator Harriet Jacobs, to "the condition of a chattel, entirely subject to the will of another" (Jacobs 55).

Christine extends the slavery metaphor:

> It's like we started out being sold, got free of it, then sold ourselves to the highest bidder.
> Who you mean "we"? Black people? Women? You mean me and you?
> (185)

The extrapolation from the singular case of "me and you" to the general category of "women" implies that Heed's situation is not unique: in a radical overthrow of the Cinderella ideal of romantic marriage as rescue and transcendence, the slave market metaphor suggests that all married women live in a power structure governed by the idea of woman-as-property: or, as Ann duCille puts it, "to be married is to be owned" (28). Morrison's subversive use of the marriage plot places it in a long line of African American antecedents, from Harriet Wilson's *Our Nig* through Zora Neale Hurston's *Their Eyes Were Watching God*, which appropriate the marriage plot "to address some of the most compelling sociopolitical issues of their era" and "to critique and reorder" the hierarchical structure of marriage (duCille 30–31).[21]

A second historical revelation similarly throws a new light on Heed's marriage to Cosey. Heed and Christine remember simultaneously—but cannot put into words even now—a moment of child abuse. Meeting the eleven-year-old Heed in the hall of the hotel at a time well before marriage was even talked of, Cosey "touches her chin, and then—casually, still smiling—her nipple, or rather the place under her swimsuit where a nipple will be if the circled dot on her chest ever changes. Heed stands there for what seems an hour but is less than the time it takes to blow a perfect bubble" (191). Immediately after, Christine sees Cosey masturbating at the window of her bedroom and vomits. The delayed disclosure of sexual abuse reveals, again, the degree of bias toward the interests of the man exercised by all the storytellers of the narrative's first part: had either the act itself or the term *pedophile* been introduced within the shifting focalizations of the first eight chapters, it would have been difficult to maintain the picture of Cosey as beneficent patriarchal figure: readers would have judged him quite differently (as we can infer from judgments on that more famous pedophile, Humbert Humbert).[22]

Morrison's description of the way Christine and Heed continue to experience the residue of the traumatic event coincides with Laplanche's (originally Freud's) explanation of the way trauma triggers the warped temporality of

Nachträglichkeit. The damage of sexual trauma comes not from the original event but from the memory of the event. Trauma cannot be processed and stored in memory in the usual way because it exceeds the cognitive resources the subject has available to understand and integrate new experiences: the image of the event "persists neither in a conscious state nor, properly speaking, in a repressed state; it remains there, waiting in a kind of limbo." What is crucial is that "it is not linked to the rest of psychical life" (Laplanche, *Life* 41), so its effects cannot be attenuated in the usual way, through integration into a stored network of signifiers drawn from previous experience. Traumatic memory goes on working inside the psychic world by releasing, again and again, the primary process responses to trauma that would have been appropriate to the initial assault. Psychic trauma overwhelms because, as Freud explained in the *Project*, the ego is armed against harm coming from the outside, its defenses trained on the external world—but the memory-trace "attacks the ego" from within. So "the ego is taken from the side on which it 'didn't expect it,'" from the side of memory rather than perception; "it is overcome, disarmed, subjected to the drive process, that primary process against which it was . . . *constituted*" (Laplanche, *Life* 47; quoting Freud, *Project* 416). The release of overwhelming primary process emotions takes place again and again, then, because "the psychical trauma—or more precisely the memory of the trauma—. . . acts like a foreign body which long after its entry . . . is still at work" (Freud and Breuer, *Hysteria* 6; qtd in Laplanche, *Life* 42).

Laplanche's explanation fits Morrison's description of sexual trauma as a foreign body within, possessed of a potent ongoing psychic life. Both Christine and Heed experience the trauma of the grandfather's sexual intervention as a "thing"—unsignifiable and inassimilable—that resides within their own bodies. The trauma fills them with overwhelming feelings of shame—still—because it is an "inside dirtiness," which they are afraid will leak out and expose them to the world (192). Since the "dirtiness" is within, each of them blames herself: "the rot was hers alone" (190). Morrison's metaphorics coincides with Laplanche's: the violation is experienced as a part of the body, inalienable but also indigestible, "a spine in the flesh" that goes on working from within (Laplanche 42).

Belatedly, then, the reader understands that the adult sexual world broke into the childhood world of Christine and Heed before the inappropriate marriage. The shame that each felt prevented her telling the other of the experience: "Even in idagay they had never been able to share a certain twin shame. Each one thought the rot was hers alone" (190). Idagay, the secret language that guaranteed the privacy of their childhood world of dialogue and play, shielding it from the penetration of uncomprehending adults, cannot integrate the pollutant from the alien world of adult sexuality; rather, the intrusion of adult sexual meanings rips through their intimate language, disrupting their communication and constituting the first rift in their childhood bond (191).

From the perspective of these final pages, the marriage of Heed and Cosey takes on a different aspect. Sexual violation of a child came first, marriage after. The marriage appears in the guise of a patriarchal structure erected to resignify and conceal a brute abuse of power: or, in Lacanian terms, the Law of the Father conceals and thus gives license to the father figure's uninhibited, unbounded exercise of sexual impulse. This legitimating process is similar to the narrative process I have been studying: as in the discourse of the first 182 pages, a patriarchal system of signifiers—here, the institution of patriarchal marriage—papers over and conceals the real (abusive) relations of power between man and woman.[23]

The new narrative dispensation is also marked by the passing of narrative authority to L, who is given the novel's last word. To our surprise, we discover that L is positioned quite differently in relation to the storyworld than we had thought: she is dead, so all along we have been hearing, unawares, her voice from beyond the grave. Instead of the partial view automatically ascribed to a character narrator who is immersed in the world she describes, L's vision is unblinkered by imprisonment in the present moment. Released from time, she, like Yeats's artist of eternity, can see with equal clarity "what is past, and passing, and to come." In addition, L acquires narrative authority from the revelation that her name, L, stands for Love (199). Speaking now with the moral authority of love itself, L recontextualizes the conventions of romantic love enshrined in popular culture, appropriating them to her description of Heed's and Christine's first meeting. "Love at first sight" becomes the instantaneous love between little girls: "It's like that when children fall for one another. On the spot, without introduction" (199). The governing cliché of romantic love is that once you have found your one and only, life without him is impossible: that becomes literally true in the case of Heed and Christine. They found a love they "can never live without": "Heed and Christine were the kind of children who can't take back love, or park it. When that's the case, separation cuts to the bone. . . . it can kill a life way before it tries to live" (199–200). L's judgment confirms Heed's and Christine's recognition that "they could have been living life hand in hand" were it not for the intervention of Bill Cosey. Separation has deprived them of lives lived fruitfully through time—"killed," destroyed, their lives before they were able even to "try to live." And the patriarchal figure, no longer shielded by the third-person narrative's disclaimers and diversions, is to blame: "I have to fault Mr. Cosey for the theft" (200).

In relocating the clichés of romance in the childhood love of "best friends," L denaturalizes the temporal schema that supports ideas of romantic love and the compulsory heterosexuality they perpetuate. According to Western cultural norms that have changed very little from what they were at the time of Freud's "Femininity" essay, girls may move through some "deviant" stages in the course of their development—such as loving females—but only in order to arrive finally at a normative heterosexuality. A female becomes a subject of interest at seventeen or eighteen—when she becomes eligible for courtship and marriage; at eleven a girl-child is not accorded the dignity of a subject whose love counts. L refers obliquely to this patriarchal paradigm of women's time: "Most people have never felt a passion that strong, that early. If so, they remember it with a smile, dismiss it as a crush that shriveled in time and on time" (199). At the same time that L takes note of the reigning dogma's force—little-girl love is dismissed "on time" according to a heteronormative schedule of female development—she overthrows that construct by locating "passion" in the love between the little girls Heed and Christine.

The radical discontinuity of Heed's and Christine's lives—the irreparably damaging break with their childhood love from which they never recover—recapitulates in extreme form the discontinuity at the heart of female development generally: the narrative of female subject-formation itself turns on a girl's separation from her first love objects, on a loss that does violence to female subjectivity.[24] Through the life-affirming reconciliation of Heed and Christine, Morrison suggests a remedy—a reclaiming of the girlfriend love that predates the heterosexual marriage plot. That Heed's and Christine's story is meant to serve as a critique of the socially induced trauma of femininity is also suggested by the course of L's life. L models a female temporality that evades the patriarchal ordering of a woman's time. Courtship, marriage, childbirth, caring for aged parents, death: L avoids all the expected phases of life—even death, in the usual sense of a disappearance from the lives of the living.[25]

From the retrospective perspective of the final chapter, L's "humming" appears to have been an alternative language of love forced to the background, unable to find full expression in the patriarchal discursive world of the first eight chapters. Always inscribed as outside the patriarchal enclosure—printed in italics, rendered in unmanageably long paragraphs—her alternative discourse takes over here. Overthrowing the norms and values central to the earlier narrators' versions of Cosey's life, L's story valorizes the relationship between young girls as love and presents patriarchal heterosexuality as a brutal intervention that stops female development cold.

"The Structure Is the Argument"

Although Morrison nowhere explicitly states an intention to shift the reader's worldview, "the structure is the argument," as Morrison says of a Faulkner novel that she admires (Schappell and Lacour 101). The two-part structure of *Love* resembles Laplanche's description of Freud's *nachträglich* temporal structure: "Two scenes are linked by associative chains, but separated from each other by a temporal barrier which inscribes them in two different spheres of meaning" (Laplanche, *Life* 40); and it may induce in the reader an intensity of revision and reevaluation similar to that experienced by Freud's hysterical subject. It is not only that the "second scene" makes the reader *nachträglich* in the sense that it enables the reader to see the textual past from a new perspective and find in it a new meaning. The final chapter's undermining of all the patriarchal norms and values of the first scene of reading also pressures the reader to turn around on her own reading practice, to question the preconceptions about love and gender that have been guiding her reading of the Cosey story. Was the reader, like the community representatives who focalize the story, suckered into accepting the terms of the patriarchal imaginary that dominate the first part of the novel and so blinded to the material damage done to the women by Bill Cosey's actions? The hooks are there in the text, but it has to be a reader's predilection for "looking for Big Daddy everywhere" that leads him or her to get hung up on them.

Speaking of her earlier fiction, Morrison acknowledges a deliberate design to provide spaces into which may "fall the ruminations of the reader and his or her invented or recollected or misunderstood knowingness" ("Unspeakable" 29). If the signposts of *Love's* first part induced the reader to fill in the blanks with his or her "knowingness" about love—that it occurs between a man and a woman, that the key to female happiness is captivating the man's desire, that women are naturally rivals for the only love worth having, the love of a man—then the final chapter reverses all such knowing. Despite the several plots of sexual love contained in the first eight chapters, the signifier "love" never appears (except once, when L, building a taxonomy of different kinds of love, defines lust as "the clown of love" [63]), and the term's absence is all the more marked because two different characters reach for the word but fail to voice it (130, 198). It is only when Heed confirms the belated mutual recognition of the relationship with Christine that the word surfaces:

"Love. I really do" (194). This articulation avoids the common phrasing, "I love you," to isolate the word *Love* and thus forge an identification with the novel's title. The alignment of true love with the deep friendship between little girls may lead a reader to recognize the narrowness of his or her conventional "knowing" about love and awaken him or her to the possibility of different love stories. As readers are jolted abruptly into the new conceptual framework of the final chapter, the surprise of sudden realization—"So that is what *Love* means!"—has the affective force of *nachträglich* recognition to create new understandings and to jostle fixed hierarchies of value—even, perhaps, to expand readers' definitions of what love is. For the revelation that it is only the love between little girls that is worthy of the name in this narrative does not necessarily mean that the reader must henceforth value only the love between children: the revelation is not prescriptive. Instead, Morrison's larger point is akin to Virginia Woolf's "Love has a thousand shapes" (*Lighthouse* 192): even as the reading experience that *Love* offers us exposes our deeply rooted cultural predilection for heterosexual romantic love, it ultimately challenges us to recognize and honor love as love even when it is enacted outside romantic convention's parameters of age and gender.

CHAPTER 5

Failed Messages, Maternal Loss, and Narrative Form in *A Mercy*

Florens, a slave girl who has been sold away from her mother in *A Mercy* (2008), is haunted by the insistent image of the mother trying to tell her something. The mother that Florens hallucinates is "saying something important to me, but holding the little boy's hand" (8); "a minha mae standing near with her little boy . . . she is always wanting to tell me something. Is stretching her eyes. Is working her mouth" (101); "she is moving her lips at me" (138).[1] Throughout Florens's narrative, the image of the hallucinated mother speaks, but nothing issues from her mouth; the daughter strains to listen but hears nothing. The theme of failed communication is central to Florens's story, and the formal elements of *A Mercy* reflect this. For Florens is a narrator as well as a character; and the damage done by the traumatic break with her mother not only to her psyche but also to her ability to communicate shows up in the distorted syntax and incomplete words of her narrative.

Readers of Morrison will inevitably think of Beloved, whose mother similarly severed their attachment abruptly in order to preserve her daughter from the evils of slavery—an act that Beloved, like Florens, could understand only as abandonment. And Beloved's speech patterns, like Florens's, are dislocated, betraying the arrest of her development at the moment of that brutal separation. But in my view the presentation of the slave daughter is quite different in the two novels. Whereas the character of Beloved keeps expanding, taking on more and more dimensions of collective meaning, Florens's story is concentrated, focused on a single point of heightened intensity: the maternal message that cannot get through, that cannot be understood.

The image of the mother straining and failing to tell is a symptom of Florens's psychic disturbances; but the image also encapsulates something that is fundamental to Florens's historical context—the distance between mother and child, across which no message can pass. The irrevocable separation of child from mother reflects a trauma that was routine under slavery: children were sold away from their mothers, "one by one, wherever [the slave-trader] could command the highest price" (Jacobs 16). *A Mercy* shows the devastating effects of these forced premature separations on a child's development. Thus Morrison, as so often, condenses psychoanalytic with historical insight to re-tell history from the inside.

In one sense the scope of *A Mercy* is broad, encompassing the several different perspectives on seventeenth-century America supplied by its multiple narrators. Each inhabitant of Jacob Vaark's farm—free, slave, indentured—gets a turn at focalizing one chapter. But the first chapter, and every alternating chapter thereafter, is narrated from Florens's first-person perspective, and it is the events of her life that I will follow. As a child slave on Vaark's farm in the Virginia of 1682, where slaves and masters labor side by side in an early, less hierarchical form of "frontier slavery,"[2] Florens is lovingly cared for by Lina, a Native American slave.[3] At the age of sixteen, in the fictional present, she falls passionately in love with the blacksmith who comes to build the gate for Jacob's mansion. Later, Florens is sent to find the blacksmith through the uncharted wilderness that is seventeenth-century America; she does find him, but the lovers' reunion is short-lived, as Florens attacks the blacksmith and his small charge, the orphan Malaik, with a violence that can be explained only through the temporally displaced logic of trauma.

The mother's original message, addressed to Jacob Vaark, was "Take the girl . . . my daughter" (7); those words effectively sold the child to Jacob. Florens is unable to interpret this message beyond its brutal surface meaning of maternal repudiation. Her misreading of her mother's message becomes the distorting lens through which she perceives her world. Florens's narrative, both what she tells about her world and how she tells it, dramatize the defects in her signifying processes that result from the mother's baffling and hurtful message.

Jean Laplanche's concept of the enigmatic message offers a way to understand the effects of the mother's message on Florens's capacity for interpreting her world and those who people it. Laplanche theorizes that a particular message from the parent, one that the child can only partially understand, both rouses a child's efforts to interpret the parent's words and has a lasting effect on the child's orientation to the world. Specifically, the part of the message that the child cannot interpret, despite many attempts to do so, becomes the nucleus of the unconscious and gives a specific direction to the drives. I make use of Laplanche's theory, first to explain the oddities of Florens's behavior as character and, second, to theorize the oddities of her language as narrator.

Laplanche explains that the parental enigmatic signifier, internalized, gives a particular distortion to the subject's approach to the world (Santner, *Psychotheology* 39–40). We can see such a distortion play out in Florens's reading of her life events. For example, she misreads the scene of her lover and the small child Malaik whom he is fostering as a repetition of the scene of maternal rejection, with tragic consequences for all three characters. As a character in the storyworld, Florens sees reality askew.

To theorize Florens's limitations as narrator, I turn Laplanche's idea of the enigmatic signifier in a direction not foreseen in his theory, toward an explanation of how a child becomes attached to language and to the process of interpreting language. In Laplanche's model, the parent's enigmatic signifier is crucial to the child's psychic development. But it is not as if the parent's message is swallowed entire and, thus intact, directly determines the child from within. Rather, an enigmatic parental signifier stimulates the child's interpretive powers, challenging him or her to make theories about the other's words, to translate and fail to translate, to interpret and misinterpret, until finally the child understands some parts of the message.

However distant from the original parental message the child's eventual understanding of its meaning is, the child's activity of translating and mistranslating and translating again is an exercise in interpreting words. This process Florens misses because the mother's enigmatic message is simultaneously the mother's dismissal. Since the mother's words evict the daughter from her presence, the mother's message is not just baffling, it is traumatizing: rather than activating the daughter's signifying processes, the mother's enigmatic speech shuts them down. It would seem, from Florens's inability to read others' words as clues to what they are thinking and feeling, that her capacity to infer meaning from people's speech is permanently lamed.

Since as narrator Florens is a reader's conduit to understanding the social world, this failure to interpret may frustrate a reader's desire to know. And Florens's language as narrator is stunted—the sentences short, the syntax distorted, and some of the words incomplete. In the act of reading, a reader has to experience a formal version of the impeded communication that is central to the novel's plot. To a degree unusual even in Morrison's carefully crafted works, form expresses content.

Misreading the Mother:
Competing Narrative Perspectives and
Mother-Love under Slavery

The narrative structure of *A Mercy* formally reproduces the thematics of mother-daughter separation. The first chapter contains Florens's memory of the traumatizing scene where her mother arranged for her sale to Jacob Vaark. The concluding chapter holds the mother's explanation for her action: on the D'Ortega plantation where Florens lived with her mother, Florens's prepubescent body was already tempting the slaveholder and his wife, and the slave mother could offer "no protection" to the child she loved (166). The position of slave mother thus imposes an unbearable contradiction: as a mother her most basic commitment is to the protection and preservation of her child; yet as a slave mother, she is powerless to protect a daughter whose body belongs to the slaveowner who would violate her.[4] The mother's "one chance" to protect and preserve her daughter was to beg Jacob Vaark to take her, as partial payment of D'Ortega's debt to him (166).

But the mother's explanation can never reach Florens. Literally, at the level of plot, the explanation cannot reach Florens because the mother lives bound to a plantation in a different state. Narrative form expresses this unbridgeable distance: the mother's explanatory narrative is placed outside the frame of the novel's action, as a coda following the daughter's story, which has already reached its painful conclusion. The mother's desperation to get the message through to Florens takes the extreme form of "staying on my knees. In the dust where my heart will remain each night and every day until you understand what I know and long to tell you" (167). But we know that this will never happen. In the absence of the mother's explanation, Florens cannot read the enigmatic love that is hidden within the mother's haunting words, "Take the girl" (7). At one end of the novel, Florens is desperately in need of her mother's words; at the other end of the novel, the mother is desperate to get the message to her daughter. But never can the transmission occur. The poignancy of irremediable separation between slave mother and child thus infuses the narrative structure, their estrangement given textual form by the distance between opening and closing chapters and the block to their communication given material form by the stuff of all the intervening pages.

Outlining the normative process of a child's encounter with the parental enigmatic signifier, Laplanche describes the grounds for misunderstanding:

[There is] an encounter between an individual whose psycho-somatic structures are situated predominantly at the level of need, and signifiers emanating from an adult. Those signifiers pertain to the satisfaction of the child's needs, but they also convey the purely interrogative potential of other messages—and those messages are sexual. These enigmatic messages set the child a difficult, or even impossible, task of mastery and symbolization and the attempt to perform it inevitably leaves behind unconscious residues. (*New Foundations* 130)

In this normative schema, the parent's words have a sexual dimension that the child cannot grasp because the child has not yet entered into the world of adult sexuality. Wrestling with the message, the child translates some of it into terms it can understand; but the lump of untranslatable signifiers becomes the "thing-presentation" that founds the unconscious. The situation is more complicated in *A Mercy*: Florens inhabits not just a world of adult sexual meanings but a plantation world of slaveholders permeated by sexuality, rife with what Jacob Vaark calls "the sweetish rot of vice" (28). As in Laplanche's paradigm—although in a different sense from Laplanche's examples—it is the sexual dimension concealed behind the mother's speech that eludes Florens.

Her mother, however, knows that "to be female in this place" is to be perpetually violated (163). The mother saw Jacob as her "one chance" to save her daughter from rape and concubinage. Without access to the mother's concluding message, Florens cannot read the enigmatic mother-love and self-sacrifice hidden within the signifier of maternal dismissal, "Take the girl . . . my daughter" (7).

It is slavery that makes the misunderstanding traumatic. It is because slaves' bodies belong to the slaveowner that the mother cannot protect her daughter in the first place, and it is because slaves' bodies are bought and sold that there is just one recourse for the mother, one avenue of escape from an abusive owner like D'Ortega—sale to a new master.[5] Then again, it is because slaves are bought and sold that the misunderstanding between mother and daughter can never be rectified: the message that would explain the mother's actions cannot get through because, once sold, the child is transported far away and held on the new owner's property. Morrison's insistence on the unending suffering caused by the irreparable separation of mother from daughter accords with historical fact, as historian Andrew Cockburn perceives it: "Family separation was the most onerous of all the miseries inflicted on enslaved blacks.

Perpetually indebted Virginia and Maryland planters were happy to breed and sell surplus bodies, regardless of family ties" (Cockburn 45).[6]

The structure of three competing narrative perspectives on Florens's sale to Jacob Vaark reveals the distortion in Florens's perception of the scene. First comes Florens's narrative:

> I see it forever and ever. Me watching, my mother listening, her baby boy on her hip. Senhor [D'Ortega] is not paying the whole amount he owes to Sir. Sir [Jacob Vaark] saying he will take instead the woman and the girl, not the baby boy and the debt is gone. A minha mae begs no. Her baby boy is still at her breast. Take the girl, she says, my daughter, she says. Me. Me. Sir agrees and changes the balance due. (7)

If we look at the discrepancies between this account of the mother's words and Jacob's account of the same scene, we can perceive the interpretive frame that Florens uses to make sense of her mother's demand. As Jacob focalizes the scene in the chapter that follows Florens's narration, D'Ortega owes Jacob money but has no cash, so he offers a slave as payment. Jacob, hating the slave trade, resists, but finally says that he will take the cook (Florens's mother) as partial payment of the debt (in part in order to nettle D'Ortega, for Jacob guesses correctly that Florens's mother is his concubine). D'Ortega refuses and the issue is closed; the idea of using a slave to pay down the debt falls away entirely. It is Florens's mother who reintroduces the idea: "Her voice was barely above a whisper but there was no mistaking its urgency. 'Please, Senhor. Not me. Take her. Take my daughter'" (26). And the mother kneels to him in silent pleading. In pity for the little girl, Jacob accedes. Because this second version of the transaction is not someone's memory but narrated in the present by an omniscient narrator and focalized by Jacob, who has little emotional stake in the scene, it strikes the reader as more credible than Florens's agonized version of the event. Moreover, the mother's account of the sale in the concluding monologue corroborates the details of Jacob's version.

The competing narratives of the sale enable a reader to perceive the frame of sibling rivalry through which Florens interprets her mother's words. In Florens's account, Jacob first proposes to "take . . . the woman and the girl, not the baby boy and the debt is gone." And—again in Florens's account—the mother responds, "No. Her baby boy is still at her breast. Take the girl, she says, my daughter, she says" (7). In both Jacob's and the mother's accounts, by contrast, the idea of Jacob's taking both Florens and her mother as payment never arises; such a possibility does not exist. Correlatively, the

mother never protests that she is still nursing her son and cannot be separated from him. As Florens construes the event, the mother has a choice:
she could go with the daughter or stay with the son. She chooses the son.
Florens configures the scene to reflect a common fantasy of sibling rivalry: a
new sibling is, at least initially, perceived as usurping the older child's place.
"Someone [is] in . . . the same position as oneself. . . . The older child is not
just displaced, but for a time is without a place—someone else *is* what she is
[the child of her parents]" (Mitchell 46–47). In Florens's account, the mother
enacts this horrific logic: there is only one place next to the mother's body
and in the mother's love; the boy is in the one contested position, next to the
maternal body (in Florens's version the mother says that he is at the breast),
so there is no space for the daughter. Although she could go with Florens, the
mother chooses the boy-child: she prefers the son to the daughter. Within the
interpretive frame of sibling rivalry, Florens can read "Take the girl" only as
the signifier of rejection in favor of the boy.

The mother's narration of the scene reveals a quite different orientation to
the situation. The mother focuses on the sexual threat to her daughter, barely
mentioning her son: it is Florens who is central to her thoughts and to her
love.

While Florens's story is linear—Jacob buys Florens, Florens grows up,
Florens tracks the blacksmith through the wilderness, finds the blacksmith,
kills (?) the blacksmith—the narrative form of Florens's narrated chapters is
not. One could call *A Mercy's* narrative shape repetitive—and so it is, reflecting Florens's traumatized obsession by coming back and back to the moment of the mother's rejection. But it is better characterized as recursive:
that is, each repetition of the original scene—focalized first by Florens, then
by Jacob, then by the mother—adds new content so that as a reader goes
back over the same incident, its meaning accumulates, building up for the
reader—but not for Florens—a fuller, multidimensional picture of the sale.
Each narrator adds a new angle on the event, but the mother's narration
does more: coming at the end of the novel, the mother's tale suddenly expands our perspective on Florens's personal tragedy by situating it within
the long historical past of the slave trade and the diasporic breadth of the
numberless women subjected to it.

The threat of rape opens the mother's narrative. She could see that the
slaveowner and his wife were lusting after Florens and would soon make
her their sexual plaything (162), so she gave her away to Jacob (163). But the
mother evidently feels that these particulars are not enough. To explain her

act she must tell Florens all the stages of her journey through the Middle Passage: from her capture in Africa to "the continue of all misery" on the slave ship (164) to the landing at Barbados and her work in the sugarcane fields to being sold to D'Ortega and shipped to Virginia's tobacco fields.

The phrase "There is no protection" occurs four times in the mother's short chapter, and only at the beginning does it apply to the impossibility of giving her daughter protection. "There is no protection" is the basic condition of all the female captives; at every stop on the Middle Passage and every stay in a plantation, slave women are vulnerable to rape. Only one rape is described in detail—when several black men followed D'Ortega's orders to "break in" the new arrivals, the mother and her friends—but it is also clear that the slavemaster and his wife have used the mother's body for their sexual pleasure (166). "There is no protection. To be female in this place is to be an open wound that cannot heal. Even if scars form, the festering is ever below" (163). The mother's image acquires its power from the collapse of metaphor into the object it represents: the vagina *is* an open wound; continually reinjured (forcibly penetrated), "it cannot heal."

Rape is in the center of the vast historical and geographical space the mother's tale opens to us in part because rape most vividly gives body to the absence of all choice, rights, and protections for the enslaved. As Naomi Morgenstern points out, it is in such spaces of ethical "wilderness," "where established legal and moral codes fail," that the most purely ethical choices emerge ("Maternal" 9). This is the space where Morrison places her mothers, Sethe as well as Florens's mother: "Morrison's mothers choose when there are no clear options. They forge a choice out of no option or choose between choice and no choice. . . . Morrison's mothers, then, might be said to invent ethics or to bring an ethical realm into being . . . through performance" ("Maternal" 23).

In a system without fine distinctions, where all slaveowners are defined by their absolute power over the enslaved, Florens's mother creates an ethical divide based on her own intuitions about human kindness: Jacob, who "never looked at me the way Senhor does," who "does not want" (163), will see Florens as a child, she thinks, rather than as sexual prey. "There is no protection but there is difference," says the mother, making moral distinctions where there are none. In a paradox befitting the contradictory conditions of female existence in slavery, the mother treats Florens as a commodity by giving her to Jacob; but in so doing she gives Florens a chance for sovereignty over her own body—a measure of freedom that the mother herself lacks. When Florens wholeheartedly enters into sexual love with the blacksmith, that act seems to be merely a fact of her adult life. But like everything in Florens's story, it goes back to her mother's creating "a choice where there are no clear options," a choice that gives Florens the chance to develop as a freely choosing sexual subject.

The Distorted Optic of Sibling Rivalry

A primary example of Florens's lack of interpretive skills is her encounter with the blacksmith, whom she has refound after an arduous journey through the wilderness of seventeenth-century America. The violence of Florens's attack on the blacksmith and the small boy in his charge seems unwarranted, but it begins to come into focus if we grant Laplanche's contention that the parental signifier, internalized, inflects the subject's drive energies and general approach to the world. In Laplanche's theory the internalized enigmatic signifier can never be metabolized, never integrated into conscious or unconscious processes: like a "spine [splinter] in the protective wall of the ego," it goes on "acting like a foreign body which long after its entry must . . . be regarded as an agent that is still at work" (Freud and Breuer, *Hysteria* 6; qtd. in Laplanche, *Life* 42). The version of the enigmatic signifier that the child internalizes gives a particular distortion, or "angle of inclination," to his or her perception of the world (Santner, *Psychotheology* 39). The way that Florens's version of the enigmatic signifier, "Take the girl, . . . my daughter," orients—or, better, disorients—Florens's perception of reality becomes clear when, after an arduous journey through the American wilderness, she finds the blacksmith.

Completing the errand on which her mistress Rebekka has sent her, Florens tells the blacksmith that Rebekka is critically ill and needs the blacksmith's healing arts. The blacksmith greets Florens joyfully and agrees to go to Rebekka. However, he says, Florens cannot go back with him because of a new development: he is fostering an orphaned child, Malaik, and while he is away he will need Florens to take care of the small boy:

> And there is another reason, you say. You turn your head. My eyes follow where you look. This happens twice before. The first time it is me peering around my mother's dress hoping for her hand that is only for her little boy. The second time it is a pointing screaming little girl hiding behind her mother and clinging to her skirts. Both times are full of danger and I am expel. Now I am seeing a little boy come in holding a corn-husk doll. He is younger than everybody I know. You reach out your forefinger toward him and he takes hold of it. You say this is why I cannot travel with you. The child you call Malaik is not to be left alone. He is a foundling. (135–36)

The sequence of Florens's narration is telling. First comes the dislocating memory through which Florens is compelled to see the present scene: the scene of hiding behind her mother's skirts when Jacob first appeared to take her away. The second memory comes from her encounter with the religious fanatics, when the little white girl cries out in terror at the sight of Florens's black skin and her elders demonize Florens's blackness as a sign that she serves the devil.[7] "Both times . . . I am expel" (136).

Thus, before we encounter what Florens is seeing in the present we are presented with the optic through which she sees—the crucial memory of rejection. When the blacksmith holds out his finger and the small boy takes it, the reader is primed to understand the gesture as a repetition of the mother's holding her "baby boy" by the hand—and thus rejecting Florens's desire for connection, her "hop[e] for her hand that is only for her little boy" (136).

Only now, after the two images from the past, does Florens give us her interpretation of the present: "I worry as the boy steps closer to you. How you offer and he owns your forefinger. As if he is your future. Not me" (136). The primitive binary of sibling rivalry reigns: if "he," then "not me." The child has usurped Florens's place, holding the blacksmith's hand and thereby ensuring that the blacksmith will choose the child for his future. It would be a mistake to dismiss Florens's subsequent actions—attacking the little boy, then attacking the blacksmith himself—as mad. On the contrary, her actions follow a terrible logic. But it is the logic of a young child, not that of a sixteen-year-old: the fantasy of being displaced by a younger sibling.

After the blacksmith leaves, Florens acts out the jealous sibling. She maliciously—and childishly—hides the boy's doll, the transitional object he clings to for security. And when he cries loudly at the loss, and then louder in his fear of Florens, she pulls his arm till she hears the shoulder crack. Florens's violence betrays her confusion of Malaik with the brother who displaced her. When does someone strike out and try to harm the other? When one feels that the other poses a threat to one's existence. We know from earlier descriptions of Florens's passion for the blacksmith that it took a symbiotic form reminiscent of a young child's dependency on the mother: "You are my shaper and my world as well" (71); "For [Rebekka], [finding the blacksmith] is to save her life. For me it is to have one" (37); "When I see you and fall into you I know I am live" (115). As in a child's early relation with the mother, Florens imagines that her own life exists only as it is enclosed within the maternal matrix of the blacksmith's love. Florens perceives Malaik's existence as a threat to her own: if he has taken the one place next to the beloved's body, there is no place for her *to be*. Juliette Mitchell, acknowledging the full measure of the displaced sibling's ontological panic, claims that "the normal reaction" is "to kill in order not to be thus obliterated" (47). In order to return to the way things were before, "the new baby must be got rid of" (48). (Of course, there are rules that prevent the child's acting out the fantasy; in most cases, "the wish to murder the sibling must be repressed" [Mitchell 135].) Although Florens, like a child caught in the act, tries to dodge culpability by disclaiming her intention—"I am trying to stop him not hurt him. That is why I pull his arm. To make him stop" (139)—her actions speak otherwise. She acts out the murderous sibling fantasy of destroying the child who threatens to replace her.

As the little boy loses consciousness after Florens has dislocated his arm, the blacksmith returns. Before he enters, Florens hears him call: "I know I am lost because your shout is not my name. Not me. Him. Malaik you shout. Malaik" (140). Again, the binary of sibling rivalry constructs the scene: If "him," then "not me." The possibility of both/and does not exist. As Florens reframed the original scene to give the mother a choice, she frames the present scene as a choice: "You choose the boy. You call his name first" (140).

Commenting on Laplanche's theory, Eric Santner says that the particularity of the parental enigmatic signifier imposes a "specific form of disorientation" on the subject's approach to the world, a specific "torsion" in "how the world is disclosed to him" (*Psychotheology* 39). This is meant to be true of everyone, of course: each of us constructs the world according to the distorting influence of his or her particular internalized parental signifier. But Morrison gives us the extreme version of disorientation caused by the trauma of separation from the mother—by the trauma of slavery. If we consider what an age-appropriate reaction to the present circumstances would be, we can better perceive just how disturbed Florens's perception of the current reality is. What Florens wants above all things is a loving connection with the blacksmith, to be "here with you always," to be "never never without you" (136). To give loving care to the blacksmith's charge would be a way to foster the blacksmith's gratitude, admiration, and love and thus move toward her goal of permanent union with him. In addition, the ethic imposed by a colonial America so chaotic and violent that orphans are produced everywhere, and are everywhere in need of adult care, is the demand that all adults care for all dispossessed children. Love and duty coincide to dictate that Florens must act the role of caregiver appropriate to her age (sixteen). But the age-appropriate fantasy structure of Florens and the blacksmith as two loving adults sharing the care of a small child is foreclosed, squeezed out by the dominating fantasy of sibling rivalry, which skews Florens's vision so that she cannot act in her own interests.

When the blacksmith angrily rebukes Florens for injuring the child, she attacks him with his own hammer and tongs. This seemingly senseless violence does make a kind of sense if we understand it through Laplanche's perspective on the drives. Differentiating his model of the drive from Freud's, Laplanche explains, "The drive is . . . not a biological force, nor a concept lying on the frontier between the mental and the physical. It is the impact on the individual and on the ego of the constant stimulation exerted from the inside by the repressed thing-presentation, which can be described as the source-object of the drive" (*Otherness* 129). The psychic representative of the parental enigmatic signifier, which Laplanche calls "the thing-presentation," goes on working from within, continually exciting and disturbing the subject, generating tension. It has the power to generate characteristic scenarios as well. "Frozen, fixed beyond the meaning that may inhabit them, . . . these frozen and fixed representations have the generative power of schemas as well as the materiality of *quasi-things*" (120; emphasis in the original). Thus, when Laplanche calls the enigmatic signifier "the source-object of the drives," he means not only that it gives a characteristic swerve to the drives but also that it can channel drive energy along the lines of a characteristic "schema," or fantasy scenario.

In *A Mercy*, the enigmatic signifier of dismissal, "Take the girl . . . my daughter," gives shape to Florens's aggressive drive energy. As the blacksmith, appalled by Florens's attack on Malaik, berates her, Florens despairs. "Are you meaning I am nothing to you? . . . Now I am living the dying inside. No. Not again. Not ever . . . the hammer is in my hand" (141–42). It is to prevent the internalized scenario of rejection from being reenacted in the present ("Not again. Not ever") that Florens attacks the blacksmith with his hammer. As he orders her to leave—"I want you to go" (141); "Leave us be" (141); "get away from me" (141)—Florens swings the tongs and hits him, trying to prevent the "expel," trying to annihilate the one who is repeating in the external world the drama of maternal rejection that dominates her internal world. First the hammer, then the tongs: Florens leaves the blacksmith bloodied and perhaps dead.

Of course, maternal abandonment would be traumatic for any child, and reenactment of the trauma is a common symptom of unresolved trauma. But I would argue that the situation of slavery gives an added intransigence to the sway of the maternal signifier over Florens's drives and desires. As the structure of the novel emphasizes, there is no possibility of repairing the breach with the mother or coming to a new understanding of the original scene. Florens cannot have a retroactive understanding of the mother's seeming rejection because, irrevocably separated by the sale, she cannot receive her mother's explanatory message.

In addition, Florens seems unable to learn from her passage into adulthood and sexuality: unlike Freud's patients who grow into a new understanding of incidents of childhood sexual abuse—when, looking back *nachträglich* from the other side of puberty, they suddenly realize "Oh! So that was sex!"[8]— Florens never acquires an adult understanding of her mother's motives. She never speculates, for example, that her mother might have arranged for her departure in order to save her from inevitable sexual violation if she remained on the D'Ortega plantation. Florens cannot gain a new perspective on the original scene because her development was arrested at the time her mother cast her aside. In Laplanche's terms, the enigmatic signifier, "the source-object of the drive, is 'stuck' in the envelope of the ego" (*Otherness* 209). Like a stuck record, the original scenario plays out without modification: Malaik *is* the younger rival for the parental figure's affections; because he is in the place next to the parent/lover's body, the place where Florens wants to be, there *is* no place for Florens, who must be cast out. Florens lives her past absolutely in her present.

Just as the mother's words to Jacob, "Take her, . . . my daughter," operated as an address to Florens, interpellating her into the social register as forsaken daughter—an identity that Lina's loving maternal care of her over eight years does nothing to ameliorate—the blacksmith's words lose their dialogic potential to take on the force of an interpellation. "You are nothing but wilderness. No constraint. No mind," says the blacksmith in anger (141). Her old self "dying inside," "lost" with the loss of her lover (142, 140), Florens takes on the identity created by the blacksmith's address: "You say I am wilderness. I am" (157). Lina once told Florens the story of an eagle mother who bravely protects her eggs until she is maimed and destroyed by a man. Her eggs hatch alone. To Florens's question, "Do they live?" Lina answers, "We have" (63), thus defining both teller and listener as orphans. Now, designated as "wild" and "wilderness" by her lover, Florens finds amid the meager resources for her identity the image of the baby eagle, orphaned but fierce. It is true that the first mention of a "clawing feathery thing" inside her follows her humiliation at the hands of the religious fanatics (115). But it is the blacksmith's words of repudiation that bring the "feathered thing" inside fully to life: "feathers lifting, I unfold"—like a baby bird emerging from the egg. "[My] claws scratch and scratch until the hammer is in my hand" (142). Condensed in the eaglet image is the rage of the orphaned child at being forsaken: once "folded up" deep in the "inside dark" (115), once suppressed beneath the surface of the docile, compliant slave Florens, the rage of the abandoned orphan child "unfolds" and strikes out against the parent/lover who fails her: "The claws of the feathered thing did break out on you because I cannot stop them wanting to tear you open the way you tear me" (160).

"I am become wilderness," says Florens (161). Confirming the transformation, Scully and Willard, the indentured servants who have long known Florens as an obedient, eager-to-please slave girl, do not recognize her when they see her returning home from killing (?) maiming (?) the blacksmith. "Stomping down the road, . . . blood-spattered," "untouchable," indifferent, she seems to them inhuman (146, 152). "The docile creature they knew had turned feral"—wild (146).

Florens's narration closes with the evocation of yet another failed message. We discover that the text we have been reading—that is, all the chapters narrated by Florens—is directed to the blacksmith (the "you" of her narrative address). But the message must fail. Florens is writing it with a nail on the walls of the big room in Jacob's newly built and abandoned mansion.[9] Although Florens imagines a moment in the future when the blacksmith might enter the house and read her message, it is clear that this will never happen. For the house is locked up; no one is allowed to enter; the blacksmith may well be dead; and even if he has survived, he is illiterate ("you don't know how to [read]" [160]).

The form of the message emphasizes its futility. "These careful words . . . will talk to themselves. Round and round, side to side, bottom to top, top to bottom all across the room" (161). A message gains its meaning only in the transmission, only as it moves from sender to receiver; this message is going nowhere. Spatialized, written on walls closed in on themselves, these signifiers are visible only to each other—and signifiers cannot read. The inscribed words are enigmatic signifiers in a sense different from Laplanche's: they lack meaning because, with no one to read them, they cannot signify; they remain merely material marks inscribed on a wall.

The novel thus closes on a double presentation of the failed message. The final two chapters align Florens and her mother in parallel positions, as tellers without a listener, messengers without a recipient. Florens's message to the blacksmith aims at explaining Florens's destructive actions, as the mother's failed message in the following (and final) chapter is meant to explain her

actions to Florens. Both Florens and her mother are inspired by an imperative need to get a message to the beloved. Florens writes to the blacksmith,
"I have need to tell you this. I cannot tell it to anyone but you" (160); the
mother pleads, in the last words of the novel, "Oh Florens. My love. Hear a
tua mãe" (167). Despite their urgency, both messages are frozen in the send-
ing. And the stasis of the messages extends to the psychic stasis of the senders.
The mother remains emotionally "on [her] knees," in a position of perpetual
supplication that her message will be received (167); and Florens is stuck in
time, unable to progress past the moment of her separation from her mother.

"Can you read?":
Florens as Narrator

"Can you read?" is an opening question of the novel; its placement signals its
thematic importance. Florens is addressing the question to the blacksmith,
but since we do not yet know that the blacksmith is the "you" of her address,
we take the question to be addressed to us readers. And as a secondary address, of course it is: the question challenges the reader's ability to read with
understanding. I would add yet a third addressee: Florens herself. Addressed
to a character narrator, the question "Can you read?" would mean, How well
can you "read"—that is, interpret—situations? How well can you read the
implications of other characters' words and gestures? Are your interpretive
skills up to the task of narrator?

While Florens writes to her narratee, the blacksmith, for her own purposes, the implied author Morrison uses both what Florens tells and, more
important, how she tells it, for *her* own purposes: the gaps and errors in Florens's interpretation of situations and the perversions of her narrative style
are evidence of how slavery's forced separation of mother from child has
damaged Florens's capacity for interpreting her world. The critique of slavery
is embedded in, and indistinguishable from, *A Mercy*'s textual practice, and
more specifically the troubled syntax of Florens as narrator.

I argue that the various peculiarities of Florens's narrative style can be
traced to the break with her mother. First and most obvious to a reader is
Florens's inability to signify temporality. She is incapable of using the past
tense; thus everything is reduced to present tense: "Lina says from the state
of my teeth I am maybe seven or eight when I am brought here" (5); "Where
they once are is nothing" (103). Florens uses words that denote temporal sequence infrequently; and when she does, the verbal disjunction is even more

striking: "When a child I am never able to abide being barefoot" (4); "At first when I am brought here I don't talk any word" (6). Because the adverbial marker of a past time sets up the expectation that a past tense will follow, the drop back into the present tense seems all the more stultifying. We could speculate that the inability to conjugate tenses is a result of English being Florens's second language: the language spoken on the D'Ortega plantation was Portuguese, and so are a few of Florens's expressions (*minha mae*, for instance, is Portuguese for "my mother"). But such a literal explanation does not seem sufficient, especially since the mother's speech at the end is delivered with few linguistic anomalies. I hypothesize, rather, that the stasis expressed by the unvarying present tense reflects the way time stopped in a single horrific moment: "I see it forever and ever. . . . Take the girl, she says, my daughter, she says. Me. Me. Sir agrees" (7).

Florens's habitual way of "reading" the world around her is through material "signs" rather than through people's words. "If a pea hen refuses to brood I read it quickly" (3); "Two hares freeze before bounding away. I don't know how to read that" (41); "The nanny goat turns to look. The billy does not. A bad sign" (114). Florens is scanning the visible world for signs of danger to her person. One could argue that she is thus participating in a code suited to her historical situation. Caroline Hunter, an ex-slave from Virginia, told a WPA interviewer that "she . . . learned to interpret everyday sights and sounds as signs of trouble to come: a turtledove's whistle was thought to warn of an impending beating" (Schwartz, *Born* 2). Slaves on large plantations live in a world governed by the unpredictable whims of their owners, so events like beatings appear arbitrary; reading the surrounding world for portents of danger is a mode of asserting control in a world where the subject has no control.

But Florens also reads humans' looks as signs of danger or no danger, and that is not so adaptive. Thus when Rebekka speaks to Sorrow, Florens doesn't listen to her words; instead, "I am only seeing how her eyes go. Their look is close to the way of the women who stare at Lina and me. . . . Neither look scares, but it is a hurting thing" (69). Rather than an affective cue to the other's feelings, the look is a concrete thing with the power to hurt her. This instance is representative: Florens reads eyes not as windows to the soul but as the source of looks that hurt.

Similarly, she is unable to read people's body language for clues to their internal states. Thus, for example, while she and Lina sit waiting for hours for the wagon that is to take Florens partway to the blacksmith, Florens observes Lina: "Lina holds her forehead in her hand, her elbow on her knee. She gives off a bad feeling so I keep my thoughts on the goatherd's hat" (38). Florens

stops at the surface of Lina's bodily gestures: she does not go further, to speculate on the feelings that might be prompting the gestures. It is not that she
is oblivious to Lina: she notices the "bad feeling." But Lina "gives off" the
unmistakable "bad feeling" in the same way that her body would "give off" a
smell; and Florens responds to it through the senses, as she would to an odor.
She does not speculate on the nature of Lina's feelings. Instead, she actively
avoids such an exploration by refocusing her perception on the goatherd's
hat, an inanimate thing that makes no demand for interpretation.

Laplanche's theory of the enigmatic signifier can help understand the effect of the break with the mother on Florens's interpretational skills. However, I take Laplanche's description in a theoretical direction not envisioned
in his work, toward an explanation of how a child acquires the desire to interpret—or, as in Florens's case, becomes averse to interpreting. Describing
a child's wrestling with the parental enigmatic signifier, Laplanche explains
that the child worries over the meaning of the words for an extended time—
translating and failing to translate, symbolizing and failing to symbolize (see
Santner, *The Neighbor* 92). While Laplanche is interested in the ways that
the residue of nonmeaning left over from this process constitutes the unconscious, I would inquire rather what this process means for the child's relation
to language.

If a child, knowing the importance of the parent's words but stymied by
their meaning, goes over and over them in an effort to extract their significance, what does she or he learn about interpreting words? Does the search
so frustrate him or her that, giving up, she is willing to settle for the obvious
in language, or even take pleasure in nonsense? Or does the child's desire
not rather become invested in discovering meaning? How does the initial encounter with the enigma of the other's speech come to inflect the subject's
adult desire to interpret?

Lacan (who was Laplanche's teacher) provides in *Seminar 11* an entry point
for thinking about the connection of desire to language:

> The desire of the Other is apprehended by the subject in that which does
> not work [in the mother's discourse], . . . and all the child's *whys* reveal not
> so much an avidity for the reason of things, as a . . . *Why are you telling
> me this?* ever-resuscitated from its base, which is the enigma of the adult's
> desire. (Lacan, *S* 11, 214; emphasis in the original)

The child's apprehension that the mother's desire "crawls" within her words
(Lacan 214) may explain why a child would cling tenaciously to the process
of deciphering them, through all its failures of interpretation. We can hy-

pothesize that a child's desire, foundationally attached to the mother and her desire, becomes enmeshed in the very process of trying to understand the parental words. The child learns not only to interpret but also to invest desire in the process of uncovering the meaning of words. Desire then becomes invested in interpreting language, so that for the grown-up child the very act of interpreting, of grasping meaning, affords pleasure.

For Florens, though, the mother's enigmatic signifier, "Take her, . . . my daughter," had a different outcome. The mother's utterance was performative in the sense of J. L. Austin's definition: "the uttering of the sentence is, or is a part of, the doing of an action" (5). The mother's words initiated the sale of Florens to Jacob Vaark, away from her mother, causing a wound in Florens's subjectivity that never heals.

Laplanche briefly describes such an outcome in an essay on "intromission":

> While implantation allows the individual to take things up actively, at once translating and repressing, one must try to conceive of a process which blocks this, short-circuits the differentiation of the agencies in the process of their formation and puts into the interior an element resistant to all metabolisation. ("Implantation, Intromission," in *Essays on Otherness* 136)

Laplanche is theorizing a type of parental signifier that, while it is enigmatic, is also violent. Instead of triggering a process of interpretation, the violent intrusion of the parental message into the psyche of the child, which Laplanche calls "intromission," shuts down the signifying apparatus (Laplanche, *Otherness* 136; see Fletcher, "Introduction" 45–46).

Laplanche does not elaborate this concept further, but Morrison's text does. Florens goes over and over the message of rejection in subsequent years, but it always returns just as it happened, without any progression toward translation. The message, "Take her, my daughter," sticks in Florens's consciousness like a foreign body that not only resists interpretation but clouds and informs her vision of all the key events of her life.

The abrupt separation from her mother robbed Florens of the leisure to weigh the words in various contexts in order to understand them, to interpret and fail to interpret, to translate and fail to translate. The mother spoke, and Florens was taken away. The enigmatic message was not registered as a signifier, suggestive of multiple meanings, but as a body blow, a threat to the survival of the self.

The lesson that Florens takes away from her mother's enigmatic message of dismissal is that what lies hidden in words is not a potentially infinite array of meanings to be discovered but a traumatic violence to be feared. As a result, Florens is more likely to think of words as material objects that can injure her than as spurs to interpretation. For example, when Lina tells Florens the story of her own brief horrific sexual experience, Florens thinks, "There is something in her voice that pricks me. Something old. Something cutting" (104). Lina's words do not lead Florens to speculate on what the words might mean about what Lina is feeling and thinking. Instead, the words are experienced as projectiles with the power to prick or cut Florens's body. Likewise, in the blacksmith's angry speech to her, "each word . . . cuts" (140). Ceasing to mean, the word loses its status as signifier and becomes a thing. Far from perceiving words as an invitation to experiment with potential meanings or to draw inferences about others' states of mind, Florens treats them as concrete things that can cause physical harm. Words are missiles without meaning— things that can hurt or, as her mother's words did, inflict irreparable injury.

Florens's will to interpret is lamed—and so is her capacity to interpret others' words as clues to their states of mind. For example, when she shares a wagon ride with some indentured servants, they tell her that they have served out their term, yet their master sends them north to work more years in a tannery. Florens is unable to grasp their feelings from what they say: "I don't understand why they are sad. Everyone has to work." Even to these casual interlocutors, Florens seems to lack ordinary powers of inference: they surmise that she is either very "young" or "daft" (40). But Florens is not daft. Rather, her ability to infer meaning from what people say is disabled.

As narrator, then, Florens cannot read others' messages properly or infer things about their mental worlds. What is the effect on a reader of perceiving the social world through a narrator who resists interpretation? To some extent, readers must have the sense that they are receiving only partial information about the other characters and their situations (although the chapters focalized by the other characters that alternate with Florens's narrated chapters to some degree make up for this deficit). Depending on how much a reader's own desire is invested in wresting meaning from words, she may be frustrated with the lack of information provided by Florens or provoked to interpret what the lack of interpretation means.

A reader's vague sense of something missing is rendered immediate and tangible by the encounter with the incompleteness of Florens's words: "I am already kill by you" (38); "sudden the moon moves" (67); "I am shock" (68); "I am live" (70); "I am expel" (136). Lacking their endings, the words themselves are stunted. A reader's impatience with a narrator whose lack of interpretation poses a screen between the fictional world and the reader's desire to know can only be exacerbated by the failure of Florens's words to complete themselves. At the level of communication between narrator and reader, the narrator's stunted words mirror the novel's thematics of impeded communication. The idea of broken communication is built into the prose we are reading.[10]

CHAPTER 6

Severed Limbs, the Uncanny, and the
Return of the Repressed in *Home*

Repression and the return of the repressed govern the narrative structure of *Home* (2012). At the level of the individual character, these structural features mirror processes of repression going on in the protagonist, Frank. At the level of national repressed memory, Frank's sister Cee's story evokes a long history of the medical establishment's use and abuse of black bodies in the name of scientific advancement. Severed body parts scattered through the text do double symbolic work. At the personal level, the intrusion of body parts into the story here and there figures the partial return from repression of Frank's traumatic memories. Images of body parts enter Frank's consciousness, and the text, as screen memories, in Freud's sense of the term: substitute images that cover over yet also distantly recall the body part that Frank wishes to forget: a severed hand. In the social dimension of the novel, the detached body parts that circulate through the narrative point toward America's treatment of black bodies as partitionable and expendable. As readers, we cannot grasp the meaning of these severed or deformed body parts, for the text withholds—or represses—their significance until near the end.

Knowledge of what is going on is then, at best, fragmentary and ambiguous, both for the reader and for the characters. Doubts about knowing pervade the formal structure of dual narration as well, impugning the veracity and completeness of the narratives told by the character-narrator Frank and by the third-person heterodiegetic narrator. Frank is barred from knowing the whole of the autobiographical story he tells because parts of his experience are repressed. And, according to Frank's frequent complaints about her, the "writer," or third-person narrator, cannot tell his story accurately either: Frank steps out of his place in the fictional world to address the "writer" directly: "I don't think you know much about love. Or me" (69).

The uncanny is one form of the return of the repressed; it produces a particular kind of equivocal knowing. According to Freud's essay "The Uncanny," the sensation of the uncanny arises when the subject perceives something in the outside world that embodies or enacts a long-repressed memory or fantasy scenario. One could say that the perception wobbles between the internal (repressed) image and the external phenomenon, producing ambiguity: one sees the uncanny manifestation in the outside world and so "knows" it as a perceived fact; but the internal analogue remains repressed or only partially evoked. We can see this puzzling, equivocal aspect of uncanny knowledge (and the anxiety that attends it) in Frank's confused perception of the young Asian girl and her seductive moves.

I will argue that a similarly uncanny half-knowing troubles a reader when he or she encounters in Cee's story fragmentary signifiers of a repressed U.S. medical history. In particular, the oblique but unmistakable parallels between Dr. Beau Scott's careless and near-fatal experiments on Cee's uterus and the similar experiments of Dr. Marion Sims on the uteruses of several slave women in the mid-nineteenth century evoke a history of unconstrained experimentation on black women's bodies in the name of scientific progress.

The central love interest in *Home* is the steady love between the siblings Frank and Cee—a relationship that gives them both comfort. But then Cee changes. Frank's encounter with Cee's different desire not only shakes up their relationship but threatens to undermine the foundation of Frank's masculine self-image. Indeed, the great love between them, which has always seemed so homey and familiar, now delivers the shock of the uncanny, together with all its psychic complications.

Beginning with the Uncanny:
Epigraph and Opening Scene

Using Freud's "The Uncanny" as a reference point can illuminate the subtleties of Morrison's conceptual play with notions of "home" and "not-home." *Home* tells the story of making a home out of an unhome, of making a home in a place (Lotus, Georgia, scene of Frank's and Cee's childhood) that had formerly withheld love, nurturing, and protection. At the most basic level, the narrative is structured by the line that goes from epigraph to epilogue—from the epigraph's evocation of estrangement from a house that is emphatically not a home to the reclaiming of home in the epilogue, which concludes: "Come on, brother. Let's go home" (147).

The novel's epigraph suggests the uncanny and so prefigures something essential both to the psychic experience of the protagonist Frank and to the novel's idea of home.

> Whose house is this?
> Whose night keeps out the light
> In here?
> Say, who owns this house?
> It's not mine.
> I dreamed another, sweeter, brighter
> With a view of lakes crossed in painted boats;
> Of fields wide as arms open for me.
> This house is strange.
> Its shadows lie.
> Say, tell me, why does its lock fit my key?[1]

If he has the key, the speaker must have known the house in some former time. The poem evokes the uncanny in the classic sense developed by Freud: it seems eerily strange, yet it must have been familiar once. The cause of this paradox, according to Freud, lies in the process of repression: "The uncanny proceeds from something familiar which has been repressed" ("The Uncanny" 247). Something in the external world mimics a long-repressed memory or fantasy, and the faint memory-trace of that repressed idea gives the real-world incident its uncanny hue. To the speaker of the poem, the house is uncanny—strange, entirely mysterious, full of "shadows" and "night" that cannot be illuminated—yet, from the fit of his key, once known and familiar.

Chapter 1 picks up the idea of the uncanny from the epigraph; and it introduces, both through explicit description and through a vivid visual image, the processes of repression and the return of the repressed. Frank recalls a childhood memory of crawling under a fence with Cee and seeing horses fight in a field: "They rose up like men . . . their forelegs around the withers of the other, we held our breath in wonder" (3–4). Crawling back through the long grass, the children observe a secret burial: "We saw them pull a body from a wheelbarrow and throw it into a hole already waiting. One foot stuck up over the edge and quivered, as though it could get out, as though with a little effort it could break through the dirt being shoveled in" (4).

At the end of the chapter, Frank steps outside the frame to address the writer (or, more accurately, the representation of the writer who is in the process of writing his story) directly: "Since you're set on telling my story, . . . know this: I really forgot about the burial. I only remembered the horses.

They were so beautiful. So brutal. And they stood like men" (5). Of all the things that the author needs to know about Frank in order to tell his story well and accurately, Frank calls out this vagary of memory—"know this"— for her special attention. Frank explains a particular ruse of repression here: what he can remember (the battle of the horses) covers over a far more disturbing memory (the burial of a body). Freud calls this trick of repression a "screen memory": what is remembered from some important event in the subject's life is not the event itself but some marginal feature of it ("Screen Memories" 307). The substitution of a benign event for the disturbing one protects the subject from distress. Beyond the level of dialogue between character-narrator and "writer," the imperative "Know this!" obliquely addresses the reader, too, with a warning to watch out for what remains "forgotten," concealed beneath the verbal surface of Frank's first-person narrative. Fair enough: for the text that lies before the reader is structured by repression.

The very example that Frank gives of repression—the forgotten scene of the burial—is itself a visual metaphor for repression and for the return of the repressed. The body is being buried, pushed down into a dark hidden space below the ground that mimics the popularly accepted Freudian model of an unconscious realm located underneath the conscious mind. What is being pushed down is that which must not be known: a corpse. The burial mimes not only the act of repression, which "turn[s] something away, and keeps[s] it at a distance from the conscious" (Freud, "Repression" 147), but also the counterforce of the repressed seeking to return. "One foot . . . quivered, as though it could get out, as though with a little effort it could break through the dirt being shoveled in" (4). The "foot" seems to be trying to "get out," in a representation of the persistent effort of the repressed to get out from under repression and gain entry into the conscious mind; the foot is trying to "break through" and emerge into the light.

So here, at the opening of the narrative, we have a double reference to repression: a vivid visual metaphor for repression and the return of the repressed; and the protagonist's explicit description of a mental process in which a harmless image (the horses) substitutes for something concealed (the repressed scene of the burial).

The foot also evokes one mode in which the repressed returns: the uncanny. In "The Uncanny," Freud lists "dismembered limbs, a severed head, a hand cut off at the wrist, . . . feet which dance by themselves . . .—all these have something peculiarly uncanny about them, especially when, as in the last instance, they prove capable of independent activity in addition" (244). The foot moving by itself in Morrison's text operates almost as a citation, referring us to a specific item on Freud's list of uncanny phenomena. More fruitful for my reading of *Home*, Freud's essay describes the uncanny as an effect of repression: "This uncanny is in reality nothing new or alien, but something which is familiar and old-established in the mind and which has become alienated from it only through the process of repression" ("The Uncanny" 241). It is just such an uncanny resurgence of the repressed, I will argue, that triggers Frank's killing of the small girl in Korea. And the autonomous foot is also the first in a series of body parts that function as uncanny reminders of a repressed national history of abusing black bodies for white purposes.

Retrieving the Repressed

From everything that we are told, regardless of which character is focalizing, we know that Frank has always been an exemplary brother to Cee: "She had been his original caring-for, a selflessness without gain or emotional profit" (34–35). I will argue, however, that his act of murder, which he has repressed and which he recovers toward the end of the novel, gives evidence of a deep-seated sexual fantasy involving Cee, a fantasy that Frank must repress in order to maintain the pure and perfect ideal of his relationship with Cee. There is a double repression, then, first of a memory—the murder of the little girl—and then, deeper still, the repression of the unconscious fantasy that motivates the killing.

What is repressed through most of the novel is Frank's traumatic memory of killing an Asian child. The memory emerges in two versions: in the first he attributes the murder to someone else, and in the second he claims the identity of the murderer as his own. During the Korean War, Frank was standing guard when he noticed a movement in the bamboo surrounding the camp's garbage dump. The hand of a child emerged, groping for anything that might be edible.

> It was a child's hand sticking out and patting the ground. I remember smiling. Reminded me of Cee and me trying to steal peaches off the ground under Miss Robinson's tree, sneaking, crawling, being as quiet as we could so she wouldn't see us and grab a belt. I didn't even try to run the girl off . . . so she came back almost every day, pushing through bamboo to scavenge our trash. (94)

The little girl's scavenging hand reminds Frank of home—of Cee, childhood, and Frank's delight in childhood adventures with Cee: these memories of home are entirely pleasant, making him "smile" and "welcome" the daily appearance of the little girl's hand. One day "she raises up . . . smiles, reaches for the soldier's crotch, touches it. It surprises him. Yum-yum? As soon as I look away from her hand to her face, see the two missing teeth, . . . he blows her away. Only the hand remains in the trash, clutching its treasure, a spotted, rotting orange" (95).

In his second telling of the story, Frank straightens out the identity of the guard:

> I shot the Korean girl in her face.
> I am the one she touched.
> I am the one who saw her smile.
> I am the one she said "Yum-yum" to.
> I am the one she aroused. (133)

What spurred Frank to shoot her? I will argue that what Frank experiences is a moment of the uncanny and that Morrison represents the experience of the uncanny very well, as the sense of shock that comes from perceiving the strange and disturbing within what is most familiar and comforting. Freud explores the ways that the German *unheimlich* (uncanny) contains its opposite, *heimlich*, or homey, in his essay "The Uncanny." Given the title of Morrison's novel, *Home*, and the love of wordplay that is evident in all Morrison's writing, we may assume that the changes Freud rings on the words *heimlich* and *unheimlich* are relevant, despite their German origin, to the present text; for it too plays on the transmutations of the homey into the uncanny and vice versa.

Freud begins "The Uncanny" by defining terms: *Heimlich* (homey) signifies "belonging to the house, not strange, familiar, . . . comfortable, homely, . . . friendly, intimate, homelike" (125–26). On the other hand, *heimlich* has a secondary meaning related to *geheimnis*, or secret: from its associations with what goes on inside a house, *heimlich* comes to mean "concealed and kept out of sight" (129). *Unheimlich*, or the uncanny, by contrast, describes something that is disquieting or frightening because of its strangeness, its eeriness. Freud, however, finds that despite the "un" that is the sign of opposition, the *unheimlich*, or uncanny, incorporates the two meanings of *heimlich*. The uncanny is what "ought to have remained hidden and secret, and yet comes to light" (130); and the uncanny is "a hidden, familiar thing that has undergone repression and then emerged from it" (153). "Thus *heimlich* is a word the meaning of which develops in the direction of ambivalence, until it finally coincides with its opposite, *unheimlich. Unheimlich* is in some way or other a sub-species of *heimlich*" (226).

Morrison stages Frank's crucial scene as an interplay and combining of the same opposites that fascinated Freud. When Frank first saw the child's hand, it gave him the pleasure of the familiar, reminding him of Cee joining with him in a childish escapade; further, the hand groping for food recalled "a bird feeding her young" as well as that even more domestic bird, "a hen scratching, scratching dirt for the worm"—images of nurturing and nature from the past and from home (94–95). The similarity of the girl's hand to Cee's hand is comforting through its familiarity. However, this very familiarity becomes horrific when the little Korean girl smiles and at the same time Frank feels that same hand on his penis, as the girl offers oral sex: "Yum-yum?" The smile vividly recalls Cee because it reveals the girl's missing front teeth and thus reproduces Cee's smile when she had lost her baby teeth—the same baby teeth that are preserved among Frank's boyhood treasures (35, 120).

The combination of innocent childhood and sexual offer may well be unsettling, but is that enough to provoke a killing? Frank's own analysis is revealing. In the first version of the incident, when he displaces the child's murder onto the other guard, Frank surmises, "I think the guard . . . felt tempted and that is what he had to kill" (96). It is then "temptation" that "the guard" (Frank) "had to kill"—something in himself rather than in the girl. But is shame over one's own temptation to respond to sexual invitation reason enough to kill? We can imagine a different soldier being so tempted, and yet, given the sensory and sexual deprivations of existing in the wasteland of a battle zone, forgive himself for the temptation. In the second version (when Frank reclaims the traumatic memory), he explains his act thus:

> A child. A wee little girl. . . .
>
> How could I let her live after she took me down to a place I didn't know was in me?
>
> How could I like myself, even *be* myself if I surrendered to that place where I unzip my fly and let her taste me . . .
>
> And again the next day and the next as long as she came scavenging.
>
> What type of man is that? (134; my emphasis)

Here Frank amplifies the description of what he had to kill: again, it is something in himself, something deep "down," in a "place" he didn't know was there. The description of an unknown "place" deep "down" inside strongly recalls the Freudian topography of the unconscious. The child pro-

vokes the anxiety of the uncanny because, as Freud describes it, "The uncanny [*unheimlich*] is something that is secretly familiar [*heimlich*], which
has undergone repression and then returned from it" ("The Uncanny" 245);
deformed over time by the processes of repression, it emerges as something
new and strange. In my view, Frank feels overwhelming anxiety in the face
of the little girl's sexual offer because it threatens to expose a fantasy hitherto
repressed. The little girl who strongly recalls Cee threatens to enact in the
external world Frank's repressed fantasy of having sex with his little sister. He
imagines what would happen "if I surrendered to that place where I unzip
my fly and let her taste me right then and there? And again the next day and
the next." It is from "that place" deep inside that this fantasy scenario begins
to unroll: how could the notion of repressed fantasy be expressed more con-
cretely? In addition, the dailiness of "the next day and the next" evokes the
daily availability, through proximity, of a sibling. Frank shoots to stop the
recognition of what has long been suppressed, the buried fantasy of incestuous sex with his little sister.

What makes the excessiveness of Frank's revulsion seem plausible is the
text's careful development of Frank's moral vision, which is tied to ideals of
masculinity. After describing the scenario of being fellated by the little girl,
Frank asks, "What type of man is that?" And he says, "How could I like
myself, even *be* myself, if I surrendered to that place?" The hitherto repressed
fantasy of predatory masculinity challenges who he *is*—challenges his very
identity as a man, which is based on a vision of himself as heroic defender of
his sister, of an innocent young girl. That positive pole of masculinity is also
linked to a fantasy scenario:

> [My sister] was the first person I ever took responsibility for. Down deep
> inside her lived my secret picture of myself—a strong good me tied to the
> memory of those horses and the burial of a stranger. Guarding her, finding
> a way . . . out of that place, not being afraid of anything—snakes or wild
> old men. I wonder if succeeding at that was the buried seed of all the rest.
> In my little-boy heart I felt heroic and I knew that if they . . . touched her
> I would kill. (104)

The remembered scene dramatizes Frank's "strong good" masculine identity.
There is then a clear and totalizing antithesis between the fantasized "bad"
masculinity, the sexual predator deep down in himself, and the fantasized
"good" masculinity dramatized in the rescue scenario.

We can see the same insistence on moral absolutes in Frank's clinging,
even as an adult, to the image of himself and Cee as Hansel and Gretel. All

innocence resides in Frank and Cee, who "like some forgotten Hansel and Gretel, locked hands" to survive the persecutions of the wicked grandmother, Lenore: "Lenore was the wicked witch" (53). Innocence and goodness are entirely on the side of Hansel and Gretel (Frank and Cee) while evil is contained in the wicked witch. Because Frank is so deeply invested in the fairy-tale distribution of good and evil, he is not able to manage the insight that he has the potential for evil, that he could even in fantasy abuse the innocence and trust of a child. Frank cannot abide the idea that the potential for incest is contiguous with the intimacy and proximity of family relations, that the potential for sex lies *within* the pure and perfect relationship between brother and sister. Such rigidity makes his self-image brittle, in need of defense. To maintain the identity of "strong good" man, the fantasy of incest has to be returned to repression, and the little girl who embodies the seduction scenario has to be "blown away." Only self-preservation is enough to explain the extreme of anxiety that leads Frank to kill.

I want to emphasize here the limits of my claim about Frank's fantasy of incest: I am not saying that he uncovers the repressed memory of an actual event but that his horror at the little girl's sexual invitation springs from its evoking an unconscious fantasy scenario. Living post-Freud, most readers are accustomed to the idea that children, including their own childhood selves, cherish fantasies of sexual intimacy with forbidden family members. Presumably because of the prohibitions on sex between family members, "repression concerns specifically sexuality" (Laplanche and Pontalis, "Fantasy and the Origins of Sexuality" 9); sexual fantasies that may begin as seemingly harmless daydreams "have since been purposefully forgotten and have become unconscious through 'repression'" (Freud, "Repression" 161, n.48, *SE* vol. 9). It is Frank's strict sense of good and evil that makes him unable to tolerate even a fantasy that mingles sex with brotherly love. Not so Toni Morrison: her presentation of incestuous sexual fantasy as integral to family relations in some ways parallels Freud's early work on the sexual underside of Victorian families: it exposes the "un-home" elements concealed beneath idealized constructions of home.

Body Parts as
Narrative Markers of Repression

Morrison incorporates both repression and the devious strategies of the repressed striving to return into the structure of *Home*. A principle like screen memory governs the text: the body parts that litter the text act as screen memories for the crucial traumatic signifier that is withheld, or repressed, by the narrative: a severed hand.

As in the first chapter, in this crucial chapter of confession a description of repression takes precedence over Frank's account of the act—as if it were as important to communicate the psychic processes that have held trauma at bay for so long as to recount the traumatic event itself. The chapter opens:

> I have to say something to you right now. I have to tell the whole truth. I lied to you and I lied to me. I hid it from you because I hid it from me. I felt so proud grieving over my dead friends. How I loved them. How much I cared about them, missed them. My mourning was so thick it completely covered my shame. (133)

First, the grammar implies the splitting of the self: one part of the self "hides" the truth of Frank's experience—the murder—from another part of the self—and hides it so effectively that this second part of the self cannot perceive it. We are remarkably close to Freud's description of the divided self and of repression, a process whereby one part of the self "intentionally turn[s] something away and [keeps] it at a distance from the conscious [mind]," safely hidden in the unconscious ("Repression" 147).

Second, Frank explains the process that maintained the disturbing memory under wraps: "I felt so proud grieving over my dead friends. How I loved them. How much I cared about them, missed them. My mourning was so thick it completely covered my shame" (133). Frank's word "cover" resonates with Freud's term for a screen memory—*Deckerinnerung*, or cover memory, derived from the German word for blanket, *Decke*. Freud describes a cover memory, or screen memory (as Strachey has translated the word), as the result of a contest between the energy of a repressed memory that pushes toward consciousness and the force of repression that keeps it down; a compromise takes place, so that an innocuous memory associated with the objectionable memory is permitted entry into consciousness; that "cover memory" effectively screens the objectionable memory from conscious knowing. Not only does Frank's wording match Freud's; his metaphor also describes the mechanism of screen memory precisely: "My mourning was so thick it completely covered my shame" (133). Sad memories of his friends Stuff and Mike "covered" over, or blanketed, the traumatic memory beneath.

Screen memory is a feature of the narrative, too. For example, the severed arm of Stuff is in plain sight; what is covered over is the severed hand of the little girl Frank killed. Indeed, isolated body parts pepper the sections focalized by Frank but narrated by the third-person narrator:

"He dreamed a dream dappled with body parts" (16);

"socks folded neatly on the rug like broken feet" (17);

"a boy pushing his entrails back in" (20);

"his dead arm" (32);

"Sleep came fairly soon, with only one image of fingered feet—or was it toe-tipped hands?" (33)

Readers likely interpret these body fragments as haunting reminders of Frank's experience in the war—and indeed, they are that as well, as I discuss in the second half of this chapter. But at the level of *Home*'s narrative structure, the intrusion of body parts into the text imitates the return of the repressed in disguised but persistent forms. The severed body parts are screen memories, signifiers that conceal what they only distantly refer to, a severed hand—that is, the hand clutching the orange that remained after Frank's gun "blew away" the Korean child's body. Condensing the shame and horror of Frank's act, the hand is the crucial signifier that the text holds back, or represses.

Through most of the novel, the reader is in the position of a subject of repression, unable to read the meaning of the part objects that appear in the text because their true referent is suppressed. Indeed, the reader is in the position of the repressed subject Frank, who can recall clearly, and mourn, the severed arm of his buddy Stuff—"Frank helped Stuff locate the arm twenty feet away," "holding his severed arm in the connected one . . . [Stuff] died" (98–99)—but not the repressed image of the severed hand that it both stands in for and hides. The object occluded by all these screen memories is revealed to the reader only when Frank accesses and narrates the memory of killing the little girl.

Is the knowledge the reader gains from Frank's recovery of the repressed memory sufficient reward for having suffered with not-knowing for so long? Insofar as Morrison plays by Freud's rules, I would say yes. That is, the image of the hand, like a node of unconscious memory, condenses many strands of the repressed in Frank's experience; so it stands as a satisfying literary representative of a repressed signifier. It is the hand—not the whole figure of the girl—that in the scene of the murder participates in the play of *heimlich* and *unheimlich*. Seeing the hand grubbing for leftovers, Frank is reminded of Cee's hand reaching for fruit, so that the hand evokes all the *heimlich* feelings attached to innocent childhood memories: comfort, nurturing, happiness (Frank smiles with pleasure). Then the same hand touches his genitals, unexpectedly combining the innocence of the child with sex and at the same time arousing his own sexuality and so confronting him with what must be kept repressed: the fantasy of sexual intimacy with "a child. A wee little girl" (134)—who is also his sister. The hand now evokes the *unheimlich*, the uncanny feeling that arises when something long repressed finds an analogue in the external world. Consequently, Frank severs the hand from the living body, killing it to stop forever the touch of the hand on his genitals and the unrolling of the incestuous sexual fantasy scenario now given embodied reality by his own arousal: more precisely, he kills to block recognition of a deep-seated predatory incestuous sexual fantasy that would contaminate his purely protective masculine identity. It is the *unheimlich* dwelling within the *heimlich* that proves unbearable.

The delayed disclosure seems aesthetically effective, then, because it has been prepared for by a narrative mode that hints at the existence of something repressed while continually reminding character, narrator, writer, and reader that they don't know what it is. The revelation of Frank's act then gives the reader the relief of understanding, as the lifting of repression might well afford the subject.

Body Parts and the History of Medical Experimentation

In the social register of the novel, isolated body parts evoke repression of a different kind: the repressions of history. I will argue that the narrative brings back what U.S. histories of various kinds have repressed: the treatment of black bodies as partitionable and expendable. And the narrative also calls attention to what gets repressed in these practices of careless violence to black bodies: the embodied subjectivity of the black persons so used.

Morrison speaks explicitly of the repressions of history when she says of *Home*,

> I wanted to rip the scab off that period. There's all this *Leave It to Beaver* nostalgia. That it was all comfortable and happy and everyone had a job. Oh, please. There was violent racism. There was [Joe] McCarthy. There was this horrible war we didn't call a war, where 58,000 people died. (Interview with Bob Minzesheimer)

According to the author, then, the text is intended to undo the repressions that support the idealized national memory of the 1950s as a time of peace, security, and prosperity. It was a time of security only for some, Morrison shows. Thus, Frank and his buddies occupy a zone of radical *in*security, the

Korean battlefield. One soldier's face is blown off, while another "push[ed] his entrails back in, holding them in his palms" (20). "Frank helped Stuff locate his arm twenty feet away. . . . Holding his severed arm in the connected one [Stuff] died" (99). In battle, Frank "dodged the scattered parts of men" (98). The repressed of history returns, assaulting consciousness with images of body parts that are unavoidably concrete: the vividly described mutilations insert into the historical record the "war we didn't call a war," the Korean War, and the radical insecurity of black bodies in that war. Body parts thus do double symbolic work in *Home*, bearing witness not only to what is repressed from Frank's individual consciousness but to what has been repressed from the national consciousness.

Of course, Frank and his buddies, Stuff and Mike, have "volunteered" for the army, it is true, and thereby knowingly put their bodies at risk; but the implication of free choice in the term "volunteer" blankets over the material conditions that push them into signing up. The United States of the 1950s offers these young black men no viable paths forward—no education, no jobs except "mindless work in fields you didn't own," as Frank says (84). With perhaps a side glance at the preponderance of people of color in the contemporary U.S. army, Morrison sketches in the material conditions that push Frank and his buddies into enlisting. She thus dramatizes the systemic racism that keeps people of color living in poverty and so ensures a steady supply of black youth willing to sign up for war.

The patriotic ideology of the armed services is color-blind: soldiers are treated as uniform, all motivated by the love of country to fight on behalf of the nation. W. E. B. Du Bois saw things differently; in 1952, writing about the Korean War from a global perspective, he said, "Today France is using the black Senegalese to conquer Vietnam, and Britain has used troops of every race and hue to hold the remains of her empire. . . . Perhaps worst of all today is the use of American Negro troops in Korea" (Du Bois, *In Battle* 179; qtd. in Green 109). It took a black critic to undo the repression of race and call attention to the worldwide exploitation of black soldiers to fight and die for white people's imperial interests. Morrison carries on that tradition of African American social critique.

Morrison's project of returning the repressed to the U.S. historical record has a larger scope than her stated aim of exposing the dark underside of the 1950s. While Frank's story brings back the wasting of black male bodies during the war, Cee's story begins to undo the repressions of U.S. medical history.

The text's critique of the medical establishment is woven into the fabric of the text, beginning with the remark of the minister with whom Frank finds shelter early in the novel. The Reverend Locke congratulates Frank on having escaped from incarceration in a nearby mental hospital:

> "You lucky, Mr. Money. They sell a lot of bodies out of there. . . . To the medical school."
> "They sell dead bodies? What for?"
> "Well, you know, doctors need to work on the dead poor so they can help the live rich." (12)

Throughout *Home* Morrison avoids using skin color to indicate race, in an attempt, apparently, to follow her desire "to enunciate race while depriving it of its lethal cling" (Morrison, "Home" 5)—that is, to avoid the racist connotations embedded in the language of "white" and "black." In *Home*, markers of class and degrees of entitlement, as well as historical context, clearly indicate who is white and who is black without those words ever appearing. Here, in the Reverend Locke's grim joke, the bodies made into dissectible corpses are "poor," but we can extrapolate from *Home's* other encodings of race as class that "poor" probably means "poor and black." In the calculus of the medical profession, as the Reverend Locke tells it, some bodies are worth more than other bodies: poor (black) bodies are worth nothing unless they can be used to enhance the health of rich (white) bodies. Black bodies acquire value only when dead—and thus partitionable in the dissection theater of medical schools. Fiction recalls history here: as dissection became an accepted feature of nineteenth-century medical education in the United States, "southern medical schools procured an illicit supply of corpses drawn disproportionately from populations of free and enslaved African Americans" (Fett 153).

This first example of the medical establishment's careless use of poor black subjects to advance medical knowledge makes visible what is repressed in the medical practices brought into question by the rest of the novel. Of the body on the dissection table, no one asks, Who was the person who inhabited this body? The focus is rather on the veins, the musculature, the liver, the pancreas, of the cadaver that medical students are dissecting. Its humanity erased, the body becomes a specimen, a collection of body parts.

In the medical experiments that Doctor Beauregard Scott practices on Cee, it is likewise a body part (her "womb") that is the focus of interest. While Frank is at war, Cee finds a job as assistant to a white doctor in a suburb of Atlanta. When Cee is hired, the doctor's wife assures Cee that Dr. Beau "is more than a doctor; he is a scientist and conducts very important experiments" (60)—namely, experiments on "wombs." He is "interested in wombs in general" (113). In the reduction of women to wombs, the organ becomes a thing apart: what is repressed is the whole body and thus the embodied subject, the black female subject to whom the womb belongs. Dr. Beau does many experiments on Cee's uterus while she is under anesthesia, as he does on many of his poor black female patients. Filtered through Cee's naïvely admiring view of the doctor, we see how many "poor people— women and girls, especially—he helped. Far more than the well-to-do ones from the neighborhood or from Atlanta proper. . . . When one or two died in spite of his care, he donated money for funeral expenses" (64–65). The text substitutes signifiers of class for signifiers of race; it is clear, however, from these women's exclusion from segregated posh neighborhoods in the suburbs and in Atlanta proper that the doctor is treating poor black women. As in the Reverend Locke's reference to dissection practices, it is the poor black body that is expendable, available for cutting up in the name of medical advancement for the majority (white) population. Cee herself is dying from Dr. Beau's experimental probings when Frank rescues her.

In the few short pages devoted to Dr. Beau Scott, historical allusions call up (at least) two different historical arenas of medical intervention into black female bodies. Since the doctor's bookshelves are full of books on eugenics, and since his "examinations" of Cee while she is sedated deprive her of the capacity to have children, we can deduce that he is tampering with black reproduction directly—and in the interests of white supremacy rather than in the interests of science.

Here the text exposes a repressed fact of U.S. social history: Americans like to associate eugenics with Nazi Germany and thus forget that eugenics flourished in the United States for the first four decades of the twentieth century, long before it became influential in Germany.[2] Eugenic beliefs resulted in laws enabling compulsory sterilization in twenty-six states. Although these statutes covered only criminal and mentally ill populations, their enactment made it easer for individual doctors to sterilize poor black and Native American women whom they considered "unfit" (Angela Davis, *Women* 216–17). Cee is effectively sterilized without her consent, calling up this history of involuntary sterilization.

However, the text does not refer explicitly to sterilization but to experimentation: the doctor is "a scientist" who "conducts very important experiments" (60). The language evokes a long history of the medical establishment's unethical use of black bodies for experiments. In the nineteenth and twentieth centuries white doctors tried out unproven medicines, experimented with surgical interventions, and perfected new medical techniques by practicing on black persons (Fett 151). As the new medical science of gynecology emerged in the mid-nineteenth century, white doctors tried out experimental procedures on black female slaves that they would not have attempted on white women.

Morrison's carefully chosen words about Dr. Beau's "interest" invoke a historical precedent. He is "interested in wombs in general, constructing instruments to see farther and farther into them. Improving the speculum" (113). The wording encodes an allusion to a historical figure, J. Marion Sims, and so evokes the history of medical experiments on black women's "wombs." J. Marion Sims hit upon a way to view the interior of a woman's genitals, which had up till then been impenetrable to the male gaze: when he bent a pewter spoon and inserted it into the vagina of a slave woman, he could see the interior of the reproductive organs. In his autobiography Sims describes the thrill of discovery: "Introducing the bent handle of the spoon I saw everything, as no man had ever seen before" (*Story of My Life* 234–35; qtd. in Kapsalis 37). The language describing Dr. Beau's scientific ambitions is marked by the same convergence of instrument invention and scopic penetration: the instruments Dr. Beau invents enable him "to see farther and farther into [wombs]" (Morrison 113). Like Dr. Marion Sims, who parcels out the womb as a virgin land for his exploration—he says in the autobiography, "I felt like an explorer in medicine who first views a new and important territory" (Sims 235; qtd. in Kapsalis 39)—Dr. Beau appropriates Cee's uterus for his own pioneering purposes. The note that Dr. Beau is in the process of reinventing "the speculum" hints even more directly at the nineteenth-century figure of the doctor who stands behind him.

Dr. Marion Sims experimented on a small group of black slave women who were bound over to him for four years (1845–49), trying out various methods for healing vesico-vaginal fistula. He used no anesthesia. One woman, Anarcha, went through thirty such exploratory surgeries. Sims eventually found a cure and thereafter operated on white women with vesico-vaginal fistula; they, unlike the slaves, were given anesthesia and charged a large sum for the surgery. History would seem to bear out the minister's pronouncement that "doctors need to work on the dead poor so they can help the live rich" (12).

Sims is remembered in medical history as the inventor of the speculum and several other gynecological instruments, for which he is acclaimed as "the father of gynecology." From medical history, we know all about Dr. Sims. Celebrated at home and abroad for his surgeries and his discoveries, Sims was heaped with glory, elected president of the American Medical Association, and given honorary titles from various European countries: "Knight Commander of the Legion of Honor of France, Knight of the Order of Isabella the Catholic of Spain, and Knight of the Order of Leopold I of Belgium" (Kapsalis 46). History has thus resoundingly recognized Dr. Sims as subject. But where can we find traces of the slave women's subjectivities? Thus Terri Kapsalis, in her recent exposé of gynecology, asks, "Who were the slave women on whom Sims experimented? . . . Did they have husbands, partners, children, and loved ones whom they were made to leave for four years while Sims worked on them? Did they agree to his experimentation? . . . What were their feelings toward their conditions?" (40). Kapsalis concludes that "the way in which Sims's surgeries related to these women's lives is left unknown"; indeed, "it is impossible to know" anything at all about their lives as subjects (40). Medical history has accounted for them only as objects of Sims's experiments—or, in Morrison's phrase, as "wombs in general."

When Cee is reduced to an object of medical study—unconscious, her womb open to Dr. Beau's explorations—her situation parallels that of the black slave women subjected to Sims's experiments. But Morrison corrects medical historiography by restoring the subject position to this object of medical experimentation. She describes at length the effects of Dr. Beau's probings on the subjectivity and subsequent life of Cee but gives no space at all to Dr. Beau's aims and accomplishments: we are (mercifully) spared an account of what he does to Cee while she is under sedation, and we are not told what instruments he invented or what his discoveries about the uterus were.

The historical allusions condensed in Cee's ordeal raise the text's critique of racism to a systemic level, indicting a national biopolitics that treats black bodies as disposable.

Love and Home

Unlike the characters in other Morrison novels (*Beloved*, *Paradise*) who yearn for, who reach for "home" without ever arriving, Frank and Cee are able to create a home together. It is, moreover, a home that holds the promise of all the traditional meanings of home: comfort, nurturing, safety, care; and it is planted in the heart of a community that is likewise supportive and nurturing. If the United States of the 1950s is so inhospitable to Frank and Cee, if both their bodies and their houses are open to violation without recourse— for their family home in Texas was taken over by white vigilantes, "both hooded and not" (10), who promised death if they did not move out—how can they establish a home that is everything a traditional home promises?

Early reviewers found fault with *Home* because of the implausibility of its happy ending—presumably because the remaking of Frank and Cee into healthy individuals after their many traumatizing experiences seems too quick and easy. An argument for the plausibility of *Home*'s happy ending hinges on uncovering credible psychological causes for the profound changes in Frank and Cee that enable them to perceive Lotus as home. Lotus, Georgia, which had seemed to them a stifling place of deprivation and entrapment—"Lotus, Georgia, is the worst place in the world, worse than any battlefield," says Frank (83)—becomes "home." What alters Frank and Cee's perception of Lotus?

Love is the agent of change. Frank changes because Cee changes. After Frank rescues the dying Cee from the house of Dr. Beau, he takes her not to the emergency room of the white medical establishment but to the black community of women in Lotus, where Cee and Frank grew up.

Morrison describes at length the women's alternative medical practices and validates their efficacy: they are able to cure Cee from the injuries inflicted by white Western medicine. "The women took turns nursing Cee and each had a different recipe for her cure" (119). The variety of the women's cures suggests a continuity with slave culture and beyond it with healing techniques from diverse parts of Africa; for, as Sharla Fett documents, "The maelstrom of the Atlantic slave trade hurled together a dazzling array of healing systems" (2). At least some of the women's treatments, like the application of "calamus root" to Cee's injuries (119), are herbal medications and thus part of what Fett describes as a "sophisticated body of knowledge" of plants' medicinal properties passed down from slavery (Fett 74). Because of their subsistence living patterns, enslaved herbalists and their descendants had an intimate knowledge of their immediate natural environment; they understood the forests where they foraged as endowed with "roots and herbs for every imaginable illness human beings might face" (Fett 79). Like their ancestors, the women of Lotus understand natural entities—plants, the sun's rays—as able to cure spiritually as well as physiologically.

As Fett explains, African American medical traditions "locate the body within the relational vision of health that acknowledge[s] physical, moral, and supernatural causes of bodily affliction" (75). Treatment then must likewise address the patient's spiritual and psychological as well as physical ills. Spiritual empowerment is indeed an integral part of the Lotus women's healing methods. It is partly the women's example—"They took responsibility for their lives and for whatever, whoever else needed them" (123)—and partly their exhortations to Cee to be a "free person" and "do some good in the world" (126) that persuade Cee to give up her sense of worthlessness and take charge of her life. "They delivered unto [Frank] a Cee who would never again need his hand over her eyes or his arms to stop her murmuring bones" (128). The biblical language solemnizes Cee's rebirth.

If Cee no longer needs Frank's protective arm to survive, what happens to a relationship based on her dependency? Rather than collapsing, as one might expect, the relation between sister and brother becomes fruitful. The novel powerfully represents love as the matrix for reciprocal change and growth.

Earlier, in perhaps the most egregious attack of the character Frank on the narrator who is telling his story, Frank accuses her of misrepresenting his thoughts on love: "Not true. I didn't think any such thing"; he ends his diatribe, "I don't think you know much about love. Or me" (69). On a first approach, Frank's accusation seems to be simply comical. He doesn't know what we know, that the "writer" to whom he speaks, Toni Morrison, has written novels explicitly entitled *Love* and *Beloved* and has consistently explored the permutations of love in all her works. To say she knows nothing of love is surely a misrecognition, and Morrison the actual author seems to be playing with dramatic irony at the expense of her character. But if we ignore the dramatic irony and take Frank's statement at face value, we can ask what there is in Frank's story of love that Morrison's previous oeuvre doesn't "know" about love: What is new here?

Love in *Home* is intersubjective in a specific sense: it rests on an interchange between what is inside—deep down—in the one and what is inside, deep down, in the other. Thus, for example, Frank locates his self-image in Cee: "She was the first person I ever took responsibility for. Down deep inside her lived my secret picture of myself—a strong good me" (104). One expects "down deep inside" to refer to Frank's own depths, where one would think to find his most cherished self-image, but the phrase refers instead to Cee's inner world: the intermingling of self and other depicts a depth of intimacy and interdependence unusual in Morrison's novels.

Frank is able to use this reciprocity between inner worlds to begin his own healing process. The doctor's experiments on Cee's uterus have destroyed this young black woman's capacity to bear children (so the forces of eugenics have triumphed here). Cee openly mourns the baby she will never have, and Frank responds with his usual effort to comfort her and prevent her suffering. "'I'm sorry, Cee. Really sorry.' Frank moved toward her. 'Don't,' she said, pushing his hand away'" (131). Cee rejects Frank's attempt to shield her from sorrow: "I can be miserable if I want to" (131).

Something goes awry here in the dynamics of Frank's and Cee's reciprocal love. From the time Frank was four and Cee a baby, Frank has sustained her with his sheltering love. In a world where there was and is no protection for black people, he fashioned an image of himself as heroic protector of his helpless sister: "guarding her, finding a way out, . . . not being afraid of anything. . . . I felt heroic" (104). His manliness is premised on her helplessness. "Who am I without her?" Frank asks, conceding the dependency of his identity on "that underfed girl with the sad, waiting eyes" who "was a shadow for most of my life, a presence marking its own absence, or maybe mine" (103). The phrase "or maybe mine" marks the lack of boundaries, the slippage between the two: Frank's identity is dependent on Cee's lack of identity, on her remaining an "absence" to herself. Admirable as the constancy of Frank's nurturing love for his sister is, it has narcissistic elements; that is, Frank can love himself through the act of loving her. When Frank surrounds Cee with his protective love, he embraces not only her but the cherished image of himself held in her deepest mind, as in the passage cited above: "Down deep inside her lived my secret picture of myself—a strong good me" (104). However, in the present Cee refuses her part in the scenario, rejecting the buffering mediation of Frank's protective comfort and claiming the right to her own feelings: "I'm not going to hide from what's true just because it hurts" (131). Affirming autonomy, Cee firmly rejects the rescue scenario: "So it was just herself . . . she wanted to be the person who would never again need rescue. . . . She wanted to be the one who rescued her own self" (129).

The effect of Cee's break with the habitual can be illuminated by one of Lacan's notions of love. While Lacan usually treats love as narcissistic, in *Seminar 8* (on transference) he describes a form of love that goes beyond the narcissistic:

> L'amour, c'est ce qui se passe dans cet objet vers lequel nous tendons la main par notre propre désir, et qui, au moment où notre désir fait éclater son incendie, nous laisse apparaître un instant cette réponse, cette autre main qui se tend vers nous comme son désir. (Lacan 216)
>
> Love is what occurs in this object toward which we hold out our hand through our own desire, and which, at the moment when our desire flames out, allows for an instant this response to appear to us, this other hand that is held out toward us as the other's desire. (my translation)

Where the lover expects to see a reflection of his own desire, what he sees instead is a glimpse of the beloved's desire—or, in Lacan's metaphor, what reaches back toward the lover is not at all a reflection of his own hand but a hand that is quite alien—a hand or a desire that, far from enhancing his self-image, delivers a shock to his habitual understanding of himself and his relation to the beloved. As Todd McGowan comments on this Lacanian passage, what comes back from the beloved "jolts the subject out of its everyday existence" (*Capitalism* 187).[3] Indeed, what comes back from Cee to Frank as she rejects his comfort is an image that, far from reaffirming his noble self-image as rescuer, creates a rupture in consciousness.

Cee, haunted by the image of the baby she will never have, tells Frank:

> It's like there's a baby girl down here waiting to be born. She's somewhere close by . . . she picked me to be born to. And now she has to find some other mother. . . . You know that toothless smile babies have? . . . I keep seeing it. (131–32)

The image of the little girl stranded outside life belongs to Cee's inner life, but it works on what is buried deep in Frank's inner world:

> Then Cee told me about seeing a baby girl smile all through the house, in the air, the clouds. It hit me. Maybe that little girl wasn't waiting around to be born to her. Maybe it was already dead, waiting for me to step up and say how.

At that moment Frank retrieves the repressed memory and faces it, in the passage quoted earlier:

> I shot the Korean girl in her face.
> I am the one she touched.
> I am the one who saw her smile.
> I am the one she said "Yum-yum" to.
> I am the one she aroused. (133)

Thus the image of the child who will never have a life migrates from the imagination of the one to the imagination of the other. Frank takes up Cee's image of the baby and processes it through his own chain of associations, so that the "toothless smile" of Cee's unborn baby links to the "toothless smile" of the Asian girl, the smile that originally recalled Cee herself and caused him to shoot. Frank borrows a specific image from Cee and follows it into his own depths: "Now the hook was deep inside his chest" (135).

Love then is an interpenetration between what is deepest in the one and what is deepest in the other; but that is not as reassuringly sweet as it sounds. In giving back to the lover the unexpected in place of the comfort of the same, love jolts the lover Frank into a traumatic dimension of repressed memory.

Indeed, it could be argued that love brings Frank into the realm of the

uncanny. To recapitulate Freud's definition, the uncanny appears to the subject as something strange, but its alienness is a product of its having been
repressed over a long period at time. That defines the memory of the killing
that the image of Cee's lost child enables Frank to call up. There is again, as
in Freud's musings on the uncanny, an interplay of *heimlich* and *unheimlich*, of the homey and the uncanny. The "toothless smile" of the lost baby
that Cee imagines evokes the toothless smile that Frank remembers in Cee,
which is *heimlich*, comforting in its well-loved familiarity; but that *heimlich* memory is intertwined with the *unheimlich* memory of the gap-toothed
smile of the girl Frank killed. Just so, in the scene that led to the killing,
the toothless smile of the Asian girl recalled Cee and so initially called up
comforting reminders of home, which turned unbearably *unheimlich* as the
Asian child touched his genitals and so released the uncanny sense that the
long-repressed scenario of incest was beginning to unfold in everyday life.
As in Freud's insistence that elements of the *unheimlich* inhabit the *heimlich*,
so in Morrison's presentation what is most homelike, most familiar and beloved, contains the uncanny.

Or, in a second approach, we could say that Frank in offering comfort to
Cee for her loss of the baby expects the *heimlich* response—the familial and
familiar response of gratitude for his solicitude that would reassure him of his
accustomed self-image of protector; instead he receives back the *unheimlich*,
the call to encounter the long-repressed, distorted image of himself, not as
heroic protector, but as cold-blooded killer of the innocent girl-child. The
closeness of Frank and Cee, the interpenetration of their deeper consciousness, brings Frank not *heimlich* comfort but the reverse.

Love that gives back the unexpected, love that disrupts the familiar to open
the way for the uncanny, is nonetheless salutary: it initiates Frank's recovery
by catapulting Frank into an encounter with repressed trauma. That enables
him to begin the long process of working through his guilt and shame or, as
he calls it, "working it loose" (135).

The Happy Ending of *Home*

The novel concludes with what seems to be a domestic idyll, and the prose
seems to reflect the uncontaminated peace of the domestic scene: "The next
morning at breakfast Cee appeared to have returned to her newly steady self,
confident, cheerful and occupied. Spooning fried onions and potatoes into
Frank's plate she inquired whether he wanted eggs too" (135). Appropriately
transparent, plain and simple, the narrator's diction describes the cheerful do-

mesticity of everyday family life. I will argue, however, that uncanny reminders of a repressed history trouble the limpid serenity of the domestic scene.
First, there is the ghostly presence of the unborn baby. Second, the economic
underpinnings of Frank's and Cee's home life both recall the oppressions of
their ancestors and show that these oppressions are ongoing. Elements of unhome disturb the *heimlich*.

The most obvious manifestation of the uncanny is the spirit of the baby
girl that embodies the child Cee will never have: "She" is "down here waiting
to be born. She's . . . in this house. . . . You know that toothless smile babies
have? . . . I keep seeing it. I saw it in a green pepper once" (131–32). The specter of what Cee has lost to medical depredations on her body is "all through
the house" (133); she permeates domestic space, the *unheimlich* troubling the
calm of the *heimlich*. As might be expected, ghosts figure prominently in
Freud's essay on uncanny phenomena. And as in Freud, ghosts in Morrison's
work often function as uncanny reminders of what has been repressed—including the national repressed. For example, Beloved at the end of *Beloved*
haunts the margins of the community (and by extension of the nation) that
has chosen to forget her. In the image that moves in a photograph of someone familiar or in the echo of the rustle of a familiar skirt, her shadowy presence makes itself felt. As uncanny signifier of the half-known, half-unknown,
repressed yet irrepressible historical fact of slavery, her presence returns and
cannot be wished away by even the most ardent disavowal of national history. If the baby ghost Beloved is "more" than the ghost of the child Sethe
lost, if she represents the masses of people lost and unaccounted for through
the Middle Passage and the vicissitudes of slavery, then the baby ghost that
haunts Cee may well represent more than Cee's own lost child. The ghost
child can be read not only as the lost potential of Cee's damaged uterus but as
the wasted potential of all the black women's bodies disabled by forced sterilization and medical experimentation.

There is indeed another ghost here at the end, and Frank and Cee do
what they can to lay it to rest. Frank and Cee return to the scene of the
secret burial they saw as children, dig up the remains, and rebury them beneath a tree overhanging their river. Cee sees, across the river, "a small man
in a funny suit swinging a watch chain. And grinning" (144). This apparition
is familiar: it is the specter of the zoot-suited man that appeared to Frank
intermittently during his journey south. As he smiles in apparent approval
at the burying taking place, we are encouraged to make the connection: he
must be the ghost of the corpse Cee and Frank originally saw disposed of in
the field. Frank has just learned that the corpse the children saw buried that

day belonged to a black man forced to provide entertainment for a white male audience by fighting his son to the death with knives. The mutilation and disposal of his body place him in the long line of historical black subjects treated as disposable bodies. Just to drive home the point, the only part of his body that remains, besides a few bone fragments, is a "skull, . . . clean and smiling" (143): the skull takes its place in the series of isolated body parts that register the unwritten history of black bodies mutilated and thrown away.

Thus at the end of the novel we realize that the opening image of a secret burial has a collective as well as a personal dimension: it represents not just the psychic repression going on in the character Frank but also the national repression of the black bodies appropriated for white projects and then thrown away as trash.

Reburying the body, Frank carves on a makeshift grave marker, "Here Stands A Man" (145). In each instance of a human reduced to a body part, what is repressed is the embodied subjectivity of the whole black person. Instead of the usual phrase, "Here lies a man," the inscription "Here stands a man" implies an intact body, standing on feet no longer severed and waving in the air, but integral to the body and supporting an embodied human being, "a man."

Traditionally, the inscription on a gravestone gives a place in the symbolic order to the dead, moving the dead from the status of corpse in the order of the real to the position of dead subject in the symbolic order. The proper burial that Frank gives the body is clearly an effort at reparation. Does it succeed? The symbolic gesture seems small, incommensurate with the cumulative symbolic weight that this final body in a string of damaged bodies is obliged to bear. And indeed, as the burial proceeds, the zoot-suited ghost lingers on in an undecidable state between being there and being at rest. The two ghosts intrude the collective traumas of a repressed history into the peaceful domesticity of Frank and Cee.

Less uncanny than these two haunting spirits but carrying implications of unhome in a different sense, the material underpinnings of Frank and Cee's domesticity quietly insert some qualifications into their domestic idyll. Cee and Frank's contentment with their re-created home is untainted by any hint of dissatisfaction or cynicism. Thus, Cee is determined to be productive and make her own way, and Frank looks forward cheerfully to going out to work every day. But exactly what kinds of work are Cee and Frank doing? Cee makes quilts that she plans to sell to a middleman from the white town of Jeffrey, who will sell them to white tourists (127). Frank will pick cotton. As if mimicking the positions of house slave and field slave, Cee will practice the craft that her slave foremothers practiced, and Frank will work the cotton fields like his enslaved forbears. While Frank, through the rose-colored lenses of his new belief in "home," now sees the cotton fields as "acres of pink blossoms" (118), in his youth these same fields looked different: "Nothing to do but mindless work in fields you didn't own, couldn't own, and wouldn't own if you had any other choice" (83–84). There is no possibility of Frank owning the land he works, any more than the house Cee and Frank live in. Just as their parents, having lost their own home to the vigilante group in Texas, worked four jobs between them to rent their house in Lotus, Frank and Cee save up enough money to rent the same house from the white landlord. So Frank and Cee's "home" is founded on elements of "unhome": dispossession, displacement, and renting from the white man.

Similarly, no taint of irony qualifies the positive picture of the community in which Cee and Frank make their home; the female community's rejection of capitalist values in favor of interdependence, mutual help, shared responsibility, and hard work is presented as totally admirable (123). However, as in the case of Cee's and Frank's work, the women's nature-based cures and herbal remedies join them to their slave ancestors. Now as under slavery, the women pull together for collective care in the face of a system that brutalizes their bodies. The unspoken point is that there is still today a need, as there was in the time of slavery, for the "rich health culture [of slaves] . . . that worked to counter the onslaught of daily medical abuse and racist scientific theories" (Fett 2). More generally, the bonding of the Lotus women for mutual help and support seems continuous with the "female slave network" that Deborah White identified as a "buffer . . . against the . . . the general dehumanizing nature of slavery" (131): as it was during slavery, the network of women is still needed for stability and survival.

The subtle echoes of slavery reinforce the dispossessions of segregation in the present setting of the 1950s South to imply an ongoing historical continuity: black people in the United States have always lived, and continue to live, in a state of exclusion from the rights, protections, and opportunities promised by liberal democracy to all its citizens.

Reviewers of the novel charged that the happy ending of *Home* is facile, unearned by the text. Thus, for example, Sarah Churchwell, reviewing the novel for the *Guardian*, says that the damage done Cee is dismissed by "a few Morrisonian perorations insisting that a woman own herself" and claims that "Frank's post-traumatic stress disorder disappears as easily, effecting one of the least satisfying 'redemptions' I can remember" (*Guardian*, 27 April 2012).

I would counter that Frank's change is credible, embedded as it is in the emotional and spiritual reciprocity between Cee and Frank that has all along been the bedrock of their relationship; it should come as no surprise that her personal growth enables his. And the ending is not uniformly happy, but fraught with sorrow. Cee mourns the child she will never have. The love that opens the way for Frank's change may be salutary, but it is deeply disturbing, confronting Frank with the buried trauma of the perpetrator, which he must work through slowly and painfully, over time. The material conditions of Frank's work and Cee's work tie their lives to the past of slavery rather than opening a path to a better future. The two ghosts, thematically connected by the white mutilation of black bodies that has robbed each of life, trouble the cheerful domesticity of Frank and Cee with echoes of the unlivability of black lives in the racist United States. Morrison's language at the end of *Home* may be simple, as the early reviewers charged, but her picture of home is complex, a contradictory mix of comfort and discomfort, of home and unhome. The one element that is wholly admirable is Cee's and Frank's determination to make a loving home in a hostile land.

Knowing, Not-Knowing,
Half-Knowing, and the Uncanny:
Home's Call on the Reader

As I have argued, repression and the return of the repressed structure two levels of the narrative: the personal and the historical. On the personal level, the repressed returns in full as Frank takes ownership of his repressed act and begins the long process of working through it. But where is a parallel retrieval and working through of the national repressed? Where is the recall of those black subjects treated as disposable bodies and erased from U.S. histories?

Because *Home* is written largely in mimetic, apparently transparent prose, it lacks the gaps and fissures that in other later Morrison novels call on the reader to do her part in constructing meaning. However, the call to a dialogue with the text is there, and in a form that foregrounds the ethical dimension. The cues to a repressed past are in the text—in the parallels between the exploratory surgeries of Dr. Beau and Dr. Sims on black women's uteruses and in the titles on Dr. Beau's bookshelves: *Out of the Night*; *The Passing of the Great Race*; *Heredity, Race and Society*. They call on the reader to bring up her own half-knowledge of subjects largely repressed from national consciousness and to struggle (through conscious research, perhaps) to add some facts about medical history or eugenics to that half-knowledge, and then to fill out the text with her own supplementary information.

I think that the hints at eugenics, forced sterilization, and medical experimentation do evoke a half-knowledge in the reader, a kind of uncanny knowing. The uncanny itself, as Freud describes it and as we have seen it play out in Frank's confused perceptions of the Asian child's seductive moves, is a mode of equivocal knowing. One encounters whatever produces the sensation of the uncanny in the external world, so one sees it and knows it exists; yet the internal analogue—the unconscious fantasy or memory—remains repressed and so cannot be known; or it is triggered by external events but recalled only in part. The uncanny exists in an ambiguous space, then, between the inner and the outer, between the known and the unknown—in the half-known, perhaps. I would say that the fragments of repressed historical knowledge in Cee's story can evoke such a sensation of not-knowing yet knowing in a reader. Most readers have probably heard vague rumors about the influence of eugenics on Americans, and we "kind of" know about sterilization abuse—but we may well not have full knowledge of these things. And there may be, as in other cases of repression, a resistance to knowing more. A white U.S. reader might well be reluctant to open up a disgraceful and disequilibrating American history of eugenic doctrine, coerced sterilization, and medical experimentation on unconsenting subjects.

The call to an ethical dialogue, then, comes in the form of these obscure signifiers of a repressed past—signifiers in the mode of the uncanny, perhaps, in that they evoke in the reader things vaguely known and vaguely familiar, yet strange—strange because they have been repressed from national consciousness for so long. The reader's participation in making meaning of the text leads to some difficult ethical choices. First, she has to decode the text by supplying appropriate historical analogs for figures in the fictional world: for Dr. Beau, with his passionate interest in "wombs in general" and in reinventing the speculum, the nineteenth-century Dr. Marion Sims, who invented the speculum by appropriating for his own use the "wombs" of black female slaves; for the titles on Dr. Beau's bookshelves, the history of surgical sterilizations practiced on women of color. That exercise in ingenuity and (in all probability) extratextual research opens onto a call for an ethical response. As at the end of *Beloved*, where the reader has to figure out exactly what the dimensions of Beloved's "claim" are and then decide whether to acknowledge that ethical claim on her or not, *Home* invites a reader to *do* something with the knowledge she has gained: to choose to acknowledge the repressed facts of a shameful history of medical abuse of black bodies and thereby recognize the tragedy of subjects robbed of their bodies' potentials by medical experimentation, or to choose ignorance. If the reader resists the call to knowledge, the cues to the past will remain, like the foot that beckons from the grave, uncanny fragments of a repressed history.

CHAPTER 7

Love, Trauma, and the
Body in *God Help the Child*

A new tone of urgency governs the story of the love between Bride and Booker in *God Help the Child* (2015). Whereas the long line of Morrison's novels shows a consistently large and compassionate patience for the lingering vicissitudes of trauma, the narration of *God Help the Child* betrays an impatience with the residues of trauma that hold back its characters from loving anew. For, as the wise woman Queen says, love is so difficult, and lovers so selfish, that loving requires the full measure of one's attention and emotional energy. The narrative forms of *God Help the Child* reflect the urgency of the message that one must get over trauma to go forward with love. The chapters of the first half of the book are short, as if the artistic aim is to capture the essence of each first-person narrator's life and the childhood trauma central to it, then move on to the next. The book as a whole is brief (178 pages), its narrative structure following the straight arrow of the quest genre that makes it seem to "fly toward its conclusion" (Michiko Kakutani, "In Toni Morrison's"). There are, however, several departures from the compressed realist prose. Excerpts from Booker's journal feature a musical prose that, in imitating jazz rhythms, reflects Booker's reliance on his trumpet to express his deepest feelings. And the surreal devolution of Bride's body into that of a little girl expresses a complex mix of temptation and resistance to remaining the "poor little black girl" traumatized by racism.

Bride and Booker and the
Narrative Forms That Express Them

In *God Help the Child*, narrative form reflects the superficiality or the complexity of the lovers, Bride and Booker. Bride, who grew up with a mother who treated her as a phobic object she "couldn't bear to look at or touch" because of her deep black skin color, remains skin-deep. That is, as a result of her mother's obsessive focus on her skin, Bride equates her self with her appearance; unloved as a child because of her color, she now counts on her gorgeous face and figure to engender love—and she is successful, to a degree. Early reviewers of the novel complain of Bride's superficiality (see Ron Charles 2; Francine Prose 13), but it is appropriate. A developmental logic governs her growth from a child treated as if she were only her skin to a beautiful adult woman whose self-image is determined by her looks.

Fittingly, Bride works for a cosmetics company, designing products for women's skin. Her style of thinking and feeling remains hostage to marketing discourse, as in this passage: "Besides, our affair wasn't all that spectacular . . . nothing like those double-page spreads in fashion magazines, you know, couples standing half naked in surf, looking so fierce and downright mean, their sexuality like lightning and the sky going dark to show off the shine of their skin. I love those ads" (9). "Love" swerves away from the actuality of her "affair" with Booker to the manufactured spectacle of love—or perhaps, as the wording suggests, to the marketing technique itself: "I love those ads." What attracts Bride is again skin—the shimmering naked skin of the lovers; or, more precisely, it is the image of skin reproduced on the glossy surface of the fashion magazine that attracts her. Bride's attachment to surfaces is compounded by the capitalist beauty industry's reliance on image without substance.

Bride's love for Booker likewise focuses on externals: "I stroked every inch of his golden skin, sucked on his earlobes. I know the quality of the hair in his armpit; I fingered the dimple in his upper lip" (37). Bride's "knowing" Booker stops at the level of skin. As the text repeatedly stresses, Bride's "lack of interest in [Booker's] personal life" is complete; she has no curiosity about what he thinks or feels or does (133). Matching her superficiality, her language as narrator is colloquial and spare, lacking the elaboration of metaphor and image. The quest that determines the sequence of her narrated chapters is similarly straightforward: abandoned by Booker, Bride sets out to find him, and in the end succeeds.

The third-person narrative focalized by Booker comes late in the novel (109) and occupies the entirety of part 3. Thus it departs from the art of brevity that governs the other chapters, perhaps reflecting the complexity of its subject, Booker. We learn that Booker grew up in a close-knit family of many children. The Saturday conference epitomized the family ethic. Each child in turn had to answer two questions: "1. What have you learned that is true (and how do you know?) 2. What problem do you have?" (112). To the problem voiced by each child, all the other children were expected to respond with advice. This is a family that encourages its children to think for themselves and question received knowledge, while also validating their innermost feelings and anxieties. It would likely produce a radically different individual from a family like Bride's, restricted to a single mother who focuses entirely on her daughter's skin.

Morrison seems to have set herself the challenge of creating a credible love relationship between very disparate adults. And the radical difference between the two characters might also encourage a reader to question the premise of the novel, that one must let go of past trauma in order to devote all one's resources to loving in the present: Is loving always a good that trumps other goods, even when the lovers are so disparate, so seemingly incompatible?

When Booker was eight, family harmony collapsed with the torture and murder of Booker's elder brother, Adam, by a sadistic pederast. While the family eventually tried to draw together and go on with their lives, Booker remained faithful to his love for the dead Adam; even now, as we learn later in the novel, his preoccupation with Adam's death gets in the way of other attachments.

The chapter that provides the backstory of Booker's life is different in every way from the other chapters: it is long; it is narrated in the third person; it presents Booker's early life and present-day preoccupations in detail; and the writing shuns the simplicity of the first-person chapters to elaborate Booker's thinking with images and metaphors that mirror the complexity of Booker's perceptions.

Why is Booker the only major character (apart from Queen) who does not have a first-person narrative voice, who does not get a turn at delivering a first-person account of his life? The answer is that Booker's innermost thoughts are written in a second narrative mode, a series of short meditations that Booker pens and sends for safekeeping to his aunt Queen. The duality of narrative form that Morrison gives to Booker reflects the multidimensionality of his character, a complexity of thinking and depth of feeling not granted to the other characters.

Booker's writings take the form of what Julia Kristeva calls "poetic language" (*Revolution in Poetic Language*). That is, syntax and sentence structure are disrupted by a word order that strives to imitate music as closely as possible. Look, for instance, at the following example:

You should take heartbreak of whatever kind seriously with the courage
to let it blaze and burn like the pulsing star it is unable or unwilling to be
soothed into pathetic self-blame because its explosive brilliance rings justifi-
ably loud like the din of a tympani. (151)

Each of Booker's prose pieces incorporates the name of a musical instrument,
usually ending like this sample with an evocation of that instrument's sound
(here, "the din of a tympani"). What connects the various pieces is their form.
Here, the sentence sequence imitates the never-ending improvisations of jazz.
The syntax of the first half of the piece makes up a full sentence ending with
the phrase, "like the pulsing star it is." But instead of the period that we expect to put a full stop to the sentence, the piece takes up "it is" as the subject
and verb of a new sentence, "it is unable or unwilling to be soothed into
pathetic self-blame." "There is no final chord," as Morrison characterizes jazz
in a 1983 interview with Nellie McKay: "Classical music satisfies and closes.
Black music does not do that. Jazz always keeps you on the edge. There is no
final chord. . . . And it agitates you" (155). Booker's syntax imitates this crucial
aspect of jazz. A sentence is not allowed to close. In the example given above,
the sentence seems to be moving toward resolution but then begins anew
with a variation suggested by the last notes of the preceding phrase, "it is."
The sentence structure "agitates you" by denying you an ordered progression
toward closure.

   Here is a second example: "It seemed a kindness in order to be able to
leave you and not fold into a grief so deep it would break not the heart but
the mind that knows the oboe's shriek and the way it tears into rags of silence" (150). According to the syntax, "the mind" ends a sentence beginning
with "It seemed"; but instead of finding closure, the wording takes "the
mind" as the subject of a new sentence, moving into a riff on "the mind that
knows the oboe's shriek." Again, as in "the din of a tympani," onomatopoeia
conveys the sound of the instrument directly to the reader's ear, encouraging
a reader to respond to the sound rather than the meaning of the words and
thus approaching the effect of a musical instrument on a listener's body.

   What Booker is striving toward, I believe, is a language that can transmit
feeling directly, as music conveys feeling by playing on a listener's corporeal
responses to sound. And what the author behind Booker is striving toward, I
believe, is the invention of a language appropriate to the character's depth of
feeling.

   For what is the content of these two textual examples? The first declares
the importance of remaining true to heartbreak through the metaphor of the

star: one must feel the full "blazing" and "burning" of passionate grief; and one must continue steadfast through the burning-up for as long as heart-break lasts—which, the image of the star suggests, might be as long as forever. From what we know of Booker's long devotion to his dead brother, Adam, the piece appears to refer to the heartbreak of losing Adam.

The second example refers again to Booker's feeling for the dead Adam. It would be a "kindness" to "leave [Bride]" rather than "fold" her into the space of Booker's inner world, which is wholly dedicated to a "grief so deep" for the dead Adam that it would "break" Bride's mind. In both examples I cite here, the wording strives to become music in an effort to convey feelings too deep for ordinary verbal expression. Even in Booker's two pieces on the larger, less personal topic of race and racism, feeling infuses thought: the first is driven by rage, the second marked by shame (150).

This new narrative mode shows us a dimension of Booker we had not seen before. However, the third-person description of Booker's life already reveals the connection between jazz and Booker's deepest feelings and thereby paves the way for Booker's attempt to incorporate jazz rhythms into his writing. After Adam's death, his father stopped playing the jazz records that Booker loved. Booker "could do without" some of them, "but not Satchmo. It was one thing to lose a brother—that broke his heart—but a world without Louis Armstrong's trumpet crushed it" (114). For he counted on jazz, and especially on Armstrong's solos, "to oil and straighten his tangled feelings" (117).

What Armstrong's playing means for Booker's feelings, and what it means for Booker's writing style, can perhaps be clarified by looking beyond *God Help the Child* to Morrison's wider oeuvre. In her preface to *Playing in the Dark*, Morrison quotes a long passage from Marie Cardinal's *The Words to Say It* that describes Cardinal's response to a performance by Louis Armstrong.

As she begins to listen, Cardinal envisions a musical structure in which each note contributes to and "contains within itself the essence of the whole." But the structuring logic of such an intellectual approach to Armstrong's music disappears as the music builds:

> The sounds of the trumpet sometimes piled up together, fusing a new musical base, a sort of matrix which gave birth to one precise, unique note, tracing a sound whose path was almost painful, so absolutely necessary had its equilibrium and duration become; it tore at the nerves of those who followed it. My heart began to accelerate, . . . shaking the bars of my rib cage, compressing my lungs so the air could no longer enter them. Gripped

by panic at the idea of dying there . . . I ran into the street like someone
possessed. (qtd. in *Playing* vi–vii)

Jazz provokes a participation in the listener so intense that life and death
seem to hinge on the sustainability of that one "precise, unique note." The
music not only "tears at the nerves" of the listener but brings Cardinal to
face her deepest fears, namely of dying. ("'I'm going to die!' she thinks and
screams" [vii].) The Cardinal text, Morrison says, has led her "to reflect on the
consequences of jazz—its visceral, emotional, and intellectual impact" (viii).

When it is used thematically in *God Help the Child*, jazz, and specifically
Armstrong's jazz, likewise represents a language of deep feeling. Booker needs
Louis Armstrong's improvisations to help him "oil and straighten" his most
"tangled feelings" at the time of Adam's death (117). Booker's first glimpse of
Bride inspires him to improvise on his own trumpet: "Still in thrall to the
sheer beauty of the girl he had seen, he put the trumpet to his lips. What
emerged was music he had never played before. Low, muted notes held long,
too long, as the strains floated through drops of rain" (131). Only music can
express the chaotic rush of Booker's emotions: "Booker had no words to describe his feelings" (131). Booker's very affinity for jazz confirms him as a man
of intense feeling. So when Booker's musings take a narrative form that ob-
scures sense to reach toward the phonics of jazz—its sounds, its rhythms, its
continuities and discontinuities, its lack of closure—he is striving toward a
language that would express his deepest, most "visceral" feelings.

Trauma and Love:
Booker

In *God Help the Child*, the protagonists must overcome the profound effects
of traumatic early loss of love in order to love again. While that may sound
like a familiar story to readers of Morrison's work, what differentiates the latest novel is the text's optimism about the human capacity to do just that.

The mothers in *God Help the Child* are terrible: each of the many diverse
female narrators reflects on a childhood made miserable by some form of
child abuse, from harsh discipline to unrelenting maternal rejection to continuous sexual exploitation. In this chapter I contend that Morrison is nonetheless optimistic in this latest book about the potential of even those who
have been cruelly unloved in childhood to develop capacities for loving as
well as the faith necessary to invest in love again. Strangers can effectively
remother a badly abused child (Rain); a woman who was utterly despised by

her colorist mother for her deep black skin (Bride) can grow past the identity of "poor little black girl" into a womanly capacity for sexual and motherly love; a melancholic (Booker) can be persuaded to give up his single-minded obsession with his dead brother in favor of loving in the present.

That optimism is accompanied by a new impatience with characters who wrap themselves around memories of early trauma and hang on to the identity of the traumatized child. Morrison's other works show that she well understands how long it takes to heal from traumatic memories. There is no easy way out for Sethe, who tries in *Beloved* to shut out past trauma only to have it come back to haunt her, or for Violet and Joe in *Jazz*, who literally move on, leaving the South for the North in order to leave behind the trauma of their lost mothers, only to replay the traumatic relation to the mother in their present-day loving. In all the later novels up to *God Help the Child*, Morrison stresses the length of time it takes for people to work through both personal and ancestral racial trauma. Thus Frank in *Home*, having finally confronted the repressed trauma of murder, notes that "the hook was deep inside his chest and nothing would dislodge it. The best he could hope for was time to work it loose" (135).

God Help the Child, however, exhibits a new impatience with the intractability of traumatic memory and with the adults who remain stuck to childhood trauma. That impatience has to do with the difficulty of loving and the concomitant need to direct all one's energies into managing those difficulties in order to keep love going. At least that is the opinion of Booker's aunt Queen, who speaks with a voice of authority that tempts the reader to hear the voice of the author speaking through her. "[Queen] knew from personal experience how hard loving was, how selfish and how easily sundered" (158). "They [Bride and Booker] will blow it, she thought. Each will cling to a sad little story of hurt and sorrow—some long-ago trouble and pain life dumped on their pure and innocent selves" (158). Mockery replaces the earlier novels' compassion for childhood trauma, as if a childhood like Bride's, marred by her mother's relentless rejection, or Booker's early loss of a beloved brother to torture and death, were only a "little" thing. To Queen, dwelling on, or working through, traumatic childhood memories is only a "wasteful" diversion of the energies needed for the difficult project of present loving. And with a few wisely chosen words she manages to persuade Booker to abandon his decade-long dedication to his dead brother in favor of returning to his love for Bride.

To a reader of Morrison's earlier novels, that resolution may seem too easy. Indeed, the images that betray the hold of past trauma on Bride and Booker are so much more interesting than the verbal exhortations of Queen that they threaten to undermine the text's explicit message that people should give up mourning and put their energies into new loving. Bride's body regresses to the prepubescent body of the "poor little black girl," victim of her mother's cruel withholding of love. And images of bodily connection imply that Booker has incorporated his dead brother Adam. So the text seems to be of two minds. On the one hand, there is the explicit message voiced by Queen that focusing on past trauma is a waste of time and should be put aside, while on the other hand there are powerful images that show how difficult such a putting aside would be, given that past trauma is woven into the trauma survivor's very body.

The images that betray Booker's melancholic strategy for holding on to his dead brother, Adam, come up in Queen's lecture to Booker, at the point in the plot when Bride has talked to Queen and through her located the runaway lover she has been tracking.

Ever the proponent of loving in the present, Queen jumps on Booker's admission that "for a while it was good, really good, being with [Bride]" (157).

> "I guess good isn't good enough for you, so you called Adam back"; "You lash Adam to your shoulders so he can work day and night to fill your brain. . . . You called Adam back and made his murder turn your brain into a cadaver and your heart's blood formaldehyde." (156, 157)

Queen moves from the picture of Adam attached to Booker's shoulders to the picture of Adam occupying a place within Booker's body. The "cadaver" is lodged in Booker's brain, and his "heart's blood" has become the formaldehyde that preserves the dead Adam intact—like a dead frog preserved in a high school biology class's beaker.

A quick look at Nicolas Abraham and Maria Torok's elaboration of Freud's description of melancholia in "Mourning and Melancholia" can reveal the implications of this imagery. Freud's essay explains melancholia as a desperate strategy to avoid the loss of a loved one: rather than giving up attachment to the dead through the laborious process of mourning—detaching oneself from each particular memory of the loved one—a melancholic identifies with the lost beloved, making him or her part of the ego. Abraham and Torok emphasize the corporeal aspects of this strategy: reverting to an oral imaginary characteristic of infantile thinking, the bereaved "incorporates" the dead, phantasmatically taking him into the body as if "swallowing" him and then preserving the dead in a kind of bodily crypt formed from the bereaved's own substance. The advantages of this strategy are, first, that the melancholic avoids loss—for the dead is not lost but preserved within; and second, he or she avoids the painful psychic reorganization that acknowledging the loss of someone profoundly connected to the self would trigger (Abraham and Torok 126–27).

According to the imagery of Queen's exhortation, the dead Adam is preserved inside Booker's body, but only through the transformation of Booker's lifeblood into a preservative to maintain the corpse. And Booker's brain has been vacated in order to house the "cadaver." The chief problem with the strategy of the melancholic is that the mourner's energy is withdrawn from external pursuits and directed toward the maintenance of the dead within. So if the dead is suspended in a kind of living death, the mourner too lives a suspended life-in-death, his or her vital energies drained away in the effort to sustain the beloved. Summing up such an exchange between the dead and the living, Queen tells Bride, "Adam's death became [Booker's] own life. I think it's his only life" (147).

Perhaps the most baffling enigma of love in the novel is Booker's love for Bride. A reader has to wonder how Booker, a man of intellect and feeling, could fall in love and stay in love with a woman trained by all her life experiences to exist at the surface of life. At a fundamental level, they seem incompatible. But if Booker is indeed following a melancholic strategy of incorporation to keep Adam with him, a relationship lived at the level of skin may fit his needs exactly. He can enjoy Bride's body in "the sexual choreography" they invent, and he can admire her looks: "If she rattled on about coworkers, products and markets, he watched her mesmerizing eyes. . . . Every feature—the ledge of her cheekbones, her invitational mouth, her nose, forehead, chin as well as those eyes—was more exquisite, more aesthetically pleasing because of her obsidian-midnight skin" (134, 133). The relationship gives him the pleasures of the surface—sexual and aesthetic. His name for her, "his Galatea" (132), attributes to Bride a perfection of form while also hinting at her inner vacuity: there is no human complexity to deal with in a statue, only an exterior that gives the observer aesthetic pleasure. "[Booker] especially liked her lack of interest in his personal life" (133). For Bride, superficial as she is, never thinks of asking Booker what he feels or thinks about. That leaves Booker free to direct all his emotional resources toward the dead within. Never, through desire or curiosity, does Bride probe Booker's inner life, allowing him to maintain intact the space of an internal world wholly dedicated to the dead.

The imagery of melancholic incorporation thus addresses and perhaps resolves the fundamentally vexing implausibility of Booker's love for Bride. But
at the same time the imagery of a traumatic loss so deep that its traces are intertwined with the subject's bodily processes raises a second question of plausibility: How can the few words of Booker's aunt, wise woman though she is,
persuade Booker to give up his hold on Adam and open body and mind to a
new love?

As a first approach, we can see that Booker might listen to Queen because
she begins from a base in melancholic logic: "You lash Adam to your shoulders so he can work day and night to fill your brain. Don't you think he's
tired? He must be worn out having to die and get no rest because he has to
run somebody else's life" (156). This appeal has force because it is grounded in
the fundamental premise of Booker's life plan: the dead is not dead and gone,
but supported and sustained by his connection with Booker's body; the dead
Adam is there. And Queen challenges the pride of a melancholic, pride in his
devotion to the dead, by suggesting that Booker's care for Adam is lacking: a
good caregiver would attend to what the dead man wants—not, presumably,
to infect his living sibling with his own deadness, but to be let go, into the
peace and rest of death.

Ruminating on Queen's words, Booker changes: "As Queen said, [Adam]
is probably weary of being my burden and my cross" (161). Respecting the
desire of the dead, Booker lets him go: "I apologize for enslaving you in order
to chain myself to the illusion of control" (161). He thus relinquishes his own
desire to keep Adam with him, to control him. And immediately—as though
cutting his connection to the dead beloved frees him up to think anew about
love, as in Freud's "Mourning and Melancholia"—Booker reexamines his
own practice of loving: "Queen's right, he thought. Except for Adam I don't
know anything about love. Adam had no faults, was innocent, pure, easy to
love. . . . What kind of love is it that requires an angel and only an angel for
its commitment?" (160). "Commitment" slips through this young man's lips
(a first in Morrison's representations of black male lovers), as he turns from
traumatic reminiscence to reloving Bride. The conflict between past trauma
and present love is resolved.

But is this not too easy? Queen's well-chosen but few wise words succeed
in persuading Booker to renounce a devotion to the dead so deep that he
has given his body over to it for more than a decade. Traumatic loss is not
usually so amenable to words and logic. What do readers make of this seeming contradiction between the text's verbal surface and the bodily images
that make a different case? Because the stubborn recalcitrance of trauma is

more fully imagined, expressed as it is through compelling images at the level of the body, a reader might well get the message that shaking trauma loose is difficult or impossible and therefore find the verbal exhortations of Queen to get over it—and get on with loving—thin and unconvincing. But a different reader, invested in hope and in the possibility of happy endings for lovers, might buy into the explicit message of the written word that one must divest from lost objects in order to free up libidinal energy for investment in new love.

Trauma and Love:
Bride

It would be a mistake to conclude, as many of the early reviewers of *God Help the Child* do, that because Bride is superficial, her story is simplistic. It is true that the plot imitates traditional patterns of romance: Bride undertakes a quest that ends in her reaching her goal (she finds Booker); and the reunited couple enacts the traditional ending of the romantic love plot in the union, after many trials, of man and woman. But I think that the surreal dimension of Bride's story, the mysterious transformation of Bride's body into the body of a prepubescent girl, offers more complex meanings. Her story ultimately rewrites some standard narratives, including the blues narrative of the woman whose man has abandoned her to sing the blues and the master narrative of some of Morrison's own novels, the tale of the child-woman locked into regression by childhood trauma.

The novel begins after Booker has broken off their passionate relationship. Soon after, Bride's body begins a devolution. First, Bride loses her pubic hair—"erased, as in never having been there in the first place" (13). Her earlobes lose their piercings (51). Then she loses the hair under her arms (52). Her body shrinks so that the child Rain's jeans fit her (93). And finally the transformation into the body of a prepubescent girl is completed by the disappearance of her breasts: "her chest was flat" (92).

The deliquescence of Bride's body begins after Booker deserts her with the words, "You not the woman I want" (8). These words come at the beginning of Bride's first narration, in the novel's second chapter; they are heavily weighted with importance because of their placement. So at first glance Bride seems to be "melting away" because Booker left her (8). However, the narrative structure suggests a more complex cause. The first chapter of the novel is narrated by Bride's mother, who is a "high yellow" woman able to pass for white (3); she explains at length and in detail how repulsive Bride was to her from birth because of her deep black skin. She enacted her horror first by denying the baby her breast and subsequently by refusing to touch her, denying any connection, however momentary, with the child's body. When Bride's chapter opens with "You not the woman I want," Booker's words follow immediately upon the mother's chapter of repudiation. I would argue that the structural sequence mirrors an emotional truth: it is the reenactment of maternal rejection that gives Booker's words their traumatic force. For her mother, too, she was "not the [girl] I want."

While Morrison provides a guide, Queen, to interpret the bodily form that Booker's grieving takes, the devolution of Bride's body remains unexplained, inviting reader interpretation. My hypothesis is that this structural degeneration embodies Bride's temptation to remain stuck in the time of trauma—to remain the little black girl cruelly unloved by a colorist mother. Indeed, Bride finally realizes that she is "changing back into a little black girl" (97). I would add the adjective *poor* "little black girl."

It is almost as if Morrison is recapitulating the "poor little black girls" of her earlier novels. Morrison often critiques systems of oppression by showing their effects on the most vulnerable—on children. In her first novel, *The Bluest Eye*, the child Pecola is assaulted from every side by racism, both by its direct effects and by its reverberations in the internalized racism of her family and community, so that, her subjectivity destroyed, she cannot move into womanhood—nor can her body produce a living child—but only slide sideways into psychosis. In *Love*, the intertwining of patriarchy and capitalism destroys the lives of the little girls Christine and Heed-the-Night by granting Bill Cosey, the hero-entrepreneur of his black community, unlimited power to exercise his pedophilic desires, first by sexually molesting the eleven-year-old Heed and then by making her his child bride. Anticipating the idea of arrested development in *God Help the Child*, Heed is not able to catch up with the temporality of her body: she has an eleven-month pregnancy that turns out to be false, and she is out of phase with menstruation, using sanitary napkins long after she has gone through menopause. Florens in *A Mercy* enacts regression in a situation similar to Bride's: when her lover berates her and tells her to leave, she can read his behavior only as a retraumatizing repetition of her mother's rejection. Fixated at the moment of her mother's (seeming) abandonment, she cannot grow into a womanly identity that would include adult sexual love (with the blacksmith) and maternal love (for his foster-child), but only project onto her adult situation the drama of the child repudiated by the mother.

Unlike her predecessors, Bride does not remain stuck in the identity of poor little black girl but moves toward a fuller subjectivity: Morrison is more optimistic here about the possibilities of overcoming even devastating, be-cause chronic, childhood trauma. On the surreal level of the plot, Bride's body enacts the arrested development experienced by Morrison's earlier child victims but only to reverse course as Bride, at the end of her quest, finds her-self again in a womanly body equipped for sexual love and maternity. What are we to make of these magical transformations? A reader might be tempted to read Bride's story as a variation on the romantic love plot of popular fiction that turns on the importance of the man to a woman's happiness: losing the man, the woman is nothing; reunited with him, she regains her self, body and soul.

However, Bride's story undercuts this simple reading in two ways. First, Bride refuses to rest in the position of victim abandoned by her man. Instead, she decides to track Booker down—and not so much to get him back as to "force him to explain why she didn't deserve better treatment from him, and second, what did he mean by 'not the woman'?" (80). Bride seeks an explana-tion more than a reunion, so she can understand better what it means to her to be, once again, the one who isn't "wanted." Later, she explains to Queen that her quest isn't about the man but about herself: "This is about me, not him! Me!" (152). Bride's quest is for knowledge—to understand her relation-ship and its abrupt ending and thereby understand more about herself and her life.

To lead the reader to understand just what narrative she is writing against, Morrison leaves a clue. As Bride hesitates, at the very end of her quest, to confront Booker, Queen begins singing "Stormy Weather":

> Don't know why
> There's no sun up in the sky . . .
> Can't go on.
> Everything I had is gone,
> Stormy weather . . . (152)

Queen uses the line "Can't go on" to address the moment of Bride's hesita-tion. But the allusion to a famous blues song places Bride's loss of nerve in a cultural history of abandoned women who sing the blues. Although we know from Angela Davis's comprehensive study of black female singers' blues lyrics that blues singers often portrayed themselves as sexual subjects who asserted their rights to sexual freedom and equality (Angela Davis, *Blues* 20–24),[1] the particular blues song that Queen's singing brings into the text, "Stormy Weather," depicts a more conventional figure. Below are the lyrics that come after the lines that Queen cites:

> Since my man and I ain't together,
> Keeps rainin' all the time . . .
> And I just can't get my poorself together,
> I'm weary all the time
> So weary all the time
> When he went away the blues walked in and met me.
> If he stays away old rockin' chair will get me.

The allusion to the song imports into the text the blues narrative that Bride refuses to enact. The woman's self is reduced to a "poorself," one with her misery. Only the blues, only sorrow for lost love, fills the vacuum of the lover's absence. And only his return can save her from total immobility in the "old rockin' chair," aged before her time.

At first Bride's self seems, like the blues woman's, to be "melting away" (8). But once she plans and begins to execute her quest to find Booker, she becomes an agent, active in her own interests. Instead of sitting immobilized in her "old rockin' chair," passive and resigned to suffering, she tracks Booker down and demands an explanation. (She thus takes the route attributed in *male* blues songs to men: "men take to the road and women resort to tears" [Angela Davis, *Blues* 20].)

When Queen sings "Stormy Weather," she is taunting Bride, at the moment when Bride's courage to confront Booker falters, by implying that Bride can only suffer for love, not act. The taunt works: Bride says, "You're absolutely right! Totally right! This is about me, not him. Me!" Recollecting her self ("Me!") and recalling her agency, she leaves to find Booker (152). At the same time, the text inserts, and resists, the cultural narrative of the forsaken woman immobilized by grief. I do not think, then, that we can read the diminution of Bride's body simply as a response to Booker's desertion, nor can we read the evolution of Bride's body back toward maturity simply as a response to getting him back. Such an interpretation would follow the emotional trajectory of the blues that the text rejects.

Instead, I would interpret Bride's transformation into the body of a little black girl as a corporeal representation of her temptation to remain the child victim of trauma. For Booker's rejection all too closely resembles her mother's, and it reawakens all the feelings associated with that original self-annihilating trauma. Bride could remain stuck in the position of traumatized child—like Pecola, like Heed, like Florens. The surreal dimension of the story thus includes a psychic dimension: to succumb to the body of poor little black girl is to rest in the position of traumatized victim.

What does it mean, then, that Bride's body not only returns to its womanly form but becomes a maternal body, pregnant with Booker's child? In interviews, Morrison offers a point of departure for tracing Bride's development: "Beauty is . . . not enough for me. You have to be a complete human being, and that has to do with your generosity. That's what I wanted for her to encounter" (*Mother Jones* 4). The most obvious act of generosity that Bride encounters is the care she receives at the hands of the strangers, Evelyn and Steve, who rescue her from an automobile accident and provide for her without question or recompense during the six weeks of her recovery. Bride in turn extends care to the young girl the couple has adopted, Rain, and thus learns to practice a matching "generosity."

When Rain tells Bride that her mother threw her out on the street when Rain was around six, Bride begins to think in a new way: "Why would anybody do that to a child? . . . As Bride imagined the scene her stomach fluttered. How could anybody do that to a child, any child, and one's own?" (101, 102). For the first time, Bride begins to imagine what a mother would feel and do. Up till now, Bride has been so focused on her own sufferings and successes that she has been incapable of empathy. But the extreme of maternal rejection recounted by Rain cuts through Bride's habitual self-absorption. She experiences fellow feeling for another's suffering—and at a deep level, as the disturbance in her stomach indicates.

Bride urges, "Tell me, . . . tell me, . . . tell me," and Rain does. Because of Bride's serious listening, Rain is able to talk about some of the pain caused by the men to whom her mother prostituted her. Bride listens like a good mother who credits her daughter's story of sexual abuse. And she cares as a mother would care about what Rain had to go through, empathizing so deeply that she had to "[fight] against the danger of tears for anyone other than herself" (103). Again a bodily response testifies to the depth of Bride's empathy; and the wording ("anyone other than herself") reminds us that Bride's habitual self-involvement makes empathy an entirely new experience. In part because of her own mother's rejection, she can listen actively to Rain's story of maternal abuse: she can, in Dori Laub's terms, serve as "witness," "actually participating in the reliving and reexperiencing" of another's trauma (Laub 62).

The text places this conversation on the edge of a forest, where Rain and Bride are observed unseen by a doe and her fawn. In a use of metonymy rare in Morrison's texts, the deer are called "mother and child," implying by proximity, or metonymic displacement, that Bride and Rain are mother and child for the moment, enacting a dialogue of maternal empathy and understanding.

Later, two boys from the neighborhood shoot at them with birdshot. Bride instinctively flings her arm and hand across Rain's face, so that the bird-shot wounds her in place of Rain. Speaking as narrator of the following chapter, Rain recognizes the novelty of being with someone who would sacrifice her own body to protect her: "My heart was beating fast because nobody had done that before. I mean Steve and Evelyn took me in and all but nobody put their own self in danger to save me. Save my life. But that's what my black lady did without even thinking about it" (105–6).

Listening, caring, and protecting, Bride practices the skills that enable her to enact the maternal role that Rain needs.[2] Rain brings out in Bride new capacities that enable her to begin the move away from the identity of abused child toward the position of maternal protector and nurturer of an abused child. And Bride's maternal listening supplies what Rain needs. Implying that the scene the text offers is only one of many conversations, Rain says that her "black lady" was the only one she could talk to. Evelyn and Steve are good to her, Rain acknowledges, but they cannot tolerate hearing "stuff about how it was in my mother's house," where her mother ran a business prostituting Rain to clients, or about how she lived on the street once her mother had evicted her (104). So Bride contributes a vital piece to Rain's remothering.

The optimism of the implied author Morrison—which allows Bride to "encounter generosity," not only in the strangers Evelyn and Steve who rescue and care for her, but in her own unexpected capacity for giving what is needed to an abused child—extends to a faith that an abused child can be reparented. The combination of strangers—Evelyn and Steve and Bride—effectively remothers Rain.

Of course, Bride's development of a maternal empathy for Rain is but one of the experiences that characterize her growth toward the recovery of a womanly body. When Queen lets Bride read the poetic, jazz-infused meditations that Booker has sent her for safekeeping, Bride wakes up to two facts about relationships. Other people, including the man she loves, have depths of emotion and complexities of thought that she has not dreamed of, and her own relationships have been skin-deep. The revelation that she has not known Booker at all—"It suddenly occurred to her that good sex was not knowledge" (146)—may awaken Bride to the possibility of a relationship that includes intimacies beyond sex. Regaining her womanly body coincides, then, with Bride's psychic growth in several directions—a change that Booker notices when he meets her again: "[Bride] had changed from one dimension into three" (173).

However, I would argue that Bride's newly acquired capacity for maternal love is more fully developed than her potential for romantic love, both in the scenes with Rain and in the surreal dimension of her bodily transformations. For when Bride's body takes back its womanly shape, it also comes equipped for motherhood. At the end of the novel, Bride is delighted to regain her full breasts, but they now have a maternal function, and so does her uterus, for it contains a fetus—Booker's baby. She moves from the prepubescent body of the "poor little black girl" to a maternal body.

That is important in a book which features mothers who are universally unmaternal and unloving. Bride's transformation to the embodiment of potential maternal love is consonant with Morrison's other efforts to show that childhood trauma can be overcome and unmothered children become loving mothers to the next generation. Or can they? The last line of the novel, and the final comment on Bride's pregnancy, comes from the cynical mouth of Bride's mother and leaves the question open: "Good luck and God help the child" (178).

Revisioning Love and Slavery

> Making it up, . . . tumbling it, creating it every moment afresh.
> VIRGINIA WOOLF, *Mrs. Dalloway*

Rather than repeating themes of love worked out in earlier novels, as one might expect in the late work of a writer now in her eighties, Toni Morrison in these latest novels (*Home* and *God Help the Child*) turns on her earlier works to critique them. Just as Morrison's late novels call on the reader to confront, examine, and reevaluate her or his established values, so *Home* and *God Help the Child* seem to call the notions of love in her prior works into question and demand a reevaluation. The form of these two novels, however, is consistent with Morrison's practice of treating novel writing as an ethical act. Dialogue, especially in *Home*, continues to be a formal mechanism for inviting multiple perspectives on ethical issues and for calling fixed ideas into question.

As I discuss at length in chapter 7, the long patience that the earlier Morrison texts—such as *Jazz*, for instance—exhibit for characters' repetitive reenactments of early scenarios of traumatic love turns in *God Help the Child* into an impatience with those who cling to traumas that drag them back into the past. The imperative in *God Help the Child* is to shake loose from old traumas and to pour the erotic energy released by that letting go into loving in the present—for love, as the character Queen authoritatively declares, is so difficult that it demands all a lover's focus and energy.

In the penultimate novel, *Home,* the character Frank steps out of the story-world to chastise the author Morrison for misrepresenting his thought processes; he ends his diatribe with the words, "I don't think you know much about love. Or me" (69). Readers of Morrison, who know more about her expertise on love than the character does, will likely see this attack as comical, a dramatic irony stemming from the character's ignorance of his interlocutor's achievements. But if we follow the example of this metalepsis to move to a meta level of interpretation, we could ask what the author herself might see in the accusation. Perhaps Morrison, through the character's protest, is questioning the wisdom of her former writings on love, wondering if she got it all wrong—as the character accuses her of doing. Now that her previous depictions of love (especially *Beloved*) have become master narratives widely disseminated throughout the culture, perhaps Morrison thinks it is time to tear down her old conceptualizations of feeling and thinking in favor of constructing new models of love. The form that Morrison's critique of her older thinking on love takes—an impossible colloquy between character and author, a transgression of the boundary sacred to literary works (Genette 236)—indicates that this demolition will not be earnest and heavy-handed but playful, engendering fun for both author and reader.[1]

The incident that provokes the character Frank to protest is itself about love, and the variety of responses that different kinds of lovers can make to incidents of racist humiliation. (In coupling love with race the novel takes up issues addressed by earlier works like *The Bluest Eye, Beloved, Love*, and *A Mercy*). In the "writer's" third-person (implicitly Morrison's) account of his thinking, Frank witnessed a scene of a man being beaten by whites at a train stop while his wife tried to defend him and then imagined how the man would beat his wife when they got home. The "writer" thus attributes to Frank's way of thinking an adherence to the stock explanation for black domestic violence: a black man humiliated in the workplace or in the social world by racial slurs or racial violence turns his rage at the white perpetrators onto his wife, an object both available and vulnerable to his dominance, to demonstrate to her, and more importantly to himself, that he is still a man. As Johnnetta Cole and Beverly Guy-Sheftall write (150), this explanation for the cause of gendered violence in black love relationships has been so often repeated that, while surely true of many domestic disputes, it has become almost a cliché. In attributing this prophecy of the man's behavior to Frank's thought, the third-person narrator (the implied Morrison) is imagining her character as a person who thinks about love relationships in clichéd terms. But it is actually the "writer" who cannot get beyond the racial stereotypes through which the world thinks about black love; for it is she who imposes this stereotype on her character's stream of consciousness. Frank's protest against her attribution of such thoughts to him is then a protest against false ways of "knowing" about love through the imposition of standard raced narratives.

Frank is here taking the position on love implied by the sequence of Morrison's novels I have been studying: there is no way of accurately preconceiving or predicting how love works in the individual instance, for love comes in a thousand different shapes. To imagine that love, when paired with racial violence, always results in the same behavior (in this example, wife-beating) is a travesty founded on racial prejudice about the way black people (always) act. The dialogue between implied author and character thus carries on Morrison's practice of bringing a reader, through subtle narrative means, to see the hidden racism implicit in certain forms of language—such as sociological studies of the black family. As she says in the essay "Home," "Eliminating the potency of racist constructs in language is the work I can do" (4).

The form of the contest over love between character and writer is continuous with Morrison's practice of fostering dialogue. Although the dialogue here is between writer and character, the reader is also invited into the conversation by unresolved enigmas: the discrepancy between two versions of what Frank thought, and the global challenge to Morrison's authority on matters of love. The character's challenge—"I don't think you know much about love"—could bring into question the notions of love a reader carries over from readings of Morrison's previous works. These points of entry challenge the reader to contribute her own opinions on how Morrison's ideas of love stack up against Frank's protest, as well as to figure out for herself the levels of metalepsis at work here. In other words, the form is consistent with the ethical concern of all Morrison's later novels to keep a dialogue on ideas going and to provoke a questioning and reevaluating of all fixed convictions and established ideas—even her own.

Contemporary Critiques of Slavery Studies: Stephen Best, *Beloved*, and *A Mercy*

Morrison's move in *Home* and *God Help the Child* toward an interrogation and critique of her earlier ideas on love, race, and trauma coincides with a similarly revisionary trend in African American cultural studies toward interrogating prevalent attitudes toward slavery. In "Failing to Make the Past Present" (2012), for example, Stephen Best makes the astonishing claim that a novel—namely, Morrison's *Beloved*—set not only the tone but also the agenda for a whole generation of African American historians of slavery. According to Best, *Beloved*'s approach to slavery influenced historians of slavery to abandon the impersonal tone of the traditional historian in favor of writing history through the lens of emotional attachment to the lost slave ancestors.

At issue in Best's essay is Morrison's emphasis on the ethical and empathic relationship between reader and character that she works to create in *Beloved*. She comments on this aspect of writing *Beloved* in "The Art of Fiction No. 134": "What I wanted [the reader] to experience . . . was what it *felt* like [to be a slave]" (77; italics in original). Similarly, in response to Marsha Darling's question about why Halle never appears in the narrative, Morrison explains:

> The loss of that man [Halle] to his mother, to his wife, to his children, to his friends, is a serious loss, and the reader has to feel it. . . . He has to *not* be there. . . . The notion of the devastation of those families is real. . . . Usually it's an abstract concept—but I and the reader have to yearn for their company, for the people who are gone, to know what slavery did. (Darling 6)

Best claims that contemporary slave historians imitate Morrison's effort to make the reader feel empathy and longing for the lost. Saidiya Hartman's *Lose Your Mother* is a particularly good example of this affective history. Hartman searches for traces of her slave ancestors in Ghana, and while acknowledging the impossibility of her mission, her writing is full of this "yearning for their company, for the people who are gone." Hartman says she wants to "resurrect the dead, . . . to redeem the enslaved" (*Lose* 54).

Best argues against this affective mode of history because he thinks it impairs African Americans' ability to build an effective politics in the present. "A sense of racial belonging rooted in the historical dispossession of slavery seems unstable ground on which to base a politics" (454). Underlying the emotional attachment to the enslaved, he claims, is the assumption that the slave past is not only continuous with the oppressions of black people in the present but also determinative: the premise is that "our present was forged when slavery and race conjoined to create a history both inevitable and determined" (466). Allegiance to such a deterministic view of the continuity between past and present, Best argues, impairs African Americans' faith in their own political agency.[2]

Best posits that Morrison recognized the problematic influence of *Beloved* and composed *A Mercy* as an antidote to *Beloved*'s approach to slavery. "I believe that there is a deliberate disjunction between [*Beloved* and *A Mercy*] and that Morrison [in *A Mercy*] demonstrates the limits and ultimate impossibility of the affective history project she has so capably inspired" (473). It is through its narrative form that *A Mercy* undermines the melancholic attachment to slavery that *Beloved* evoked. The text discourages reader identification with the characters through a variety of means, including the nongrammatical, halting, broken speech of the first-person narrator Florens, which, says Best, seems calculated by the author to "disorient readers." A reader's inclination toward identification with a first-person narrator is blocked by a narrating discourse that "builds a set of 'defenses against being read,' seeking no given assembly of hearers or readers, and repelling every approach" (Best 471, quoting Stanley Cavell [12]). Best implies that the final epistle from the mother is similarly cut off from the reader: "this last chapter . . . is unanchored, without identification of source or recipient, which leaves the reader wondering where this bit of writing *is*" (469). The text itself, he says, is "isolated," "with no place in the world" (468).

I think that Best approves of *A Mercy*'s "abandonment" of the reader because it leaves the text of slavery, minus all attachments to the reader and therewith to the present, in "a world of its own"—cut off from affective ties to present readers, discontinuous with the present, over and done and complete in itself. Rather than demanding an ethical relation to the past through empathy, as *Beloved* does, *A Mercy* "raises a bulwark . . . against that very possibility," demanding that we occupy instead "a more baffled, cut-off, foreclosed position with regard to the slave past" (472). And rather than the "logic of racial slavery" "capturing racial injustice in the present," slavery would be "appreciated in the failure to make its racial legacy present" (474). In Best's opinion, that detachment would enable a more effective political agenda.

I leave an assessment of the validity of Best's claims about the effects of *Beloved* and *A Mercy* on scholars of slavery to the slave historians themselves. What Best's article contributes to my project here is a sense of how *Beloved*'s call to readers to confront, acknowledge, and work through the traumas of slavery reverberated in the culture, shifting the perspective through which Americans, and especially African American scholars, write, read, and think slavery. Additionally, Best's claim that *A Mercy* radically revises the affective and ethical dialogue on slavery that *Beloved* offered its reader adds yet another text to my list of late Morrison novels that challenge, overthrow, and replace central ideas of the novels that came before.

Love in Morrison's Later Novels

While Best's article highlights perhaps the most visible example of how Morrison's novels have shifted cultural attitudes, one can speculate that the long sequence of her late novels' surprising models of love may have similarly opened minds to new and different approaches to love. To review just two of the novels covered in this study: We can infer Morrison's pedagogical designs on readers from looking at the ways in which the narrative forms of *Love* and *Jazz* provoke a reader into ethical dialogues about love. After the main body of *Love* draws out and exposes a reader's conventional assumptions that the title refers to heterosexual romance, the novel ends by showing that the signifier of true love refers to the deep friendship between eleven-year-old girls. That concluding surprise has the potential not only to unsettle a reader's heterosexual model of romantic love—together with its assumption that male desire is necessarily the center of a love story—but also to open a reader's mind to accepting, honoring, and recognizing a multiplicity of different kinds of love and lovers.

Jazz celebrates the notion of love as creative innovation. When Violet wonders aloud to Alice what she should do about her flagrantly unfaithful husband, Joe, Alice responds, "You got anything left to you to love, anything at all, do it" (112). Violet objects, "You saying take it? Don't fight?" Alice responds, "Nobody's asking you to take it. I'm sayin' make it, make it!" (113). The suggestion is that love is something you improvise, or make up: you pour your imaginative resources into making something new of the old love, some new form of loving relationship. Thus Violet and Joe revitalize their relationship by making up a new family formation that includes a surrogate "daughter," Felice, and a new bird.

At the end of *Jazz* the narrator exuberantly joins this erotic creativity by making up an unprecedented song of love that reaches across the impassable barrier between printed page and flesh-and-blood reader to declare the narrator's love for her reader. And then she proposes that the reader "make me, remake me!" (229). The narrator may well be punning on the sexual meaning of "make me," but more importantly she is inviting the reader to love her in a specific way, by retelling in her own original fashion the love story the narrator has just finished.

Throughout the later novels, Morrison has been subtly invoking the call-and-response tradition of African American storytelling and jazz by calling on her reader, through various narrative twists and tricks, to complete the text with her own ideas—her own "politics" on love, gender, and race ("Home" 7). Here, as the narrator calls on the reader to pick up the tale and improvise her own version, the African American call-and-response tradition underlying Morrison's various textual exchanges with the reader becomes visible.

Jazz's call to create innovative new ways of loving reverberates through the sequence of later novels—and perhaps through the life experiences of Morrison's readers.

NOTES

INTRODUCTION
Love and Narrative Form

1. Morrison seems to admire the skill with which psychoanalysis captures a basic human process and presents it, together with its interpretation, in compact narrative form: "The narrative into which life seems to cast itself surfaces most forcefully in certain kinds of psychoanalysis," she says in *Playing in the Dark* (v).

2. Cathy Caruth describes a related but different model of the belated temporality of trauma. Her theory of the unwilled intrusions of images from past trauma, trauma that remains inaccessible to conscious memory, has been used to good interpretive effect by many critics writing on Morrison. According to Caruth's model of trauma, the traumatic event escaped understanding even as it was happening: it becomes "fully evident only in connection with another place, and in another time" ("Trauma and Experience" 8). In PTSD (post-traumatic stress disorder), "the repetitions of the traumatic event—which remain unavailable to consciousness but intrude repeatedly on sight"— recur unbidden in "repeated flashbacks, nightmares, and other repetitive phenomena" (*Unclaimed* 92, 91). Brooks Bouson, Gurleen Grewal, Jill Matus, and Laurie Vickroy use Caruth's theory of "historical trauma" to broaden the concept of trauma from the personal to the collective and from the idea of a single overwhelming event to the chronic trauma experienced by marginalized groups and by those subject to domestic abuse. According to this more inclusive definition of trauma, trauma may be collective (as in slavery or the Holocaust), or it may take the form of "'insidious trauma,' which refers to the 'traumatogenic effects of oppression that are not necessarily overtly violent or threatening to bodily well-being at the given moment but that do violence to the soul and spirit'" (Laura Brown 107; qtd. in Jill Matus 28). These literary critics use contemporary trauma theory perceptively to address Morrison's central concern with collective African American memory and historical trauma.

3. Katherine Nash's definition of rhetorical narrative theory in *The Encyclopedia of the Novel* is cogent and useful: "The rhetorical approach defines narrative as a communicative act . . . and examines the nuanced roles of both speaker (real author, implied

author, narrator) and audience (real reader, authorial audience, narrative audience, narratee)" (548). Further, rhetorical narrative theory emphasizes the interaction of plot dynamics with "readerly dynamics: the audience's cognitive, affective, ethical, and aesthetic experiences as they arise from the audience's sequence of interpretive, ethical, and aesthetic judgments" (549).

Nash develops her own model of rhetorical narrative ethics, in relation to modernist novels and the history of feminism, in *Feminist Narrative Ethics*.

4. Valerie Smith eloquently describes this aspect of Morrison's work. "This quality of engagement is also important to her work because it is a means through which she dismantles the hierarchies that undergird systemic forms of oppression" (4).

5. Jennifer Heinert's *Narrative Conventions and Race in Toni Morrison's Novels* (1995) likewise sustains a focus on narrative structure, but she is most interested in Morrison's revisions of genre. She analyzes how Morrison's work disrupts the conventions that govern both fiction in general (narrator, setting, characters, plot) and specific generic forms. Her aim is to show how Morrison's subversions of genre interrupt dominant discourses of race.

6. The full quotation from Woolf's diary reads: "It took me a year's groping to discover what I call my tunneling process, by which I tell the past by installments, as I have need of it. This is my prime discovery so far" (*Writer's Diary* 61). Mitchell Leaska comments, "It was essentially discovering how to render the backwardness of *mind time* while simultaneously moving the narrative forward" (227).

CHAPTER I
Maternal Language and
Maternal History in *Beloved*

1. See the introduction, section entitled "*Beloved* as Turning Point" (pages 9–11 above), for a discussion of the ways in which *Beloved* marks a radical departure from the style of the early novels.

2. Rafael Pérez-Torres ascribes the complexities of *Beloved*'s style and structure to its mixture of oral tradition and postmodern linguistic play: "There is a crossing of genres and styles and narrative perspectives in *Beloved* that suggests it filters the absent or marginalized oral discourse of a pre-capitalist black community through the self-conscious discourse of the contemporary [postmodern] novel" (690). Eusebio Rodrigues comments, "The structural ordering of this 'aural' novel is not spatial but musical." Thus "the language, slow moving, will be thick with history. . . . The oral-aural mode will use repetition to intensify the experience. Words will be repeated; . . . to generate rhythmic meaning" ("Telling" 154, 155).

3. Molly Abel Travis makes a powerful argument that, on the contrary, it is our inability to identify fully with Sethe (because the narrative strategy prevents our taking a fixed position on her act of murder) that puts the reader into ethical space: "By keeping readers at a distance and preventing too easy an empathy with [her] protagonist, Morrison's . . . novel pose[s] searing ethical questions" (232).

4. Another narrative strategy that keeps reader judgment in suspension is, as Maggie Sale argues, the telling of the infanticide from several different perspectives. The lack of a single definitive account "challenges readers to examine their own responses" both to Sethe's act and to the circumstances that force her to it (44). Philip Page and James

Phelan (*American*) have thoroughly and well described the multiple narrative perspectives on the infanticide. Page understands the novel's structure to be circular: repetitions govern the novel's style (*Dangerous* 140); and attempts to form family circles and community circles dominate the novel's content. Circles and metaphors of circles "reveal the subtle relationships between the novel's content and its form" (*Dangerous* 135).

5. Hazel Carby make the point that "slave narratives by women, about women, could mobilize the narrative forms of adventure and heroism normally constituted within ideologies of male sexuality" (*Reconstructing* 38).

6. Lorraine Liscio writes a sophisticated analysis of the hazards of using the pre-Oedipal mother-daughter bond to disrupt the master discourse. "What I see Toni Morrison doing in *Beloved* [is] . . . speaking the unspeakable process of signification associated with the mother—what I call writing mother's milk—to tell the invisible 'unofficial history' of blacks during slavery and 'wreaking havoc upon the signified,' the language of the white father that relegates them to this invisibility or namelessness" (34). However, this literary strategy risks "reinstating essentialist beliefs about maternal discourse" (35).

7. Mae Henderson points out that "the first full representation of the events surrounding the infanticide [is] figured from a collective white/male perspective, represented by schoolteacher and the sheriff" (78). So Sethe's infanticide is constructed in "the dominant metaphors of the master's narrative—wildness, cannibalism, animality, destructiveness" (Henderson 79). Henderson argues, however, that when Sethe explains to Paul D that "I took and put my babies where they'd be safe" (*Beloved* 164), she "creates a counternarrative that reconstitutes her humanity and demonstrates the requirements of motherlove. . . . Sethe effectively changes the plot and meaning of the story. . . . A story of inhumanity has been overwritten as a story of higher humanity" (79–80). I maintain, however, that although Sethe does put the motivation for her act into words in this passage, she never tells the story of the infanticide itself (she leaves the trauma unnarrativized).

8. Doreen Fowler's article on *Beloved* focuses on the father as the figure who sets boundaries for the child that both differentiate selves and provide a site of connection between self and other. When Paul D leaves 124 Bluestone Road, Fowler says, the principle of differentiation disappears with him, precipitating Beloved's and Sethe's "narcissistic regression to a former unmarked unity" and "dramatizing the breakdown of subjectivity that occurs when . . . a desire to return to a totalizing identification is not checked" ("Nobody" 23).

9. Reading *Beloved* through a Lacanian lens, Sheldon George identifies Beloved as the object a, the source-object of Sethe's desire. Once Sethe "embrac[es] Beloved as the object a that fills her lack, . . . Sethe becomes a *full*, desireless subject." That is, possessing the object a makes her feel whole and thus "eliminates the dimension of desire and all subjective aspirations" ("Approaching" 119).

10. For Linda Krumholz, "Beloved is Sethe's 'ghost,' the return of her repressed past, and she forces Sethe to confront the gap between her motherlove and the realities of motherhood in slavery. But Beloved is also everyone's ghost. . . . Beloved initiates the individual healing processes of the three characters [Sethe, Paul D, and Denver]. . . . And Beloved is the reader's ghost, forcing us to face the historical past as a living and vindictive presence" ("Ghosts" 400). Similarly, Linda Koolish regards Beloved as the embodiment of the split-off parts of all the characters' selves—for all the characters in

Beloved, Koolish states, suffer from dissociation—so Beloved is a force for healing. She forces the characters to confront their own split-off selves. Rebecca Ferguson uses D. W. Winnicott's essay "Mirror-Role of Mother and Family in Child Development" to explain Beloved's fixation on her mother's face (117–18). Jennifer FitzGerald reads Beloved's ambivalence toward Sethe through Melanie Klein's notion of infantile oscillations between dependency on and aggressivity toward the mother figure (684). See also Jean Wyatt's 1993 *PMLA* article, which, in addition to a discussion of Sethe and Beloved, has an extended discussion of Denver's relation to Sethe, to the community, and to the symbolic order.

Stephanie Demetrakopoulos focuses on the destructive effects of Sethe's mothering, especially the destructive effects on her own growth as an individual. She argues that the infanticide is Sethe's attempt "to return the babies to perhaps a collective mother body, to devour them back into the security of womb/tomb death . . . as the ultimate act of protection" (52). Andrea O'Reilly reads Sethe's ways of mothering, including the infanticide, as positive acts of maternal nurturance: "In her motherlove, Sethe seeks to foster in her children a loved sense of self, and through the infanticide protect them from harm and deliver them to safety" (136–37).

La Vinia Delois Jennings claims that in creating Beloved, Morrison is drawing on two figures in Yoruba religion. In her initial form as the amorphous spirit that fills the house, Beloved is "the abiku, . . . the child that dies in infancy . . . but returns to earth usually because . . . it is drawn by 'the deep evocative desire of its mother,' which in Beloved's case is Sethe's 'too thick love'" (*Idea of Africa* 65). As the revenant, however, Beloved embodies "the Haitian-created loa, Erzulie Ge-rouge" and is malevolent; like Erzulie, she "exact[s] vengeance upon those who betray her in love" (*Idea of Africa* 65, 66). Teresa Washington uses the system of Yoruba cosmology to describe the mother-daughter relationship between Beloved and Sethe. Baby Suggs, Sethe, and Beloved are all endowed with *Àjé*, a spiritual force "inherent in Africana women" (171). In her view, the infanticide is a matter of establishing an *ojubo*, or praisehouse, in the woodshed, where Sethe "returns" her progeny to "the Great Mother," the only force "that can ensure her children's safety" (177). According to Deborah Horvitz, Beloved is "the powerful corporeal ghost who creates matrilineal connection between Africa and America. . . . She is the haunting symbol of the many Beloveds—generations of mothers and daughters—hunted down and stolen from Africa" (157–58).

See Pelagia Goulimari for helpful summaries of many articles on *Beloved* (201–17).

11. As I show in the introduction to this work, the four Morrison novels that precede *Beloved* repeat the message that possessiveness strangles love and damages both the lover and the beloved. Calling the character Beloved "a literal manifestation of memory as body," Kevin Quashie writes, "For me, the key question of *Beloved*/Beloved is of possession: that is, who possesses, or can possess Beloved or who possesses, can possess, the body memory. . . . Beloved has been possessed (or owned), . . . possesses (haunts) the characters . . . and is possessed by . . . other characters in the novel" (102).

12. Cathy Caruth posits a different model of belatedness for the temporality of trauma ("Recapturing," "Trauma," *Unclaimed Experience*). Critics of Morrison have made good use of her theories, together with those of Dori Laub and Onno Van der Hart and Bessel Van der Kolk, to analyze trauma in Morrison's novels. See, for example, Laurie Vickroy's description of trauma narratives and her analysis of Morrison's "dia-

logical conceptions of witnessing" in *Beloved*, where "many voices" combine to give a shape to repressed collective trauma (174–75). See note 2 in the introduction for a more complete account of recent trauma theory.

13. Cynthia Dobbs's close reading of Beloved's monologues is detailed and perceptive (570–73).

14. Barbara Schapiro also generalizes the damaging intergenerational effects of Sethe's deprivation to all those damaged by the system of slave mothering: "the emotional hunger, the obsessive and terrifying narcissistic fantasies" are not Beloved's alone; they belong to all those denied both mothers and selves by a slave system that "either separates [a mother] from her child or so enervates and depletes her that she has no self with which to confer recognition" (194). Reading Sethe's deprivation through the lens of attachment theory, Schreiber also comments on the intergenerational transmission of a traumatic lack of mothering in a slave child's life: "Sethe's early trauma, as well as her mother's, passes on to Denver" (35).

15. This meditation on Beloved's claim is inspired by James Phelan's reading of *Beloved*'s ending ("Toward a Rhetorical"). His methodology comes closer to capturing the actual experience of reading *Beloved* than any other analysis of reader response I have read.

16. For a more recent call to remember those lost in the Middle Passage and excluded from history, see historian Saidiya Hartman's *Lose Your Mother*. Hartman explores Ghana, from the slave holds of Elmina Castle and Cape Coast Castle to a reimagining of life on the slave ships, looking for traces of her slave ancestors. Her wish is "to resurrect the dead, . . . to redeem the enslaved" (54). From the meager records of the British trial of a slave-ship captain for the murder of one of the young African captives, Hartman reconstructs the events of the dead girl's final days aboard the slave ship. Hartman tells the story "to save the girl from oblivion." But she simultaneously admits, "Hers is a life impossible to reconstruct, not even her name survived" (137). So Hartman's vivid reconstruction of the events onboard the slave ship is framed, like Morrison's telling of Beloved's story, by the paradoxical truth that the story of the Middle Passage can be told, but the story cannot be (fully) told.

CHAPTER 2
Riffing on Love and
Playing with Narration in *Jazz*

1. Matthew Treherne discusses "the protean nature of the narrative voice—varying between seeming to be one of the characters at the start of the novel, and a position close to that of the author herself at the end." He takes "the novel's project" to be "questioning the very nature of narrative itself" (210).

2. John Duvall writes that "The narrator of *Jazz* encodes the multiple paradoxes of Morrison's own relation to authority. . . . The author seems to use her narrator to comment on the psychic determinism of her early fiction in which the individual often is doomed to repeat later in life the prior insult and injury that defines his or her subjectivity" (133). In *Jazz*, by contrast, the early authoritative prediction of the narrator that Joe and Violet are doomed to repeat their earlier traumas proves false, as "Joe, Violet and Felice form a felicitous relationship" (133).

3. Veronique Lesoinne's essay considers the identity of the narrator from a range of perspectives. She arrives at the conclusion that the narrator is "the voice of the whole

African American community. . . . Here, we are listening to the voice of Toni Morrison as the *griot*, the storyteller of the African diaspora" (158).

4. Henry Louis Gates supplies a historical context for this feature of African American writing: "Black people have always been masters of the figurative: saying one thing to mean something quite other has been basic to black survival in oppressive Western cultures. Misreading signs could be, and indeed often was, fatal. 'Reading,' in this sense, was . . . an essential aspect of the 'literacy' training of a child. This sort of metaphorical literacy, the learning to decipher codes, is just about the blackest aspect of the black tradition" ("Criticism" 6).

5. Justine Tally sees *Jazz* as a "narrativiz[ation] of Bakhtinian theory" (85). Jazz music, with "its plan of call and response, [its] ongoing dialogue of music as process rather than product," functions as "a trope for dialogic discourse" (85).

6. Richard Hardack understands this statement to be true of *Jazz*'s characters: according to him, they lack agency and control over their own actions, while "a series of impossibly personified and conscious inanimate agencies preside over human will through most of Morrison's text" (462). The City is one of these forces: "Personified agency in *Jazz* resides not with characters but with Nature, the City, Music, or the Narrator, each of which feeds off the characters to achieve existence. The appetites of these impersonal yet personified forces . . . determine our destinies" (454). Rather than take the passage at face value as Hardack does, I take the narrator's complacency to constitute Morrison's parody of any authority figure—city administration or narrator—who claims omniscient control of its subjects. Such a claim is delusional, as we see when the characters depart from script and from external control to originate innovative designs for their own lives and loves.

   Anne-Marie Paquet-Deyris reflects on the double-faced nature of the City: "Harlem's fundamentally constructive/destructive ambiguity seems to be built into a text which alternately reflects the open space of romantic possibility and, at the same time, re-presents, literally embodies the reality of physical defeat and death" (230).

7. Although Madhu Dubey does not identify the narrator as the City, she comments insightfully and extensively on the relation of the narrator to the City. She conceives the narrator to be someone in the city, whose "unreliability" stems from her "limited first-person viewpoint, which . . . is a consequence of the narrator's urban location" (303). As an inhabitant of the City, the narrator is "locked within the confining limits of an urban frame of signification" that keeps her from seeing the "'original, complicated, changeable' humanity of her characters" (304).

8. I am borrowing the language of determinism and contingency from the ancient (fourth century B.C.) debate between Democritus and Epicurus. Both understood the universe to be composed of material atoms. Democritus believed the atoms fell in straight lines through the cosmos. His thought was likewise governed by a strict logic of cause and effect: he held that one can always find a long chain of causality determining any event. Epicurus posited a swerve—a random shift of an atom away from the straight. Stephen Greenblatt has recently revived interest in Epicurus in *The Swerve*, his study of Lucretius's *On the Nature of Things*, which expounds the philosophy of Epicurus.

9. Caroline Brown analyzes the Golden Gray episode at length, foregrounding both Golden Gray's ambivalence and the ambivalence of the narrator in creating his story as well as commenting on reader response to these ambiguities (634–39). Philip Page

comments on the narrator's telling and retelling different versions of the Golden Gray story: "The discrepancies, and the mere fact of the juxtaposition of two competing accounts by the same narrator, calls into question the status of each account and of the narrator's accounting in general. Such an unraveling of the means of narrative transmission calls attention to the narrative and therefore to the act of reading, reminding readers of their roles and requiring their active participation" (*Dangerous* 172). Carolyn Jones understands the Golden Gray story to be "the centerpiece of the novel." She comments on the narrator's interventions into the story and claims that "Writing Golden Gray . . . is a way of reclaiming [the narrator's] own self" (481, 488). Reading the character of Golden Gray through a comparison with Faulkner's character Charles Bon in *Absalom! Absalom!*, Doreen Fowler charts Golden's changing attitudes toward blackness ("Reading").

10. As Naomi Morgenstern writes, "If there is an 'original' trauma in *Beloved*, . . . it is the trauma of Middle Passage, which establishes a pattern of separation and desertion" ("Mother's Milk" 113).

11. Evelyn Schreiber writes that Golden Gray's pain at the loss of his father marks the first of a long line of parental losses in the novel, going back to "the disruptions of family life associated with slavery" (109).

12. *The Return of the Water Spirit*, by the contemporary Angolan novelist Pepetela (1995), powerfully evokes the water spirit Kwandai, who brings down building after building of the city built by Portuguese colonizers on land that used to hold Kwandai's lagoon; finally, in a tidal wave, he wipes out the city, reclaiming the land for his waters.

13. Cutter's analysis of the possibilities inherent in the Wild-Beloved connection shows how complex the interaction between textual ambiguity and a reader can be. "Morrison's point is not to convince us of the fact [of Wild being Beloved]; rather, her point is to play a sophisticated literary game of 'what if': 'What if Beloved was not a ghost, but an actual pregnant woman?' and 'What if she appears in my next novel as a physical being, gives birth to a child, and then disappears?' . . . How does such a series of questions . . . force us to read intertextually and metatextually, and to reread and recreate the two textual worlds?" (67). Cutter's analysis provides insight into the complexities of inference that a Morrison ambiguity (if it works) can inspire in a reader.

14. I am indebted to Eugene Victor Wolfenstein's *Talking Books: Toni Morrison Among the Ancestors* (404) for this insight. More generally, some of the ideas on Golden Gray and Wild in this paragraph were developed in personal conversation with the late Wolfenstein.

15. Doreatha Drummond Mbalia articulates in precise detail the many ways that the relationship between Alice and Violet is healing for both. And she elaborates the meaning of that relationship as a model for the bonding that should exist among all African women: "Sisterhoods, groups of African women bonding together, help clear things up" and "help one another to live healthy, wholesome lives" (632).

CHAPTER 3
Displacement—Political, Psychic,
and Textual—in *Paradise*

1. Shirley Stave, connecting Dovey's speech to Julia Kristeva's *sémiotique*, also calls Dovey's babbling jouissance. Stave writes insightfully about the Ruby men's desires for

dominance and the fears inspired by women (like Fairy and Lone) who operate in a sphere beyond male control ("Separate Spheres?" 36–37).

2. Stéphane Robolin offers a useful anthropological account of the reasons for the control of female sexuality in societies governed by rigid racial and caste hierarchies like Ruby's (307–8).

3. Commenting on the counterpoint of Patricia's radical counternarrative to the patriarchal historical narrative, Rob Davidson writes, "*Paradise* complicates every version of history it presents, continually urging broader contexts that undermine and problematize the conservative approach of the men" (363, 361). Davidson gives a detailed analysis of Patricia's situation and her setting fire to her historical manuscript. See Akoma, Gauthier, and Hilfrich for insightful readings of Patricia's production of "countermemory" (Hilfrich 336) as well as analyses of the various Ruby women's critical views of their men's historical narrative.

4. Morrison recounts that when she found the newspaper account of twenty families who were denied entry into an all-black community in Oklahoma, which later became the nucleus of *Paradise*, she became "interested in what on earth that must have felt like, to have come all that way and look at some other Black people who said you couldn't come in" (McKinney-Whetstone 3; qtd. in Bouson 192). As Morrison reimagines the incident, it "felt," above all, humiliating.

5. See Cherrie Moraga for an account of the historical Malintzin Tenepal (La Malinche) and the ongoing influence of this figure of female sexual betrayal on male attitudes toward Latina and Mexican women. "There is hardly a Chicana growing up today who does not suffer under her name even if she never hears directly of the one-time Aztec princess" (175).

6. Thus in *Three Essays on the Theory of Sexuality*, women's nature is hidden, inaccessible to research, "partly owing to their conventional secretiveness and insincerity" (*SE* 7, 151; qtd. in Gilman 37). The pejorative tone as well as the specifics of this description, according to Gilman, parallel descriptions of the hidden nature of the Jew in Freud's Vienna: "[Jews] engage in hidden practices and conspiracies; they lie as a natural reflex of their character" (Gilman 37). The inferiority of a woman's genitalia to the penis of the man was a rewriting of the commonplace attribution of inferiority to "the circumcised ('truncated') penis of the Jewish male" (39). In the scientific writing of the time, the Jewish male was characterized as prone to disease and especially at risk for mental illness (95). The quintessential hysteric was the male Jew (Gilman 114–15). After Freud and Breuer wrote *Studies in Hysteria*, woman replaces the male Jew as the figure of the hysteric. The biology of race disappears from Freud's writing, to leave just two categories of difference: male and female.

7. For an insightful reading of the novel's spiritual dimension, see Megan Sweeney's analysis of the Convent women's healing rituals; Sweeney views them as Morrison's alternative telling of "the Last Supper, crucifixion, resurrection, and redemption" ("Racial House" 57).

8. Ambiguity in *Paradise* has yet another political use, suggested by Katrine Dalsgård's "The One All-Black Town Worth the Pain." According to Dalsgård, Morrison is destabilizing the American narrative of exceptionalism as well as the African American variant story of exceptionalism. Conflicting and fragmented stories of Ruby's origins throw into question the patriarchal master narrative of Ruby's origins. And the Oven,

the sacred symbol and soul of the community's ideal pure community, has an inscription that is hallowed yet enigmatic. Its ambiguity undermines the patriarchal leaders' insistence on remaining loyal to the singular directive Word of the founding fathers and the founding myth of ancestral heroism.

9. At the end, the women who were apparently killed at the Convent seem to inhabit physical bodies, for they feel hunger, they feel pain, they eat, and they bleed; yet they appear and disappear with the ease of ghosts for whom the laws of the physical world do not apply. The antinomy is irreducible to a single reality: it is a parallax. The full quotation from the 1998 interview of Morrison is as follows: "The part that I want the reader to decide for his or her self is whether or not they want this redemption to take place [the women are alive] . . . or do they prefer the more 'realistic approach' [the women are dead]" ("Interview with Toni Morrison"; qtd. in Page, "Furrowing" 638).

CHAPTER 4
Love's Time and the Reader

1. I will be using the term *Nachträglichkeit* in the specific configuration that Jean Laplanche develops from Freud's usage, not in the more general way that Freud sometimes employs *nachträglich* to mean "the assignment of new meaning to memory traces": "the form of memory traces [is] . . . subjected from time to time to a re-arrangement in accordance with fresh circumstances—to a re-transcription" (Freud to Fliess, 6 December 1896, in *The Origins of Psychoanalysis* 233); nor as contemporary theorists sometimes use the term, to refer to the retroactive conferral of meaning, through the lens of the present, on past events. Thus, for example, Haydee Faimberg makes interesting use of *Nachträglichkeit* or, as she more often labels it, *après-coup*, to designate the double movement of anticipation and retroaction in the analytic experience. Dana Birksted-Breen usefully explores the several meanings of *Nachträglichkeit* and how they figure in analysis. See Eickhoff for a comprehensive history of the term in Freud's writings and in the theories of D. W. Winnicott, Wolfgang Loch, and Haydee Faimberg. See also Mather and Marsden for an alignment of Freud's *Nachträglichkeit* with Derrida's notion of "*différance*" and Puhl for the parallels between Freud's *Nachträglichkeit* and Wittgenstein's "perspicuous representation." Thoma and Cheshire offer a contrarian reading of *Nachträglichkeit*'s causal sequence.

2. Some critics have used *Nachträglichkeit* to explicate literary texts. Greg Forter brilliantly describes reading Faulkner's *Absalom! Absalom!* as an experience of "biphasic textuality" akin to the "biphasic sexuality" of Freud's *Nachträglichkeit* (35). Charles Bernheimer describes his reading of Kafka's "Ein Landarzt" as *nachträglich*: he finds the moment of reading always "displaced, shifted, postponed, hindered," unable to coincide with the text's presence (4). James Mellard deploys Freud's *Nachträglichkeit* to explain the structure of Faulkner's "A Rose for Emily" ("Faulkner's Miss Emily"). Cynthia Chase and John Fletcher ("Scenography") give new and insightful readings of *Oedipus the King* by developing its *nachträglich* thematic dimensions.

3. I use the term *patriarchy* to mean, according to Gerda Lerner's definition, "the manifestation and institutionalization of male dominance over women and children in the family and the extension of male dominance over women in society in general" (239).

4. Anissa Wardi, in an essay on the function of hands in *Love*, persuasively argues that "Morrison's novels can be read through the paradigm of healing hands, an embodied

form of love and nurturance" ("A Laying On" 204). In *Love*, love is an action rather than an emotion: "Morrison's repeated use of hands as a leitmotif in *Love* foregrounds the action of love, the materiality of love, love as verb, not as noun" ("A Laying On" 202).

5. J. Brooks Bouson complicates this gender dynamic by focusing on class, namely the color/caste system within African American communities. "In *Love* [Morrison] deliberately pairs the dark-skinned, lower-class Heed with the light-skinned, upper-middle-class Christine as she examines the damaging impact of the color caste hierarchy on black identity" ("Uncovering" 358); "Morrison emphasizes . . . the shaping and deforming influence of deeply entrenched middle-class prejudices against lower-class blacks" ("Uncovering" 363).

6. I draw this (imagined) exclamation of Emma's from Cynthia Chase's perceptive explanation of the parallels between the *Nachträglichkeit* model and *Oedipus Rex* (58).

7. Forter argues that the widespread influence of Cathy Caruth's model of trauma has produced a body of literary criticism that privileges texts that transmit the effects of trauma directly to the reader rather than merely representing traumatic events. Taking their cue from Caruth's insistence that respect for trauma has to include a respect for trauma's essential incomprehensibility, these critics value depictions of trauma that confound the reader's understanding—and thus respect trauma's "affront to understanding" (Caruth, "Recapturing the Past" 154)—over texts that merely convey the knowledge of trauma. That practice, Forter says, tends to equate the reading experience with the experience of trauma and thus to trivialize the latter; and it depreciates the value of understanding the historical forces that produce trauma and so discourages attempts to resist them. Forter rejects Caruth's model of trauma for Freud's *Nachträglichkeit,* which, he says, better serves his purpose of revealing the cumulative effects of chronic socially induced traumas such as patriarchal gender identity formation.

8. The notion of implied author is under siege in current theoretical debates: as Shlomith Rimmon-Kenan says, "the values (or 'norms') of the implied author are notoriously difficult to arrive at" (101; qtd. in Nünning, "Unreliable" 56); and Gérard Genette is representative of those who claim that "the concept is unnecessary because the categories of author and narrator are sufficient to account for the complexities of narrative communication" (Phelan, *Living* 41). The notion of implied author is useful, however, when a writer, as in the present case, sets up norms and values that she does not share as the ruling conventions of a text. See Phelan (*Living* 38–49) and Nünning ("Unreliable" 55–66) for clarifying overviews of narratologists' theories of the implied author.

9. Messages about domestic felicity and romantic love have historically been addressed to white middle-class readers. However, in *Black Sexual Politics,* Patricia Hill Collins claims that contemporary African Americans are influenced by ideologies of courtship, romantic love, and marriage, even as she documents the difficulties that African American men and women have in successfully implementing them, given the economic and social effects of racism—for example, the high rates of incarceration among young African American men and the discrepant rates of higher education among black women and black men (see especially 249–60).

10. Carden quotes W. E. B. Du Bois's "The Talented Tenth" to show the rigid class division he assumes between the "aristocracy of talent and character" he calls the "Talented

Tenth" and the ignorant masses of black people (Du Bois, "Talented" 139, 133; qtd. in Carden 132). On the subject of Cosey and the community, Evelyn Schreiber writes, "In order to maintain his position of power, Cosey himself has created an 'other' within his community by treating blacks at the bottom of the economic heap much like whites treat him and other blacks: by asserting control over them" ("Power and Betrayal" 98). And Herman Beavers observes that "*Love* pays strict attention to the black community's presumption that racial progress can only occur when someone in its midst replicates the hierarchy and exclusivity found in the white community" (115). Beavers argues persuasively that "Cosey's Resort is . . . created within the dominion of white supremacy by the intersection of pleasure and betrayal. The Coseys' prosperity rests on the presumption that blacks will always opt to pursue pleasure rather than confront the realities of segregation and discrimination. The system is a product of white supremacy" (120).

11. Evelyn Hammonds is commenting here on the ethic of race loyalty in relation to African Americans' complicated responses to the Clarence Thomas hearings: "Black women must always put duty to the race first. No mention was made of how Clarence Thomas had failed in his duty to the race, especially to Black women. This deeply held ethic that Black women have a duty to the race while Black men are allowed to have a duty only to themselves can only be challenged by a Black feminist analysis that emphasizes the importance of Black women's lives" (Hammonds 7–8; qtd. in Cole and Guy-Sheftall 99). I would argue that *Love* emphasizes the overlooked importance of black women's lives (Heed's and Christine's) and so contributes to the airing and critique of this race-loyalty ethic.

Tessa Roynon argues that *Love* is "structured around acts of rape and is unified by anxiety about rape." She sees the male-female relations of *Love* as an allegory of the standard trope of the conquest of America "as a kind of glorious sexual assault," with Cosey as "an allegorical representation of America itself" and Heed as "a parodic version of the configuration of America as the innocent virgin despoiled by the all-conquering hero" (33).

12. In her essay on the uses of silence in *Love*, Carolyn Denard locates L's hum within a range of African American women's traditional self-expressions: the hum indicates a "knowledge and understanding that go deeper than the open-mouthed voicing of the words could reveal." Humming also has cultural overtones of the "'nobody-knows-the-trouble-I've seen' refrain that black women have used to articulate sadness" (87).

13. Palladino presents the interesting thesis that L (who at the end [199] reveals that L stands for Love) is a modern embodiment of Aphrodite: "she is a personification of love, a new Aphrodite" (338). As Aphrodite emerged from sea foam, so L is born into water: "the two of them delivered me in a downpour. You could say going from womb water straight into rain marked me"; and L continues to be connected to water: "The ocean is my man" (*Love* 64, 100; qtd. in Palladino 338). Further, Palladino reads Junior as L's alter ego, a "junior" version of L and thus of Aphrodite, goddess of love (344, 347). She finds narrative evidence for this doubling in the italicization of the passages that convey Junior's thoughts; Junior's use of L's "idiosyncratic italics" signals the merging of the two characters (346).

14. In *Toni Morrison: Writing the Moral Imagination*, Valerie Smith writes, "While the titled chapters in roman font are comparatively straightforward and accessible, they

exemplify L's view of late twentieth-century discourse where *'all is known and nothing understood'* (*Love* 4). In those sections reside accessible, convenient explanations for complex emotions . . . [and] characters attribute unfathomable suffering to 'outside evil' (*Love* 5). . . . In contrast, L's sections are allusive and indirect; harder to comprehend, they are the places where difficult, hidden truths may be found" (111–12).

15. The questions of the newcomer Junior do jog free some of Christine's memories of her early friendship with Heed, but Christine's understandable resentment of being displaced by Heed—literally displaced, for Christine is sent away from home soon after the marriage—warps the memories even as they emerge: "to have your best and only friend leave the squealing splash in your bathtub, trade the stories made up and whispered beneath sheets in your bed for a dark room at the end of the hall reeking of liquor and an old man's business, doing things no one would describe but were so terrible no one could ignore them" (132). Each memory of girlfriends together gives way to friendship's betrayal, each remembered pleasure superseded by a memory of its corruption: "One day we were playing house under a quilt; next day she slept in his bed. One day we played jacks; the next she was fucking my grandfather" (131–32). James Mellard's description of Heed's and Christine's girlhood relationship as one of narcissistic identification provides one explanation of why their mutual hatred is so intense: as Lacan theorizes, in mirror-stage identifications there is a tension between love—"I want to be you"—and aggressivity—"I want to be you but I cannot be." Hence the intimate connection between "love and hate, care and violence" (Mellard, "Families" 706).

16. Megan Sweeney perceptively analyzes Morrison's critique of standard legal discourses in *Love*: her novels "experiment with forms of narration that . . . unbalance the presumed equations undergirding the dominant economy of justice" ("Something Rogue" 443). Sweeney's analyses of L's monologues are particularly insightful, showing how they rewrite dominant disciplinary and legal narratives ("Something Rogue" 447, 456–57).

17. Evelyn Schreiber's sympathetic reading of Christine's situation emphasizes the severity of Christine's childhood trauma: she experiences not just separation from Heed but "rejection from her mother . . . and her grandfather, as well as a loss of home" when her mother sends her away shortly after Heed's marriage to Cosey and then "throws her away" again (*Love* 133) when she returns home at sixteen. From then on, according to Schreiber, Christine struggles to "recapture her place in her family," so that "Christine's claim on Cosey's property is a claim on her own subjectivity" (*Race* 149, 150).

18. Speaking with Anne-Marie O'Connor, Morrison says of *Love*: "Patriarchy is assumed, but women have to agree to the role. You have to say, 'This is the most important person in my life.' It's not that [Cosey] gobbles them up, but they allow themselves to be eaten" (e1).

19. Ghosts contribute to the temporal disorder of *Love*'s fictional world, to the pervading sense that time is out of joint. By definition, ghosts bring the past to which they rightly belong into the present, disrupting the temporal order. The ghosts of Cosey and L are particularly inappropriate to the present moment, since they interact with the living in a sensual or sensuous way that would have been more appropriate to a past time when they had bodies. Many of Morrison's novels draw on African temporalities in which the line between the living and the dead is porous. In African cosmologies, the

"living-dead"—the most recently dead, up to four or five generations—appear to their families. The smell of L's baking bread suggests a link with the African tradition of the family dead who return to break bread with family members and to monitor their activities, as "the guardians of family affairs, traditions, ethics, and activities" (Mbiti 82).

20. Undergraduate Occidental College student Alison Reed pointed out to me the absence of quotation marks in Heed's and Christine's dialogue and gave me the idea of a dual voice: "the voices echo each other and ultimately merge as one" (13).

21. Heather Duerr Humann writes that "The fact that marrying the young girl [whom Cosey] desires sexually is a way to sanction his pedophilic and abusive desires suggests that Morrison is attacking the institution of marriage" and that "Morrison wants to critique America's value system. . . . [S]he places the blame on society for domestic abuse" (253–54, 252).

22. Opinions about the aesthetic and ethical value of Nabokov's *Lolita* are varied (and heated, as James Phelan's review of reader responses indicates [*Living* 101]). But Phelan's own judgment is I think representative of many readers' responses to Humbert Humbert and to acts of pedophilia more broadly: "Humbert treats the young and innocent Dolores as a sex object and uses her for his sexual gratification, transforming her from a child into a sexual toy" (*Living* 105). See also Eichenwald for a sampling of contemporary attitudes toward pedophiles.

23. Carden argues forcefully that Morrison is debunking the (white) U.S. norm of the father-dominant family structure that is often prescribed as a panacea for the economic and social ills of African American families: "*Love* challenges the status of the father-dominant family as measure of respectability, civilization, and equality" by showing up its real nature as "male ownership" (143).

24. In the course of her seminal analysis of Virginia Woolf's *Mrs. Dalloway*, Elizabeth Abel describes female development as a psychic history of discontinuity and disruption, remarking that Freud too lamented the losses incurred in a woman's progress toward "normalcy"—for example, in the tone of such phrasings as the following: "If too much is not lost in the course of [development] through repression, this femininity may turn out to be normal" (Freud, "Femininity" *SE* 22:128; qtd. in Abel, *Virginia Woolf* 36).

25. I owe this insight into L's alternative temporality to University of Kansas graduate student Chloe Jones's unpublished paper, "Opposing Patriarchal Temporalities." See Judith Halberstam for an analysis of hegemonic time frames—such as women's reproductive time, "ruled . . . by strict bourgeois rules of respectability and scheduling" (5). Halberstam theorizes "queer" temporalities that would evade the dominant paradigm.

CHAPTER 5
Failed Messages, Maternal Loss, and
Narrative Form in *A Mercy*

1. Cathy Waegner takes the first instance of this vision to "encode the entire Atlantic slave trade triangle in this picture" (91). She focuses on the words, "I see a minha mae standing hand in hand with her little boy, my shoes jamming the pocket of her apron" (*A Mercy* 8). Rather than seeing the hallucination as the mother's enactment of failed communication, she follows the significance of pocket, shoes, and feet through the rest of the novel (95–96, 104–5).

2. In the "frontier period" of American slavery, slaveholdings were small and their eco-

nomic success uncertain. So, as on Jacob Vaark's farm, "slaveowner and enslaved person were mutually dependent upon one another for survival"; and that made for a "tenuous equalitarianism that 'tempered white domination and curbed slavery's harshest features'" (Morgan 78, quoting Berlin 55). In addition, slavery was not yet indissolubly linked to race: as Toni Morrison emphasizes whenever she is interviewed on *A Mercy*, slaves in this period of American history might be black, white, of European descent, or Native American: "That was, I suppose, the central project of the book. I wanted to see what it might have been like to remove race from slavery" (Norris; see also Jennings, "*A Mercy*" 645). As Valerie Babb and Jessica Cantiello assert, the purpose is to "expose the sociohistorical construction of racial categories" (Cantiello 170).

The link between blackness and slavery was established only gradually, and state by state. A turning point came with the Virginia law of 1662 that "reversed the English practice by which children followed the condition of their father" (Brown 132) by declaring that "all children borne in this country shalbe held bond or free only according to the condition of the mother" (*Norfolk Wills and Deeds D*, 15 August 1992; qtd. in Brown 132). As Kathleen Brown says, "The 1662 law represented a bold attempt to naturalize the condition of slavery by making it heritable and embedding it in a concept of race" (133). A series of laws followed that cemented the link between slave status and African descent. Valerie Babb shows that Morrison weaves the language of early American legal statutes into her prose in order to deconstruct U.S. origin myths. "Evoking the statutes makes plain that the synonymity of *white* and *American* was a construction enacted and reenacted by law" (152).

3. Maxine Montgomery, emphasizing the diasporic, ocean-crossing diversity of the characters who make up the Vaark household, writes that in this transnational space on the margins, these "pre-colonial migratory subjects" have "an unprecedented level of freedom" to invent their own self-fashioned identities, outside the reach of social constructions and roles (629, 631). Valerie Babb writes that the plurality of voices in *A Mercy* (and in Vaark's household) reminds readers of the marginalized subjects "erased" from U.S. origin histories (147): "Morrison enlists such marginalized voices to rewrite the origins narrative as a cautionary tale warning of the dangers of selfish individualism to any form of community" (148). Similarly, Mina Karavanta sees the narratives of the various dispossessed "orphans" in the Vaark household as a "countermemory" to the official narrative of U.S. origins: "they symbolically represent the histories that the discourses of American exceptionalism have . . . omitted" (725).

4. The cornerstone of maternal thinking, as Sara Ruddick has written, is the imperative to protect and preserve the life of one's child; and Ruddick, although she is speaking from the standpoint of contemporary white middle-class motherhood, makes the claim that this interest is universal, across cultures (215). But, as Harriet Jacobs points out from the position of slave mother, protection is not always an option. "The mother of slaves . . . knows that there is no security for her [female] children. After they have entered their teens she lives in daily expectation of trouble" (56). As if citing the clash between these two classic texts on maternal subjectivity, Morrison has Florens's mother repeat four times, "There is no protection" (162, 163, 166), indicating that the imperative to protect and preserve her child is and was uppermost in her mind, together with the impossibility of implementing it.

5. Steven Deyle, in a revealing chapter on African American resistance to the domestic

slave trade (245–75), mentions that slaves were sometimes able to "force their own sale to get away from abusive owners" (245).

6. Steven Deyle likewise reports that "as a prevalent form of collateral, [many young children] were commonly sold to settle debts" (249). Deyle includes many firsthand accounts by adult slaves who remembered the "traumatic experience" of being sold away from their families as children: "Sale meant that they would almost certainly never see their families or friends again, and in many respects, it brought the same type of finality as death" (250, 252). "It has been estimated that at least half of all slave families in the Upper South were broken through . . . the sale of either a spouse or a child" (246).

7. The child who cries out in fear at the sight of Florens's skin recalls Franz Fanon's traumatic induction into a racial symbolic order through a child's cry: "Mama, see the Negro! I'm frightened!" (Fanon 112). The allusion imports into Florens's experience Fanon's terror at feeling his body transformed under the demonizing gaze of the white child, as his "corporeal schema crumbled, its place taken by a racial epidermal schema" (Fanon 112). Likewise, the Puritan child's terror interpellates Florens as black and therefore repellant, terrifying, evil. It is the white gaze—"eyes that do not recognize me, eyes that examine me for a tail, an extra teat . . . eyes that stare and decide if my navel is in the right place if my knees bend backward" (114–15)—that, as in Fanon's case, takes away her body and gives it back as the signifier of inferiority and evil. Up until this moment, race has not been a determining issue for Florens. Morrison is repeating a classic trope of African American autobiography and fiction, the moment of interpellation into a racial hierarchy that suddenly and shockingly redefines the African American subject and imposes on him or her a negative identity. Shirley Stave points out that it is Florens's precarious sense of self, or "lack of self," that makes her especially vulnerable to the townspeople's gaze, which defines her as less than human ("Across Distances" 145).

8. The sudden retroactive understanding of a childhood incident is characteristic of Freud's case studies of hysterics: he named the phenomenon *Nachträglichkeit*. See Laplanche, *Life* 38–41; Chase 57–59; Wyatt, chapter 4 of the present study.

9. Evelyn Schreiber understands Florens's inscribing her story on the walls of the house as an effective self-therapy; verbalizing her experience is a means of freeing herself from the traumatic past (*Race* 170). Anissa Wardi asserts that Florens's writing on the wall is an act of claiming a place for herself, who as a slave has no place, in the master's house, "the space of power" ("Politics" 35).

10. See the conclusion to this book for a discussion of Stephen Best's provocative argument, in "On Failing to Make the Past Present," that the broken prose of Florens's narration is designed to alienate readers and thus cut off a reader's empathy and emotional identification with the slave character and to distance a reader from slavery itself.

CHAPTER 6
Severed Limbs, the Uncanny, and
the Return of the Repressed in *Home*

1. Christopher Benfey, in his review of *Home* in the *New York Review of Books* (12 July 2012), points out that the epigraph is a song lyric written by Morrison and set to music by André Previn in 1992. Benfey also mentions in a passing but suggestive comment the relevance of Freud's uncanny to Morrison's "twilit region of ghosts" (25).

2. In the early twentieth century popular eugenic beliefs seeped into presidential discourse, as Teddy Roosevelt tried, in his 1906 State of the Union speech, to raise the white birth rate by accusing white women who would avoid bearing children of "race suicide," of "willful sterility—the one sin for which the penalty is national death, race suicide" (Roosevelt 1906, qtd. in Davis 209). And the discouragement of reproduction among poor women of color infiltrated the discourse of Margaret Sanger's birth control movement in, for example, the Birth Control Federation of America's 1939 proposal for their "Negro project": "the mass of Negroes, particularly in the South, still breed carelessly and disastrously, with the result that the increase among Negroes, even more than among whites, is from that portion of the population least intelligent and fit, and least able to rear children properly" (Sanger and Smith; qtd. in Gordon 235). Here, as Linda Gordon comments, "The eugenic disguise fell off to reveal overt white supremacy" (235).

3. As Mari Ruti, building on Lacan's formulation of love, writes: "Allow[ing] ourselves to be touched by the unknowable otherness of the other [enables us] to transform the basic parameters of our being" (177). According to Ruti, true intimacy and personal change come about through exposing oneself to the strangeness at the core of the lover (176–77). See Frances Restuccia's *Amorous Acts* for an insightful explanation of Lacan's several models of love, including self-shattering love.

CHAPTER 7
Love, Trauma, and the Body in *God Help the Child*

1. Angela Davis's encyclopedic review of women's blues songs shows that classic blues singers like Ma Rainey and Bessie Smith rarely "evoke women so incapacitated by their lovers' infidelity, desertion, or mistreatment that they are bereft of agency or driven to the brink of self-destruction" (*Blues* 20). Their lyrics more often "launch a brazen challenge to dominant notions of women's subordination" by "drawing parallels between male and female desire, between their similar inclinations toward intoxication, dance, and sex" (Davis, *Blues* 22).

2. I am indebted to Mirin Fader for suggesting that mothering Rain is key to Bride's reformation (personal conversation).

CONCLUSION
Revisioning Love and Slavery

1. Valorie Thomas understands "Frank's signifying on the narrator's limitations" to constitute "an Eshu move that destabilizes authority and control of knowledge" (201). Eshu is the divine trickster in West African cosmologies, "master of 'Signifyin(g)' rhetorical play, hybridity, transgressing borders" (195). Thomas traces Morrison's use of African archetypes drawn from "Yoruba-Bantu-Kongo spiritual systems" (194) to construct "a space of knowledge and healing" (194). Thomas's references to African healing methods (198–99) are especially relevant to the Lotus women's approaches to healing Cee.

In Jan Furman's reading of *Home*'s narrative structure, first-person and third-person narrative voices express different sides of Frank: "That the voices are not in accord suggest Frank's unresolved psychic conflict" (231). Furman understands that trajectory

of the novel as a movement from Frank's split subjectivity, as reflected in the dual narration, to an integration of his "bifurcated vision" as Frank moves into maturity (232).

2. See Sheldon George's *Trauma and Race* for a psychoanalytic perspective on the same
issue. George shares Best's view that attachment to slavery (the "real" in George's Lacanian terminology) weakens African Americans' political strategies. As he says, "*Trauma
and Race* seeks to articulate a notion of agency and identity that distances itself" from
"the traumatic past" of slavery (*Trauma* 36).

WORKS CITED

Abel, Elizabeth. "Black Writing, White Reading: Race and the Politics of Feminist
  Interpretation." In *Female Subjects in Black and White: Race, Psychoanalysis, Feminism*,
  ed. Elizabeth Abel, Barbara Christian, and Helene Moglen, 102–31. Berkeley and Los
  Angeles: University of California Press, 1997.
———. *Virginia Woolf and the Fictions of Psychoanalysis*. Chicago: University of Chicago
  Press, 1989.
Abraham, Nicolas, and Maria Torok. "Mourning *or* Melancholia: Introjection *versus*
  Incorporation." In *The Shell and the Kernel*, trans. Nicholas Rand, 125–38. Chicago:
  University of Chicago Press, 1994.
Akoma, Chiji. "The 'Trick' of Narratives: History, Memory, and Performance in Toni
  Morrison's *Paradise*." *Oral Tradition* 15.1 (2000): 3–25.
Allen, Brooke. "The Promised Land." Review of *Paradise,* by Toni Morrison. *New York
  Times*. 11 January 1998. Sec. 7, 6.
Ashbrook, Tom. "Toni Morrison." Interview. *On Point with Tom Ashbrook*, WBUR, Boston,
  11 May 2012. Radio. http://onpoint.wbur.org/2012/05/11/toni-morrison.
Austen, Jane. *Emma*. New York: Norton, 1972.
Austin, J. L. *How to Do Things with Words*. 2nd ed. Cambridge, Mass.: Harvard University
  Press, 1977.
Babb, Valerie. "E Pluribus Unum? The American Origins Narrative in Toni Morrison's *A
  Mercy*." *Toni Morrison: New Directions*. Ed. Kathryn Nicol and Jennifer Terry. Spec.
  issue of *MELUS* 36.2 (2011): 147–64.
Baker, Houston. *Workings of the Spirit: The Poetics of Afro-American Women's Writing*.
  Chicago: University of Chicago Press, 1991.
Bakerman, Jane. "The Seams Can't Show: An Interview with Toni Morrison." In
  Conversations with Toni Morrison, ed. Danille Taylor-Guthrie, 30–42. Jackson:
  University Press of Mississippi, 1994.
Beavers, Herman. "The Power in 'Yes': Pleasure, Dominion, and Conceptual Doubling in
  Love." In *Toni Morrison: Paradise, Love, A Mercy*, ed. Lucille P. Fultz, 107–25. London:
  Bloomsbury, 2013.

Bellour, Raymond. *The Analysis of Film*. Ed. Constance Penley. Bloomington: Indiana University Press, 2000.

Benfey, Christopher. "Ghosts in the Twilight. A Review of *Home* by Toni Morrison." *New York Review of Books* 59.12 (12 July 2012): 25–26.

Berlin, Ira. "Time, Space, and the Evolution of Afro-American Society on British Mainland North America." *American Historical Review* 85 (1980): 44–78.

Bernheimer, Charles. "Kafka's *Ein Landarzt*: The Poetics of *Nachträglichkeit*." *Journal of the Kafka Society of America* 11.1–2 (1987): 4–8.

Best, Stephen. "On Failing to Make the Past Present." *Modern Language Quarterly* 73.3 (2012): 453–74.

Birksted-Breen, Dana. "Time and the *après-coup*." *International Journal of Psychoanalysis* 84 (2003): 1501–15.

Boone, Joseph Allen. *Tradition Counter Tradition: Love and the Form of Fiction*. Chicago: University of Chicago Press, 1987.

Bouson, Brooks J. *Quiet as It's Kept: Shame, Trauma, and Race in the Novels of Toni Morrison*. Albany: State University of New York Press, 2000.

———. "Uncovering 'the Beloved' in the Warring and Lawless Women in Toni Morrison's *Love*." *Midwest Quarterly* 49.4 (2008): 358–73.

Braidotti, Rosi. *Nomadic Subjects: Embodiment and Sexual Difference in Contemporary Feminist Theory*. New York: Columbia University Press, 1994.

Brenkman, John. "Politics and Form in *Song of Solomon*." *Social Text* 39 (1994): 57–82.

Brooks, Peter. *Reading for the Plot*. New York: Vintage Books, 1984.

———. *Realist Vision*. New Haven: Yale University Press, 2005.

Brown, Caroline. "Golden Gray and the Talking Book: Identity as a Site of Artful Construction in Toni Morrison's *Jazz*." *African American Review* 36.4 (2002): 629–42.

Brown, Kathleen M. *Good Wives, Nasty Wenches, and Anxious Patriarchs: Gender, Race, and Power in Colonial Virginia*. Chapel Hill: University of North Carolina Press, 1996.

Brown, Laura. "Not Outside the Range: One Feminist Perspective on Psychic Trauma." In *Trauma: Explorations in Memory*, ed. Cathy Caruth, 100–112. Baltimore: Johns Hopkins University Press, 1995.

Cantiello, Jessica Wells. "From Pre-Racial to Post-Racial? Reading and Reviewing *A Mercy* in the Age of Obama." Ed. Kathryn Nicol and Jennifer Terry. Spec. issue of *MELUS* 36.2 (2011): 165–83.

Carabi, Angels. "Nobel Laureate Toni Morrison Speaks about Her Novel *Jazz*." *Belles Lettres*. 1995. Reprinted in Denard, *Toni Morrison*, 91–97.

———. "Toni Morrison's *Beloved*: 'And the Past Achieved Flesh.'" *Revista de Estudios Norteamericanos* 2 (1993): 105–15.

Carby, Hazel. "It Jus Be's Dat Way Sometime: The Sexual Politics of Women's Blues." *Radical America* 20.4 (1986): 9–24. Rpt. in *Gender and Discourse: The Power of Talk*, ed. Alexandra Dundas Todd and Sue Fisher, 227–42. Norwood, N.J.: Alex, 1988.

———. *Race Men*. Cambridge, Mass.: Harvard University Press, 1998.

———. *Reconstructing Womanhood: The Emergence of the Afro-American Woman Novelist*. New York: Oxford University Press, 1987.

Carden, Mary Paniccia. ""Trying to find a place when the streets don't go there': Fatherhood, Family, and American Racial Politics in Toni Morrison's *Love*." *African American Review* 44.1–2 (2011): 131–47.

Cardinal, Marie. *The Words to Say It: An Autobiographical Novel.* Trans. Pat Goodheart. Cambridge, Mass.: Van Vactor and Goodheart, 1983.

Caruth, Cathy. "Recapturing the Past: Introduction." In *Trauma: Explorations in Memory*, ed. Cathy Caruth, 151–57. Baltimore: Johns Hopkins University Press, 1995.

———. "Trauma and Experience: Introduction." In *Trauma: Explorations in Memory*, ed. Cathy Caruth, 3–12. Baltimore: Johns Hopkins University Press, 1995.

———. *Unclaimed Experience: Trauma, Narrative, and History.* Baltimore: Johns Hopkins University Press, 1996.

Cavell, Stanley. "Finding as Founding: Taking Steps in Emerson's 'Experience.'" In *This New Yet Unapproachable America: Lectures after Emerson after Wittgenstein.* Albuquerque, N.M.: Living Batch, 1989.

Charles, Ron. "Toni Morrison's Familiar, Flawed 'God Help the Child.'" Rev. of *God Help the Child*, by Toni Morrison. *Washington Post*, 4 April 2015, www.washingtonpost.com /entertainment/books/toni-morrisons-familar-flawed-god-help-the-child/2015/04/14 /6cde0cfe-dec6-11e4-a500-1c5bb1d8ff6a_story.html.

Chase, Cynthia. "Oedipal Textuality: Reading Freud's Reading of *Oedipus*." *Diacritics* 9.1 (March 1979): 54–68.

Christian, Barbara. "Fixing Methodologies: *Beloved*." In *Female Subjects in Black and White: Race, Psychoanalysis, Feminism*, ed. Elizabeth Abel, Barbara Christian, and Helene Moglen, 363–70. Berkeley: University of California Press, 1997.

Churchwell, Sarah. "*Home* by Toni Morrison—Review." Guardian.co.uk, 27 April 2012.

Cockburn, Andrew. "Washington Is Burning." *Harper's Magazine*. Sept. 2014. 44–48.

Cole, Johnnetta Betsch, and Beverly Guy-Sheftall. *Gender Talk: The Struggle for Women's Equality in African American Communities.* New York: Random House, 2003.

Collins, Patricia Hill. *Black Sexual Politics: African Americans, Gender, and the New Racism.* New York and London: Routledge, 2004.

Culler, Jonathan. "Omniscience." *Narrative* 12.1 (2004): 22–34.

———. *Structuralist Poetics: Structuralism, Linguistics, and the Study of Literature.* Ithaca: Cornell University Press, 1975.

Cutter, Martha. "The Story Must Go On and On: The Fantastic, Narration, and Intertextuality in Toni Morrison's *Beloved* and *Jazz*." *African American Review* 34.1 (2000): 61–75.

Dalsgård, Katrine. "The One All-Black Town Worth the Pain: (African) American Exceptionalism, Historical Narration, and the Critique of Nationhood in Toni Morrison's *Paradise*." *African American Review* 35.2 (2001): 233–48.

Darling, Marsha. "In the Realm of Responsibility: A Conversation with Toni Morrison." *Women's Review of Books* 5 (March 1978): 5–6.

Davidson, Rob. "Racial Stock and 8-Rocks: Communal Historiography in Toni Morrison's *Paradise*." *Twentieth Century Literature* 47.3 (2001): 355–73.

Davis, Adrienne. "'Don't Let Nobody Bother Yo' Principle': The Sexual Economy of American Slavery." In *Sister Circle: Black Women and Work*, ed. Sharon Harley, 103–27. New Brunswick, N.J.: Rutgers University Press, 2002.

Davis, Angela. *Women, Race and Class.* New York: Random House, 1983.

———. *Blues Legacies and Black Feminism.* New York: Pantheon Books, 1998.

Davis, Christina. "Interview with Toni Morrison." 1988. In *Toni Morrison: Critical*

Perspectives Past and Present, ed. Henry Louis Gates Jr. and K. A. Appiah, 412–20. New York: Amistad Press, 1993.

de Certeau, Michel. *The Practice of Everyday Life*. Trans. Steven Rendall. Berkeley: University of California Press, 1984.

de Rougemont, Denis. *Love in the Western World*. Trans. Montgomery Belgion. Greenwich, Conn.: Fawcett, 1966.

Demetrakopoulos, Stephanie. "Maternal Bonds as Devourers of Women's Individuation in Toni Morrison's *Beloved*." *African American Review* 26.1 (1992): 51–60.

Denard, Carolyn. "'Some to Hold, Some to Tell': Secrets and the Trope of Silence in *Love*." In *Toni Morrison: Paradise, Love, A Mercy*, ed. Lucille P. Fultz, 77–91. London: Bloomsbury, 2013.

Deyle, Steven. *Carry Me Back: The Domestic Slave Trade in America*. New York: Oxford University Press, 2005.

Dobbs, Cynthia. "Toni Morrison's *Beloved:* Bodies Returned, Modernism Revisited." *African American Review* 32.4 (1998): 563–78.

Du Bois, W. E. B. *In Battle for Peace: The Story of My 83rd Birthday*. New York: Masses and Mainstream, 1952.

———. "The Talented Tenth" (1903). In *The Future of the Race*, ed. Henry Louis Gates Jr. and Cornel West, 131–57. New York: Vintage, 1997.

Dubey, Madhu. "Narration and Migration: *Jazz* and Vernacular Theories of Black Women's Fiction." *American Literary History* 10.2 (1998): 291–316.

duCille, Ann. *The Coupling Convention: Sex, Text, and Tradition in Black Women's Fiction*. Oxford: Oxford University Press, 1993.

Duvall, John. *The Identifying Fictions of Toni Morrison: Modernist Authenticity and Postmodern Blackness*. New York: Palgrave Macmillan, 2000.

Eckard, Paula Gallant. "The Interplay of Music, Language, and Narrative in Toni Morrison's *Jazz*." *College Language Association Journal* 38.1 (1994): 11–19.

Eckstein, Lars. "A Love Supreme: Jazzthetic Strategies in Toni Morrison's *Beloved*." *African American Review* 40.2 (2006): 271–83.

Eichenwald, Kurt. "From Their Own Online World, Pedophiles Extend Their Reach." *New York Times*, 21 August 2006, A1, A14.

Eickhoff, Friedrich-Wilhelm. "On *Nachträglichkeit:* The Modernity of an Old Concept." *International Journal of Psychoanalysis* 87 (2006): 1453–69.

Eliot, George. *The Mill on the Floss*. New York: New American Library, 1965.

Ellison, Ralph. "The Charlie Christian Story." In *Living with Music: Ralph Ellison's Jazz Writings*. Ed. Robert G. O'Meally. New York: Modern Library, 2002.

Engels, Frederick. *The Origin of the Family, Private Property, and the State*. 4th ed. Moscow: Foreign Languages Publishing House, 1891.

Evans, Dylan. "From Kantian Ethics to Mystical Experience: An Exploration of Jouissance." In *Key Concepts of Lacanian Psychoanalysis,* ed. Dany Nobus, 1–28. New York: Other Press, 1998.

Faimberg, Haydee. *The Telescoping of Generations: Listening to the Narcissistic Links between Generations*. London and New York: Routledge, 2005.

Fanon, Frantz. *Black Skin, White Masks*. Trans. Charles Markman. New York: Grove Press, 1967.

Ferguson, Rebecca. "History, Memory and Language in Toni Morrison's *Beloved*." In

Feminist Criticism: Theory and Practice, ed. Susan Sellers, 109–27. Toronto: University of Toronto Press, 1991.

Fett, Sharla. *Working Cures: Healing, Health, and Power on Southern Slave Plantations.* Chapel Hill: University of North Carolina Press, 2002.

Fielding, Helen. *Bridget Jones's Diary.* New York: Penguin, 2001.

FitzGerald, Jennifer. "Selfhood and Community: Psychoanalysis and Discourse in *Beloved.*" *Modern Fiction Studies* 39.3&4 (1993): 669–87.

Fletcher, John. "Introduction: Psychoanalysis and the Question of the Other." In *Essays on Otherness,* by Jean Laplanche, 1–51. London: Routledge, 1999.

———. "The Scenography of Trauma: A 'Copernican' Reading of Sophocles' *Oedipus the King.*" *Textual Practice* 21.1 (2007): 17–41.

Forter, Greg. "Freud, Faulkner, Caruth: Trauma and the Politics of Literary Form." *Narrative* 15.3 (October 2007): 259–85.

Fowler, Doreen. "Nobody Could Make It Alone": Fathers and Boundaries in Toni Morrison's *Beloved.*" *MELUS* 36.2 (2011): 13–33.

———. "Reading Faulkner through Morrison." In *Critical Insights: William Faulkner,* ed. Kathryn Stelmach Artuso, 68–93. Ipswich, Mass.: Salem Press, 2013.

Fraile-Marcos, Ana María. "Hybridizing the 'City upon a Hill' in Toni Morrison's *Paradise.*" *MELUS* 28.4 (2003): 3–33.

Freud, Sigmund. *Beyond the Pleasure Principle.* Trans. James Strachey. New York: Norton, 1961.

———. "Femininity" (1933). In *The Standard Edition of the Complete Psychological Works of Sigmund Freud,* ed. and trans. James Strachey, 22: 116–35. London: Hogarth Press, 1953–73.

———. *The Interpretation of Dreams* (1900). In *The Standard Edition of the Complete Works of Sigmund Freud,* ed. and trans. James Strachey, 4–5. London: Hogarth Press, 1953–73.

———. *The Origins of Psycho-Analysis.* New York: Basic Books, 1954.

———. *Project for a Scientific Psychology* (1895). In *The Origins of Psycho-Analysis.* New York: Basic Books, 1954.

———. "Repression." In *The Standard Edition of the Complete Psychological Works of Sigmund Freud,* ed. and trans. James Strachey, 14: 141–58. London: Hogarth Press, 1953–73.

———. "Screen Memories." In *The Standard Edition of the Complete Psychological Works of Sigmund Freud,* ed. and trans. James Strachey, 3: 299–322. London: Hogarth Press, 1953–73.

———. "The Uncanny." In *The Standard Edition of the Complete Psychological Works of Sigmund Freud,* ed. and trans. James Strachey, 17: 217–56. London: Hogarth Press, 1953–73.

Freud, Sigmund, and Josef Breuer. *Studies on Hysteria* (1893–95). In *The Standard Edition of the Complete Psychological Works of Sigmund Freud,* ed. and trans. James Strachey, 2. London: Hogarth Press, 1953–73. Reprinted in *Studies on Hysteria,* ed. Irvin Yalom. New York: Basic Books, 2000.

———. "Three Essays on the Theory of Sexuality." In *The Standard Edition of the Complete Psychological Works of Sigmund Freud,* ed. and trans. James Strachey, 7: 135–243. London: Hogarth Press, 1953–73.

Friedman, Susan Stanford. "'Beyond' White and Other: Narratives of Race in Feminist Discourse." In *Mappings: Feminism and the Cultural Geographies of Encounter,* ed. Friedman, 36–66. Princeton: Princeton University Press, 1998.

Fultz, Lucille. *Toni Morrison: Playing with Difference.* Urbana and Chicago: University of Illinois Press, 2003.

Furman, Jan. "Telling Stories: Evolving Narrative Identity in Toni Morrison's *Home.*" In *Toni Morrison: Memory and Meaning*, ed. Adrienne Seward and Justine Tally, 231–42. Jackson: University Press of Mississippi, 2014.

Gates, Henry Louis, Jr. "Criticism in the Jungle." In *Black Literature and Literary Theory*, ed. Gates, 1–24. New York: Methuen, 1984.

———. "Introduction: The Language of Slavery." In *The Slave's Narrative*, ed. Charles T. Davis and Henry Louis Gates Jr., xi–xxxiv. New York: Oxford University Press, 1985.

Gauthier, Marni. "The Other Side of *Paradise*: Toni Morrison's (Un)Making of Mythic History." *African American Review* 39.3 (2005): 395–414.

Genette, Gérard. *Narrative Discourse: An Essay in Method.* Trans. Jane Lewin. Ithaca: Cornell University Press, 1981.

George, Sheldon. "Approaching the Thing of Slavery: A Lacanian Analysis of Toni Morrison's *Beloved.*" *African American Review* 45.1/2 (2012): 115–30.

———. *Trauma and Race: A Lacanian Study of African American Racial Identity.* Waco, Tex.: Baylor University Press, 2016.

Gilman, Sander. *Freud, Race, and Gender.* Princeton: Princeton University Press, 1993.

Gordon, Linda. *The Moral Property of Women: A History of Birth Control Politics in America.* Urbana and Chicago: University of Illinois Press, 2007.

Goulimari, Pelagia. *Toni Morrison.* London: Routledge, 2011.

Goyal, Yogita. "The Gender of Diaspora in Toni Morrison's *Tar Baby.*" *Modern Fiction Studies* 52.2 (2006): 393–414.

Green, Michael Cullen. *Black Yanks in the Pacific: Race in the Making of American Military Empire after World War II.* Ithaca, N.Y.: Cornell University Press, 2010.

Greenblatt, Stephen. *The Swerve: How the World Became Modern.* New York: W. W. Norton, 2011.

Grewal, Gurleen. *Circles of Sorrow, Lines of Struggle: The Novels of Toni Morrison.* Baton Rouge: Louisiana State University Press, 1998.

Halberstam, Judith. *In a Queer Time and Place: Transgender Bodies, Subcultural Lives.* New York: New York University Press, 2005.

Hall, Cheryl. "Beyond the 'Literary Habit': Oral Tradition and Jazz in *Beloved.*" *MELUS* 19.1 (1994): 89–95.

Hammonds, Evelynn. "Who Speaks for Black Women?" In *Sojourner: The Women's Forum* (November 1991): 7–8.

Hardack, Richard. "'A Music Seeking Its Words': Double-Timing and Double-Consciousness in Toni Morrison's *Jazz.*" *Callaloo* 18.2 (1995): 451–71.

Hartman, Saidiya. *Lose Your Mother: A Journey Along the Atlantic Slave Route.* New York: Farrar, Straus and Giroux, 2007.

Heinert, Jennifer. *Narrative Conventions and Race in the Novels of Toni Morrison.* New York: Routledge, 2009.

Henderson, Mae. "Toni Morrison's *Beloved:* Re-membering the Body as Historical Text."

In *Comparative American Identities: Race, Sex, and Nationality in the Modern Text,* ed. Hortense Spillers, 62–86. London: Routledge, 1991.

Hilfrich, Carola. "Anti-Exodus: Countermemory, Gender, Race, and Everyday Life in Toni Morrison's *Paradise.*" *Modern Fiction Studies* 52.2 (2006): 321–49.

Holloway, Karla. "*Beloved:* A Spiritual." *Callaloo* 13 (1990): 516–25.

Horvitz, Deborah. "Nameless Ghosts: Possession and Dispossession in *Beloved.*" *Studies in American Fiction* 17 (1989): 157–67.

Humann, Heather Duerre. "Family and Violence in *Love.*" *Women's Studies: An Interdisciplinary Journal* 43.2 (2014): 246–62.

Jacobs, Harriet. *Incidents in the Life of a Slave Girl* (1861). Cambridge, Mass.: Harvard University Press, 1987.

Jennings, La Vinia Delois. "*A Mercy:* Toni Morrison Plots the Formation of Racial Slavery in Seventeenth-Century America." *Callaloo* 32.2 (2009): 645–49.

———. *Toni Morrison and the Idea of Africa.* Cambridge: Cambridge University Press, 2008.

Jones, Carolyn. "Traces and Cracks: Identity and Narrative in Toni Morrison's *Jazz.*" *African American Review* 31.3 (1997): 481–95.

Jones, Chloe. "Opposing Patriarchal Temporalities." Unpublished graduate seminar paper, University of Kansas, June 2007.

Jones, Jacqueline. *Labor of Love, Labor of Sorrow: Black Women, Work, and the Family, from Slavery to the Present.* New York: Perseus, 2010.

Jones, W. T. *The Classical Mind: A History of Western Philosophy.* 2nd ed. New York: Harcourt, Brace & World, 1969.

Kakutani, Michiko. "In Toni Morrison's 'God Help the Child,' Adults Are Hobbled by the Pain of the Past." Rev. of *God Help the Child,* by Toni Morrison. *New York Times,* 17 April 2015, C1.

———. "Worthy Women, Unredeemable Men." Review of *Paradise,* by Toni Morrison. *New York Times,* 6 January 1998.

Kapsalis, Terri. *Public Privates: Performing Gynecology from Both Ends of the Speculum.* Durham, N.C.: Duke University Press, 1997.

Karavanta, Mina. "Toni Morrison's *A Mercy* and the Counterwriting of Negative Communities: A Postnational Novel." *Modern Fiction Studies* 58.4 (2012): 723–46.

Koenen, Anne. "The One Out of Sequence." In *Conversations with Toni Morrison,* ed. Danille Taylor-Guthrie, 67–83. Jackson: University Press of Mississippi, 1994.

Kolbenschlag, Madonna. *Kiss Sleeping Beauty Good-Bye: Breaking the Spell of Feminine Myths and Models.* New York: Doubleday, 1979.

Koolish, Lynda. "'To Be Loved and Cry Shame': A Psychological Reading of Toni Morrison's *Beloved.*" *MELUS* 26.4 (2001): 169–95.

Kristeva, Julia. *Revolution in Poetic Language.* Trans. Margaret Waller. New York: Columbia University Press, 1984.

Krumholz, Linda. "The Ghosts of Slavery: Historical Recovery in Toni Morrison's *Beloved.*" *African American Review* 26.3 (1992): 395–408.

———. "Reading and Insight in Toni Morrison's *Paradise.*" *African American Review* 36.1 (2002): 21–34.

Lacan, Jacques. "The Function and Field of Speech and Language in Psychoanalysis." 1953. Lacan, *Ecrits,* 30–113.

————. *Le Séminaire, livre VIII: Le transfert, 1960–1961.* Ed. Jacques-Alain Miller. Paris: Seuil, 2001.

————. *Le Séminaire X: L'Angoisse* (1962–63). Unpublished manuscript, session of June 19.

————. *Seminar XI: The Four Fundamental Concepts of Psychoanalysis.* Ed. Jacques-Alain Miller. Trans. Alan Sheridan. New York: Norton, 1981.

————. *The Seminar of Jacques Lacan: On Feminine Sexuality. The Limits of Love and Knowledge* (1972–73). Book 20. Ed. Jacques-Alain Miller. Trans. Bruce Fink. New York: W. W. Norton, 1998.

————. *The Seminar of Jacques Lacan.* Book 2. *The Ego in Freud's Theory and in the Technique of Psychoanalysis* (1954–55). Trans. Sylvana Tomaselli. New York: Norton, 1991.

Laplanche, Jean. *Essays on Otherness.* Trans. John Fletcher. London: Routledge, 1999.

————. *Life and Death in Psychoanalysis.* Trans. Jeffrey Mehlman. Baltimore: Johns Hopkins University Press, 1976.

————. *New Foundations for Psychoanalysis.* Trans. David Macey. London: Basil Blackwell, 1989.

Laplanche, Jean, and Jean-Bertrand Pontalis. "Fantasy and the Origins of Sexuality." In *Formations of Fantasy*, ed. Victor Burgin, James Donald, and Cora Kaplan, 5–34. London and New York: Methuen, 1986.

Laub, Dori. "Truth and Testimony: The Process and the Struggle." In *Trauma: Explorations in Memory*, ed. Cathy Caruth, 61–75. Baltimore: Johns Hopkins University Press, 1995.

Leaska, Mitchell. *Granite and Rainbow: The Hidden Life of Virginia Woolf.* New York: Picador, 1998.

Lerner, Gerda. *The Creation of Patriarchy.* Oxford: Oxford University Press, 1986.

Lesoinne, Veronique. "Answer Jazz's Call: Experiencing Toni Morrison's *Jazz*." *MELUS* 22.3 (1997): 151–66.

Lewis, Helen. "Introduction." In *The Role of Shame in Symptom Formation*, ed. Lewis, 1–28. Hillsdale, N.J.: Lawrence Erlbaum, 1987.

Li, Stephanie. *Signifying without Specifying: Racial Discourse in the Age of Obama.* New Brunswick, N.J.: Rutgers University Press, 2012.

Liscio, Lorraine. "*Beloved*'s Narrative: Writing Mother's Milk." *Tulsa Studies in Women's Literature* 11.1 (1992): 31–46.

Lucretius. *On the Nature of Things.* Trans. Martin Ferguson Smith. London: Sphere Books, 1969; rev. trans., Indianapolis: Hackett, 2001.

Marx, Karl, and Frederick Engels. "Difference Between the Democritean and Epicurean Philosophy of Nature" (1835–43). In *Collected Works.* New York: International, 1975. 1: 25–105.

Mather, Ronald, and Jill Marsden. "Trauma and Temporality: On the Origins of Post-Traumatic Stress." *Theory and Psychology* 14.2 (2004): 205–19.

Matus, Jill. *Toni Morrison.* Manchester: Manchester University Press, 1998.

Mbalia, Doreatha Drummond. "Women Who Run with Wild: The Need for Sisterhoods in *Jazz*." *Modern Fiction Studies* 39.3&4 (1993): 623–46.

Mbiti, John S. *African Religions and Philosophy.* 2nd ed. Oxford: Heinemann, 1969.

McGowan, Todd. *Capitalism and Desire: The Psychic Cost of Free Markets.* New York: Columbia University Press, 2016.

———. *The End of Dissatisfaction? Jacques Lacan and the Emerging Society of Enjoyment.* Albany: State University of New York Press, 2004.

McKay, Nellie. "An Interview with Toni Morrison." *Contemporary Literature* 24.4 (1983): 413–29. Reprinted in Danille Taylor-Guthrie, *Conversations with Toni Morrison*, 138–55. Jackson: University Press of Mississippi.

McKinney-Whetstone, Diane. "The Nature Of Love: Novelist Diane McKinney-Whetstone Talks with Toni Morrison About Her New Novel, the Literary Scene and What Comes Next." *Essence*, Oct. 2003.

Mellard, James. "'Families make the best enemies': Paradoxes of Narcissistic Identification in Toni Morrison's *Love*." *African American Review* 43.4 (2009): 699–712.

———. "Faulkner's 'Miss Emily' and Blake's 'Sick Rose': Invisible Worm, *Nachträglichkeit*, and Retrospective Gothic." *Faulkner Journal* 2.1 (1986): 37–45.

———. "The Jews of Ruby, Oklahoma: Politics, Parallax, and Ideological Fantasy in Toni Morrison's *Paradise*." *Modern Fiction Studies* 56.2 (2010): 349–77.

Mitchell, Juliet. *Siblings: Sex and Violence.* Cambridge: Polity Press and Blackwell, 2003.

Mobley, Marilyn Sanders. "Call and Response: Voice, Community, and Dialogic Structures in Toni Morrison's *Song of Solomon*." In *New Essays on Song of Solomon,* ed. Valerie Smith, 41–68. Cambridge: Cambridge University Press, 1995.

Montgomery, Maxine. "Got on My Traveling Shoes: Migration, Exile, and Home in Toni Morrison's *A Mercy*." *Journal of Black Studies* 42.4 (2011): 627–37.

Moraga, Cherríe. "From a Long Line of Vendidas: Chicanas and Feminism." In *Feminist Studies: Critical Studies*, ed. Teresa de Lauretis, 173–90. Bloomington: Indiana University Press, 1986.

Morgan, Jennifer. *Laboring Women: Reproduction and Gender in New World Slavery.* Philadelphia: University of Pennsylvania Press, 2004.

Morgenstern, Naomi. "Maternal Love / Maternal Violence: Inventing Ethics in Toni Morrison's *A Mercy*." *MELUS* 39.1 (2014): 7–29.

———. "Mother's Milk and Sister's Blood: Trauma and the Neoslave Narrative." *Differences: A Journal of Feminist Cultural Studies* 8.2 (1997): 101–26.

Morrison, Toni. *Beloved.* New York: Alfred A. Knopf, 1987.

———. "A Bench by the Road: *Beloved* by Toni Morrison." In *The World: The Journal of the Unitarian Universalist Association.* January/February 1989. Reprinted in Denard, *Toni Morrison*, 44–50.

———. *The Bluest Eye* (1970). New York: Penguin (Plume), 1994.

———. *Conversations with Toni Morrison.* Ed. Danille Kathleen Taylor-Guthrie. Jackson: University Press of Mississippi, 1994.

———. *God Help the Child.* New York and Toronto: Alfred A. Knopf, 2015.

———. "Home." In *The House That Race Built: Original Essays by Toni Morrison, Angela Y. Davis, Cornel West, and Others on Black Americans and Politics in America Today,* ed. Wahneema Lubiano, 3–12. New York: Random House, 1998.

———. *Home.* New York and Toronto: Alfred A. Knopf, 2012.

———. Interview by Bob Minzesheimer. "New novel 'Home' brings Toni Morrison back to Ohio." *USA Today,* 7 May 2012, www.usatoday.com/life/books/news/story /2012-05-07/toni-morrison-home-books/54814002/1.

———. "Interview with Toni Morrison." *America Online.* 22 February 1998. Quoted in Page, "Furrowing All the Brows," 638.

———. *Jazz*. New York: Alfred A. Knopf, 1992.

———. *Love*. New York: Alfred A. Knopf, 2003.

———. *A Mercy*. New York: Alfred A. Knopf, 2008.

———. *Paradise*. New York: Alfred A. Knopf, 1998.

———. *Playing in the Dark: Whiteness and the Literary Imagination*. New York: Vintage Books, 1992.

———. "Recitatif." In *Confirmation: An Anthology of African American Women,* ed. Amiri Baraka and Amina Baraka, 243–61. New York: William Morrow, 1983.

———. "Rootedness: The Ancestor as Foundation." In *Black Women Writers (1950–80): A Critical Evaluation,* ed. Mari Evans, 339–45. New York: Doubleday, 1984.

———. *Song of Solomon* (1977). New York: Penguin (Plume), 1987.

———. *Sula*. New York: Random House, 2004.

———. "Toni Morrison: The Art of Fiction 134." *Paris Review*. 1992. Reprinted in Denard, *Toni Morrison*, 62–90.

———. *Toni Morrison: Conversations.* Ed. Carolyn C. Denard. Jackson: University Press of Mississippi, 2008.

———. "Toni Morrison Knows All About the 'Little Drop of Poison' in Your Childhood." Interview in *Mother Jones*, 21 April 2015, www.motherjones.com/media/2015/04/toni-morrison-interview-god-help-the-child.

———. "Unspeakable Things Unspoken: The Afro-American Presence in American Literature." *Michigan Quarterly Review* 38.1 (Winter 1989): 1–34.

Muller, John. "Language, Psychosis, and the Subject in Lacan." In *Interpreting Lacan,* ed. Joseph Smith and William Kerrigan, 21–32. New Haven: Yale University Press, 1983.

Nash, Katherine. *Feminist Narrative Ethics: Tacit Persuasion in Modernist Form*. Columbus: Ohio University Press, 2013.

———. "Narrative Structure." In *The Encyclopedia of the Novel*, ed. Peter Melville Logan, 2: 545–49. London: Wiley-Blackwell, 2011.

Nelson, Dana. *The Word in Black and White: Reading "Race" in American Literature, 1638–1867*. New York: Oxford University Press, 1993.

Neroni, Hilary. "Jane Campion's *Jouissance*: *Holy Smoke* and Feminist Film Theory." In *Lacan and Contemporary Film*, ed. Todd McGowan and Sheila Kunkle, 209–32. New York: Other Press, 2004.

Nicol, Kathryn. "Visible Differences: Viewing Racial Identity in Toni Morrison's *Paradise* and "Recitatif." In *Literature and Racial Ambiguity*, ed. Teresa Hubel and Neil Brooks, 209–31. Amsterdam and New York: Rodopi, 2002.

Norris, Michele. "Toni Morrison Finds 'A Mercy' in Servitude." *All Things Considered*, 27 October 2008, www.npr.org/templates/story/story.php?storyId=96118766.

Nünning, Ansgar. "Deconstructing and Reconceptualizing the Implied Author: The Resurrection of an Anthropomorphized Passepartout or the Obituary of a Critical Phantom?" *Anglistik* 8 (1997): 95–116.

———. "Unreliable, Compared to What? Toward a Cognitive Theory of Unreliable Narration: Prolegomena and Hypotheses." In *Grenzüberschreitungen: Narratologie im Kontext*, ed. Walter Grünzweig and Andreas Solbach, 53–73. Tübingen: Gunther Narr Verlag, 1999.

O'Connor, Anne-Marie. "*Love* and the Outlaw Women: Toni Morrison's Latest Explores the Relationship between the Sexes and Segregation's End." *Los Angeles Times*, 15 October 2003, e1.

O'Reilly, Andrea. *Toni Morrison and Motherhood: A Politics of the Heart*. Albany: State University of New York Press, 2004.

Page, Philip. *Dangerous Freedom: Fusion and Fragmentation in Toni Morrison's Novels*. Jackson: University Press of Mississippi, 1995.

———. "Furrowing All the Brows: Interpretation and the Transcendent in Toni Morrison's *Paradise*." *African American Review* 35.4 (2001): 637–49.

Palladino, Mariangela. "Aphrodite's Faces: Toni Morrison's *Love* and Ethics." *Modern Fiction Studies* 58.2 (2012): 334–52.

Paquet-Deyris, Anne-Marie. "Toni Morrison's *Jazz* and the City." *African American Review* 35.2 (2001): 219–31.

Pepetela. *The Return of the Water Spirit*. Trans. Luís R. Mitras. Portsmouth, N.H.: Heinemann, 1995.

Pereira, Malin. "Periodizing Toni Morrison's Work from *The Bluest Eye* to *Jazz*: The Importance of *Tar Baby*." *MELUS* 22.3 (1997): 71–82.

Pérez-Torres, Rafael. "Knitting and Knotting the Narrative Thread: *Beloved* as Postmodern Novel." *Modern Fiction Studies* 39.3&4 (1993): 689–707.

Peterson, Christopher. "Beloved's Claim." *Modern Fiction Studies* 52.3 (2006): 548–69.

Phelan, James. "The Beginning of *Beloved*: A Rhetorical Approach." In *Narrative Beginnings: Theories and Practices*, ed. Brian Richardson, 195–212. Lincoln: University of Nebraska Press, 2008.

———. *Living to Tell About It*. Ithaca: Cornell University Press, 2005.

———. "Narrative as Rhetoric and Edith Wharton's *Roman Fever*: Progression, Configuration, and the Ethics of Surprise." In *A Companion to Rhetoric and Rhetorical Criticism*, ed. Walter Jost and Wendy Olmsted, 340–54. Malden, Mass.: Blackwell, 2004.

———. "Narrative Judgments and the Rhetorical Theory of Narrative: Ian McEwan's *Atonement*." In *A Companion to Narrative Theory*, ed. James Phelan and Peter J. Rabinowitz, 322–36. Malden, Mass.: Blackwell, 2005.

———. "Toward a Rhetorical Reader-Response Criticism: The Difficult, the Stubborn, and the Ending of *Beloved*." *Modern Fiction Studies* 39.3&4 (1993): 709–28.

Phelan, James, and Peter Rabinowitz. "Narrative as Rhetoric." In *Narrative Theory: Core Concepts and Critical Debates,* by David Herman et al., 3–8. Columbus: Ohio State University Press, 2012.

Prose, Francine. "Growing Up Too Black." Rev. of *God Help the Child*, by Toni Morrison. *New York Review of Books,* 7 May 2015.

Puhl, Klaus. "Only Connect . . . Perspicuous Representation and the Logic of *Nachträglichkeit*." *Grazer Philosophische Studien* 71 (2006): 23–38.

Quashie, Kevin. *Black Women, Identity, and Cultural Theory: (Un)Becoming the Subject*. New Brunswick, N.J.: Rutgers University Press, 2004.

Radway, Janice. *Reading the Romance: Women, Patriarchy, and Popular Literature*. Chapel Hill: University of North Carolina Press, 1984.

Rawick, George. *The American Slave: A Composite Autobiography*, part 3, vol. 13. Westport, Conn.: Greenwood, 1973.

Reed, Alison. "Dual Narration in Morrison's *Love*." Unpublished undergraduate seminar paper, Occidental College, May 2007.

Restuccia, Frances. *Amorous Acts: Lacanian Ethics in Modernism, Film, and Queer Theory.* Stanford: Stanford University Press, 2006.

Rimmon-Kenan, Shlomith. *Narrative Fiction: Contemporary Poetics.* New York: Methuen, 1983.

Robolin, Stéphane Pierre Raymond. "Loose Memory in Toni Morrison's *Paradise* and Zoë Wicomb's *David's Story.*" *Modern Fiction Studies* 52.2 (2006): 297–320.

Rodrigues, Eusebio. "Experiencing *Jazz.*" *Modern Fiction Studies* 39.3&4 (1993): 733–54.

———. "The Telling of *Beloved.*" *Journal of Narrative Technique* 21.2 (1991): 153–69.

Rody, Caroline. "Impossible Voices: Ethnic Postmodern Narration in Toni Morrison's *Jazz* and Karen Tei Yamashita's *Through the Arc of the Rain Forest.*" *Contemporary Literature* 41.4 (2000): 618–41.

Rose, Jacqueline. *The Last Resistance.* London and New York: Verso, 2007.

Rothstein, Mervyn. "Toni Morrison, in Her New Novel, Defends Women." Rev. of *Beloved*, by Toni Morrison. *New York Times,* 26 August 1987, C17.

Roynon, Tessa. "A New 'Romen' Empire: Toni Morrison's *Love* and the Classics." *Journal of American Studies* 41.1 (2007): 31–47.

Rubenstein, Roberta. "Singing the Blues / Reclaiming Jazz: Toni Morrison and Cultural Mourning." *Mosaic* 31.2 (1998): 147–64.

Ruddick, Sara. "Maternal Thinking." In *Mothering: Essays in Feminist Theory,* ed. Joyce Trebilcot, 213–30. Totowa, N.J.: Rowman and Allanheld, 1984.

Rushdie, Salman. "An Interview with Toni Morrison." *Brick: A Literary Magazine.* 1992. Reprinted in Denard, *Toni Morrison,* 51–61.

Ruti, Mari. *The Singularity of Being: Lacan and the Immortal Within.* New York: Fordham University Press, 2012.

Said, Edward. "Thoughts on Late Style: A Lecture." *London Review of Books* 26.15 (2004): 3–7.

Sale, Maggie. "Call and Response as Critical Method: African-American Oral Traditions and *Beloved.*" *African American Review* 26.1 (1992): 41–50.

Sanger, Margaret, and Ellen Smith. "Birth Control and the Negro." In Birth Control Federation of America pamphlet, 1939.

Santner, Eric. "Miracles Happen: Benjamin, Rosenzweig, Freud, and the Matter of the Neighbor." In *The Neighbor: Three Inquiries in Political Theology*, by Slavoj Žižek, Eric Santner, and Kenneth Reinhard. Chicago: University of Chicago Press, 2005.

———. *On the Psychotheology of Everyday Life: Reflections on Freud and Rosenzweig.* Chicago: University of Chicago Press, 2001.

Schapiro, Barbara. "The Bonds of Love and the Boundaries of Self in Toni Morrison's *Beloved.*" *Contemporary Literature* 32 (1991): 194–210.

Schappell, Elissa, and Claudia Brodsky Lacour. "Toni Morrison: The Art of Fiction." *The Paris Review* 128 (1993): 83–125.

Scholes, Robert. *Fabulation and Metafiction.* Urbana: University of Illinois Press, 1979.

Schreiber, Evelyn. "Power and Betrayal: Social Hierarchies and the Trauma of Loss in *Love.*" In *Toni Morrison: Paradise, Love, A Mercy,* ed. Lucille P. Fultz, 92–106. London: Bloomsbury, 2013.

———. *Race, Trauma, and Home in the Novels of Toni Morrison.* Baton Rouge: Louisiana State University Press, 2010.

Schwartz, Marie Jenkins. "'At Noon, Oh How I Ran': Breastfeeding and Weaning on Plantation and Farm in Antebellum Virginia and Alabama." In *Discovering the Women in Slavery: Emancipating Perspectives on the American Past*, ed. Patricia Morton, 241–59. Athens: University of Georgia Press, 1996.

———. *Born in Bondage: Growing Up Enslaved in the Antebellum South*. Cambridge, Mass.: Harvard University Press, 2000.

Seward, Adrienne, and Justine Tally. *Toni Morrison: Memory and Meaning*. Jackson: University Press of Mississippi, 2014.

Shaw, Stephanie. "Mothering under Slavery in the Antebellum South." In *Mothering: Ideology, Experience, and Agency*, ed. Evelyn Nakano Glenn, Grace Chang, and Linda Rennie Forcey, 237–58. New York: Routledge, 1994.

Sims, J. Marion, M.D. *The Story of My Life*. Ed. H. Marion-Sims, M.D. New York: Appleton, 1884.

Smallwood, Stephanie. *Saltwater Slavery: A Middle Passage from Africa to American Diaspora*. Cambridge, Mass.: Harvard University Press, 2007.

Smith, Valerie. *Writing the Moral Imagination*. Chichester, West Sussex: Wiley-Blackwell, 2012.

Spillers, Hortense. "Mama's Baby, Papa's Maybe: An American Grammar Book." *Diacritics* 17 (1987): 65–81.

Stave, Shirley. "Across Distances without Recognition: Misrecognition in Toni Morrison's *A Mercy*." In *Toni Morrison's A Mercy: Critical Approaches*, ed. Shirley Ann Stave and Justine Tally, 137–50. Cambridge: Cambridge Scholars, 2011.

———. "Separate Spheres? The Appropriation of Female Space in *Paradise*." In *Toni Morrison: Paradise, Love, A Mercy*, ed. Lucille Fultz, 23–39. London: Bloomsbury, 2013.

Stave, Shirley, and Justine Talley, eds. *Toni Morrison's A Mercy: Critical Approaches*. Cambridge: Cambridge Scholars, 2011.

Suzuki, Shunryu. *Zen Mind, Beginner's Mind*. Boston: Shambhala, 2010.

Sweeney, Megan. "Racial House, Big House, Home: Contemporary Abolitionism in Toni Morrison's *Paradise*." *Meridians* 4.2 (2004): 40–67.

———. "'Something Rogue': Commensurability, Commodification, Crime, and Justice in Toni Morrison's Later Fiction." *Modern Fiction Studies* 52.2 (2006): 440–69.

Tally, Justine. "The Morrison Trilogy." In *The Cambridge Companion to Toni Morrison*, ed. Tally, 75–91. Cambridge: Cambridge University Press, 2007.

Thoma, Helmut, and Neil Cheshire. "Freud's *Nachträglichkeit* and Strachey's 'Deferred Action': Trauma, Constructions, and the Direction of Causality." *International Review of Psycho-Analysis* 18 (1991): 407–27.

Thomas, Valorie. "'A Kind of Restoration': Psychogeographies of Healing in Toni Morrison's *Home*." In *Toni Morrison: Memory and Meaning*, ed. Adrienne Seward and Justine Tally, 194–204. Jackson: University Press of Mississippi, 2014.

Travis, Molly Abel. "Beyond Empathy: Narrative Distancing and Ethics in Toni Morrison's *Beloved* and J. M. Coetzee's *Disgrace*." *Journal of Narrative Theory* 40.2 (2010): 231–50.

Treherne, Matthew. "Figuring In, Figuring Out: Narration and Negotiation in Toni Morrison's *Jazz*." *Narrative* 11.2 (2003): 199–212.

Turow, Scott. "By the Book." *New York Times Book Review*. 10 October 2013. 8.

Van Der Kolk, Bessel A., and Onno Van Der Hart. "The Intrusive Past: The Flexibility of

Memory and the Engraving of Trauma." In *Trauma: Explorations in Memory*, ed. Cathy Caruth, 158–82. Baltimore: Johns Hopkins University Press, 1995.

Vega-Gonzalez, Susana. "Toni Morrison's Water World: Watertime and Writing in *Love*." *The Grove: Working Papers on English Studies* 11 (2004): 209–20.

Vickroy, Laurie. *Trauma and Survival in Contemporary Fiction*. Charlottesville: University of Virginia Press, 2002.

Waegner, Cathy Covell. "Ruthless Epic Footsteps: Shoes, Migrants, and the Settlement of the Americas in Toni Morrison's *A Mercy*." In *Post-National Inquiries: Essays on Ethnic and Racial Border Crossings,* ed. Jopi Nyman, 91–112. Cambridge: Cambridge Scholars, 2009.

Wardi, Anissa. "A Laying on of Hands: Toni Morrison and the Materiality of *Love*." *MELUS* 30.3 (2005): 201–18.

———. "The Politics of 'Home' in *A Mercy*." In *Toni Morrison's A Mercy: Critical Approaches*, ed. Shirley Ann Stave and Justine Tally, 23–41. Cambridge. Cambridge Scholars, 2011.

Washington, Teresa. "The Mother-Daughter Àjé Relationship in Toni Morrison's *Beloved*." *African American Review* 39.1/2 (2005): 171–88.

Weinstein, Philip. *What Else But Love? The Ordeal of Race in Faulkner and Morrison*. New York: Columbia University Press, 1996.

White, Deborah. *Ar'n't I a Woman? Female Slaves in the Plantation South*. 2nd ed. New York: Norton, 1999.

Winnett, Susan. "Coming Unstrung: Women, Men, Narrative, and Principles of Pleasure." *PMLA* 105.3 (1990): 505–18.

Wolfenstein, Eugene Victor. *Talking Books: Toni Morrison Among the Ancestors*. CreateSpace, 2010.

Woolf, Virginia. *Mrs. Dalloway*. New York: Harcourt Brace, 1981.

———. *To the Lighthouse*. New York: Harcourt Brace, 1981.

———. *A Writer's Diary: Being Extracts from the Diary of Virginia Woolf*. London: Hogarth Press, 1965.

Wyatt, Jean. "Failed Messages, Maternal Loss and Narrative Form in Toni Morrison's *A Mercy*." *Modern Fiction Studies* 58.1 (Spring 2012).

———. "Giving Body to the Word: The Maternal Symbolic in Toni Morrison's *Beloved*." *PMLA* 108.3 (May 1993): 474–88.

———. "*Love*'s Time and the Reader: Ethical Effects of *Nachträglichkeit* in Toni Morrison's *Love*." *Narrative* 16.2 (May 2008).

———. *Risking Difference: Identification, Race, and Community in Contemporary Fiction and Feminism*. Albany: State University of New York Press, 2004.

Wyndham, John. *Myths of Ifè*. (1921). Reproduction by Berkeley: University of California Press, William and Berta Bascom Collection, n.d.

Yeats, William B. "Sailing to Byzantium." In *The Collected Poems of W. B. Yeats*. New York: Macmillan, 1963.

INDEX

CPSIA information can be obtained
at www.ICGtesting.com
Printed in the USA
LVHW020104090819
627063LV00001B/241/P